HIGH PERFORMANCE HEALTHCARE

HIGH PERFORMANCE HEALTHCARE

Using the Power of Relationships
to Achieve Quality, Efficiency
and Resilience

JODY HOFFER GITTELL

New York   Chicago   San Francisco   Lisbon   London
Madrid   Mexico City   Milan   New Delhi   San Juan
Seoul   Singapore   Sydney   Toronto

The McGraw·Hill Companies

1 2 3 4 5 6 7 8 9 0   FGR/FGR   0 1 0 9

ISBN: 978-0-07-162176-2
MHID: 0-07-162176-8

This publication is designed to provide accurate and authoritative information in regard to the subject matter covered. It is sold with the understanding that the publisher is not engaged in rendering legal, accounting, or other professional service. If legal advice or other expert assistance is required, the services of a competent professional person should be sought.

—From a Declaration of Principles Jointly Adopted by a Committee of the American Bar Association and a Committee of Publishers and Associations

McGraw-Hill books are available at special quantity discounts to use as premiums and sales promotions, or for use in corporate training programs. To contact a representative, please visit the Contact Us pages at www.mhprofessional.com.

This book is printed on acid-free paper.

Contents

Acknowledgments

Of the many people who have contributed to this book, first and foremost are the care providers, managers, and patients who participated in data collection. Some of those participants were from hospitals in Boston: Beth Israel Deaconess, Brigham and Women's, Massachusetts General, New England Baptist, and Newton-Wellesley; in New York City: Beth Israel Hospital, the Hospital for Joint Diseases, and the Hospital for Special Surgery; and in the Dallas area: Baylor University Medical Center and Presbyterian Plano. Other participants were from nursing homes throughout Massachusetts: Beaumont, Chapin, D'Youville, German Center, Harborside Healthcare, Hathaway Manor, Hebrew Rehab, Neville Manor, New England Deaconess, Loomis House, Lutheran Home, Orchard Cove, Penacook Place, Radius Healthcare, and South Cove Manor.

I am particularly thankful to Dr. Benjamin Bierbaum of New England Baptist, Dr. William Head of Presbyterian Plano, Dr. Robert Jackson of Baylor University Medical Center, Dr. Michael Kelly of Beth Israel New York, Dr. Richard Laskin of the Hospital for Special Surgery, Dr. Stephen Lipson of Beth Israel Deaconess, Dr. John Siliski of Massachusetts General, Dr. Thomas Thornhill of Brigham and Women's, and Dr. Joseph Zuckerman of the Hospital for Joint Diseases, who were my coinvestigators in the original study of surgical care coordination and who provided their insights as well as access to many of the interviews and outcomes data presented in this book.

I am also indebted to others who collaborated with me on the research underlying this book, with whom I have published many of the results in academic journals. I especially thank Julian Wimbush, who worked with me on every aspect of the original study of surgical care coordination, gathering patient outcomes data, surveying providers, and interviewing hospital administrators. I also thank Dr. Adrienne Bennett, Joseph Miller, and Dana Weinberg, with whom I collaborated on the study of medical care coordination; Cori Kautz, Will Lusenhop, Dana Weinberg, and Dr. John Wright, with whom I collaborated on the study of postdischarge care coordination; and Christine Bishop, Lisa Dodson, Almas Dossa, Susan Eaton, Walter Leutz, Susan Pfefferle, Dana Weinberg, and Rebekah Zincavage, with whom I collaborated on the study of long-term care coordination.

For helping to test out my early ideas regarding the coordination of patient care, I thank the participants in the Quality of Care Seminar at the Harvard School of Public Health, led by Heather Palmer, and the participants in the Alfred P. Sloan Foundation's Managed Care Industry Group at Harvard, led by Joseph Newhouse, who pushed me to sharpen my questions and find better methods for answering those questions. I thank Anne-Marie Audet of the Commonwealth Fund of New York as well as the Robert Wood Johnson Foundation, Atlantic Philanthropies, and the Harvard Business School Division of Research for funding the studies that are reported in this book. As always, I thank Gail Pesyna and the Alfred P. Sloan Foundation for their ongoing support of industry studies.

I am grateful to Susan Edgman-Levitan and Paul Cleary, founders of the Picker Institute, who taught me to assess the patient's experience from the patient's perspective, and to Dr. Jeffrey Katz of Brigham and Women's Hospital, who taught me to measure and risk-adjust patient outcomes. For ongoing insights into healthcare management and the health policy environment, I thank my colleagues at Brandeis University's Heller School, particularly Stuart Altman, Christine Bishop, Sarita Bhalotra, Jon Chilingerian, Michael Doonan, Deborah Garnick, Connie Horgan, Stan Wallack, and other members of the Schneider Institutes for Health Policy. For their thorough comments on this book, I thank my colleagues Thomas Kochan, Robert McKersie and Earll Murman at the Massachusetts Institute of Technology. I thank the Families First Health and Support Center staff with whom I have worked as a board member to improve the quality and efficiency of care for patients and the work environment for staff. I am indebted to leaders of the Service Employees International Union for including me in a working session on the U.S. healthcare system in which we sought solutions to meet the needs of multiple stakeholders.

This book is dedicated to my brother Ed Hoffer and to those at St. Luke's Roosevelt in New York City who provided care for him in his final months. I thank my friends and neighbors, brothers, sisters, and extended family, especially my parents, John and Shirley Hoffer, and my parents-in-law, Marilyn and Irwin Gittell, for their love and support over the years. Most of all, I thank my husband, Ross Gittell, and our daughters, Rose and Grace Hoffer Gittell, for sharing with me in the adventures of everyday life.

Preface

This book explores how healthcare organizations can harness the power of relationships to achieve and sustain high performance over time, building on ideas that first emerged from a study of the flight departure process. While studying American, Continental, United, and Southwest Airlines in the 1990s, I found stark differences in how pilots, flight attendants, mechanics, gate agents, ticket agents, operations agents, ramp agents, and fueling agents worked together to ensure the safe on-time departure of flights. At the time, many people in the northeastern United States, including myself, had never heard of Southwest Airlines. But I soon discovered that the way employees worked at Southwest was dramatically different from the other airlines, particularly the ways they communicated and related with one another regarding the coordination of flight departures.

I called this *relational coordination:* coordinating work through relationships of shared goals, shared knowledge, and mutual respect. With the help of colleagues at the MIT Sloan School of Management, I created a method for measuring relational coordination. With the help of colleagues in the MIT Flight Transportation Laboratory, I found ways to measure the quality and efficiency outcomes of flight departures. I discovered that relational coordination was a powerful driver of both quality and efficiency outcomes and that the high levels of relational coordination found at Southwest Airlines enabled employees to shift out the quality-efficiency frontier that constrained their competitors. Furthermore, I found Southwest had achieved its relational coordination advantage by adopting a unique set of high performance work practices. These findings were documented in *The Southwest Airlines Way: Using the Power of Relationships to Achieve High Performance*, a book that has been read by employees and managers in the airline industry and beyond.

The relevance of relational coordination is not limited to the airline industry, however. While studying the airlines, I found myself in the hospital for the first time as a patient, with my husband, giving birth to our first child. The day after I gave birth, care providers were in and out of my room constantly. One nurse would come into the room and explain something. Another would come in later and say: "I know you just heard about a, b, and c, and I want to reiterate some of that, but also to let you know about x, y, and z." After this had happened several times, I said to one nurse: "I am really impressed with your coordination. Have you been working on this?" She told me: "Yes, we've been doing total quality management." I was even more impressed, but when I asked, "When is my doctor coming?" I was told, "Oh, we don't know; they never tell us anything!"

Clearly, something was wrong with this picture. It was the same problem I had observed in the airlines. There, flight attendants, pilots, mechanics, ramp agents, and customer service agents tended to have a relatively easy time coordinating with their colleagues in their individual functions, but when it came to coordinating with colleagues in other functions, it was a different story. Whether or not they liked each other on a personal level, their lack of shared goals, shared knowledge, and mutual respect undermined the quality of their communication and created barriers to effective coordination.

At that moment, I was determined to explore relational coordination as a potential driver of healthcare performance and explore how healthcare organizations could foster it. What I discovered is summarized in this book. The bottom line is that relational coordination is indeed a powerful driver of quality and efficiency for healthcare organizations. Consistent with my experience that day in the hospital, however, physicians are often a missing piece of the puzzle. This is not due to the personal failings of physicians but rather to the way healthcare work is organized. Organizations that want to strengthen relational coordination will have to assess their work practices as they relate to all care providers, including physicians, and transform those practices that are creating barriers to relational coordination. This book will show them why and how.

Part I

Transforming Healthcare

Chapter 1

The Challenges We Face

Coordination of care, for which personnel are constantly striving but know they are not often attaining, is something of a mirage except for the most standardized of trajectories. Its attainment is something of a miracle when it does occur.[1]

We could easily become discouraged. Despite having some of the best clinicians and health policy analysts in the world, the U.S. healthcare industry is failing to deliver cost-effective quality care. The McKinsey Global Institute found recently that "even after adjusting for its higher per capita income levels, the United States spends some $477 billion more on healthcare than its peer countries" per year.[2] Meanwhile we suffer from an epidemic of medical errors that threatens our well-being—even our lives—with medical errors that cause 44,000 to 98,000 deaths annually, at a cost of $17 billion to $29 billion.[3] To add insult to injury, a growing number of our fellow citizens live with the fear that they will not have access to care when illness strikes.[4]

Some of these problems, such as the prevalence of medical errors and the costs associated with them, can be addressed in part through improved clinical training and expanded information systems. Other problems, such as lack of access and the associated costs, are likely to be addressed under our new political leadership as we finally garner the will to ensure universal access to healthcare. But many of our cost and quality problems are more fundamental and cannot be resolved by these means alone.

Indeed, the source of our cost and quality problems goes deeper into the very work processes through which healthcare is delivered. Healthcare is complex, with high levels of specialization that are driven—perhaps inevitably—by the complexity of the human body, the human mind, and the social world in which we live. The complexity and fragmentation of healthcare make coordination exceedingly difficult.[5] Patients are often required to sort their way through the system, receiving diagnoses and treatments from a fragmented, loosely connected set of providers. Patients with diabetes typically see 8 distinct physicians belonging to five distinct medical practices, and patients with coronary artery disease typically see 10 distinct physicians belonging to six distinct medical practices.[6] Even within the hospital setting, where resources presumably are brought together within a single organization to improve the coordination of their deployment, the responsibility for coordination often falls to the patient and his or her family members.

Coordination problems appear to have gotten worse rather than better over the years. The Institute of Medicine identified coordination as one of the most critical problems plaguing the U.S. healthcare system: "In the current system, care is taken to protect professional prerogatives and separate roles. The current system shows too little cooperation and teamwork. Instead, each discipline and type of organization tends to defend its authority at the expense of the total system's function."[7] A recent study by the Commonwealth Fund found that the most common quality problems reported by physicians are related to problems of coordination.[8] A physician leader at Brigham and Women's Hospital explained: "The communication line just wasn't there. We thought it was, but it wasn't. We talk to nurses every day but we aren't really communicating." Nurses tend to agree. A nurse administrator at Massachusetts General Hospital explained: "Miscommunication between the physician and the nurse is common because so many things are happening so quickly. But because patients are in and out of the hospital so quickly, it's even more important to communicate well."

Coordination is not a problem that is unique to the U.S. healthcare system. Even in countries such as England, Canada, and Belgium, whose systems for ensuring access to care are dramatically different from ours, healthcare providers are working hard to overcome fragmentation and achieve better-coordinated patient care. In Belgium, a consortium of healthcare providers has been meeting to figure out how to coordinate care between primary care, home care, and acute care, particularly for patients who are elderly or who have chronic conditions. The fragmentation they describe sounds remarkably similar to the U.S. system. Thus, it is not just the peculiar U.S. approach to healthcare financing that makes coordination such a challenge, though policy changes can certainly help, as I argue in the final chapter of this book.

Instead, coordination is a fundamental problem of work process that requires a process-level solution. Work process improvements can help organizations achieve high performance healthcare, for example, by using the reengineering, total quality improvement, and lean strategies that have helped other industries streamline and coordinate their work. Don Berwick and his colleagues at the Institute for Healthcare Improvement have transformed healthcare by redesigning work flows for hospitals and primary care practices, often starting from the patients' point of view.[9] Although these steps are useful, healthcare administrators who have engaged in work process redesign often point out that by themselves they are often not sufficient. As Robert Hendler, regional chief medical officer and vice president of clinical quality for Tenet Healthcare, explained:

> *We've been doing process improvement for several years, and we think we're on the right track. But we've tried a number of tools for process improvement, and they just don't address the relationship issues that are holding us back.*

The biggest challenge for coordinating work—how we work together and, more often, how we *fail to* work together—cannot be addressed solely through reengineering or total quality management. In complex systems such as healthcare (or airlines or auto manufacturing or professional services), work is divided into areas of functional specialization. As we will see in Chapter 2, these areas of specialization often become the basis for dividing colleagues into distinct thought worlds with distinct goals, distinct knowledge, and distinct levels of status. Although this division of labor can be a powerful source of quality and efficiency, as Adam Smith taught over 200 years ago, it can also lead to fragmentation and a breakdown of coordination.[10] Healthcare organizations benefit from the division of labor but they also suffer from the fragmentation that can result from it.

When doctors, nurses, therapists, case managers, social workers, other clinical staff, and administrative staff are connected by shared goals, shared knowledge, and mutual respect, their communication tends to be more frequent, timely, accurate, and focused on problem solving, enabling them to deliver cost-effective, high quality patient care. More often, however, these diverse providers lack shared goals, shared knowledge, and mutual respect, even when they are working with the same patients, so that their communication with one another is infrequent, delayed, inaccurate, and more often focused on finger-pointing than on problem solving. When this happens, everyone's best efforts to deliver high-quality care without wasting resources are frustrated. Relationships are an essential ingredient of any workable solution to the coordination problem because they drive the communication through which coordination occurs.

High quality relationships between care providers also require high quality collaborative labor-management relationships. Even though healthcare is the most rapidly growing union sector in the United States, it has inherited a long history of adversarial relationships between unions and employers. Yet there is an alternative. Labor-management partnerships that promote coordination and engagement among care providers have developed in a small number of healthcare settings such as Kaiser Permanente. American labor policy will need to support these types of labor-management partnerships if it is to make sustainable progress toward improving the quality and efficiency of healthcare delivery.

These insights are not new. In an earlier study of the airline industry, I found that shared goals, shared knowledge, and mutual respect—key elements of relational coordination— were at the heart of the longstanding success of Southwest Airlines, which continues to be the most successful airline in the United States and by many measures the most successful in the world. Southwest is also the most highly unionized company in the U.S. airline industry. However, unlike most others, it accepted unionization without a fight with its workers and has treated union leaders as partners from the beginning. Despite the stresses of September 11, 2001, ever-rising fuel costs, a well-compensated workforce, and constant growth, Southwest Airlines continues to have nearly the lowest unit costs in the industry (just above the unit costs of the much younger JetBlue Airways), the best on-time performance, and the lowest customer complaints of any major airline, resulting in an unbroken record of profitability for 38 years. As I demonstrated in

The Southwest Airlines Way, these impressive results are driven by the relational coordination that Southwest has built and sustained through the ups and downs of the airline industry.[11]

The good news is that healthcare organizations are waking up to the reality that they need to improve the coordination of care. Their leaders understand that cost pressures have increased the importance of achieving well-coordinated patient care. Payers have reduced the number of days they will reimburse for any specific episode of care, often by more than one-half, from 12 to 5 days for a hip replacement, for example, and are pressing for faster discharge from acute care to get patients into subacute care more quickly. As the director of patient care and quality management at the Hospital for Special Surgery explained: "Managed care companies are pushing acute care to the subacute providers to save money. They are pushing out the boundary between acute and subacute." Hospitals are able to keep patients longer than the number of reimbursed days if they choose to do so, but at a financial loss. Alternatively, payers provide a fixed fee to the hospital for a patient with a particular diagnosis so that a hospital earns money if the patient is discharged quickly and loses money if the patient stays longer. Shorter lengths of stay increase the need for coordination within the hospital setting to move patients quickly through testing and treatments to achieve the target dates of discharge.

Hospitals are also under pressure to reduce staffing costs and have been working to achieve those reductions through a combination of leaner staffing and staffing with a lower skill mix, assigning some previously high-skilled tasks to lower-skilled aides. But these changes often increase the number of handoffs, further increasing the need for coordination.

Pressures to increase quality have grown alongside of pressures to reduce costs. Hospitals compete for managed care contracts and referrals not only on the basis of their cost-effectiveness but also on the basis of the quality of care they provide, measured by their quality ratings. In addition to being accountable to patients, clinical personnel, and their professional associations for the quality of patient care, hospitals increasingly are being held accountable by accreditation boards such as Joint Commission for the Accreditation of Healthcare Organizations as well as by managed care organizations that rate hospitals on the quality of care they deliver to patients. The former chief operating officer of the Hospital for Special Surgery Lou Harris argued: "In airlines, you had downsizing but customer expectations were going down too. In healthcare, you have patient expectations going up. We are getting squeezed between patient expectations and payer pressures."

These pressures have motivated intensive efforts to improve the coordination of patient care. The chief of social work at Beth Israel Deaconess described her hospital's efforts:

> *We didn't used to focus on processes, just on individual clinician responsibility. As the screws have tightened, we've had to look at processes. We've moved from patients experiencing individuals as caregivers to experiencing systems as caregivers. Our length of stay is 4.9 or 5.0 days now, while it was 8.0 in the recent past. Because of the reduction in length of stay and downsizing, you have to substitute many more caregivers, and there's less time to build individual relationships. Handoffs have become much more critical. ... It's not just individual brilliance that matters anymore. It's a coordinated effort.*

Pressures from managed care have intensified the focus on coordination at Baylor University Medical Center. Baylor's director of case management explained:

> *As managed care has evolved in our market, the need to achieve both quality and efficiency has become greater. There's the need to show that you have high quality care and that it's cost-effective—that's the whole challenge that we face now. The market demands that in order to get business, you have to create the value. So the demand*

to think in terms of care processes is greater because you have to manage the processes to get both quality and efficiency results.

From the point of view of a social worker at Beth Israel Deaconess, coordination has helped fill the gap created by the loss of one-on-one relationships:

Caregivers can't have that totally personal relationship with the patient anymore. There isn't the time. ... Since we can't have strong one-on-one relationships with our patients, they need to feel that we are talking with each other behind their backs.

Increased coordination is particularly important from the patient's point of view, according to the CEO of Brigham and Women's Hospital:

First and foremost, improving coordination is better for the patient. That is number one—the quality and the experience that people have in the healthcare system are much improved when everything is integrated. Especially as people get more specialized in the healthcare industry, the need to assimilate and integrate and oversee all of the information about a person's healthcare has become more and more important. It becomes more important that somebody is there integrating all of the data and all of the opinions and all of the consultants' reports into a whole, because all of these things are interrelated in somebody's body and their state of mind and their state of health.

Coordination has even risen to the attention of the board in some healthcare organizations. A board member of Massachusetts General Hospital explained:

Coordination is a huge subject, the big thing. Our strategic plan is all about operations improvement. The whole business about delivering patient care. The need to be more efficient and more pleasing to patients. Outpatient links. Providing a continuum of care. ... The end result is that we hope we can live within the limits of managed care and federal government cutbacks without jeopardizing teaching and research.

Due to their tradition of independence, physicians have in some cases been the last group to recognize the need for greater interdisciplinary coordination. One physician leader explained:

We are finally beginning to recognize that healthcare is a multidisciplinary process, with the need to communicate with people inside and outside the discipline. We have to recognize that each discipline has its own track but that they have to go in the same direction.

But while many healthcare organizations are now seeking to improve the coordination of care among physicians, nurses, therapists, social workers, and other members of the care provider team, some have achieved far more success than others by investing in work practices that support relational coordination. The remainder of Part 1 will explain what relational coordination is and how it drives healthcare performance. Part 2 will describe a unique high performance work system that enables care providers to achieve relational coordination consistently every day—and show how the wrong work practices, however well intended, will have the opposite effect. Part 3 shows how relational coordination helps care providers respond resiliently to the pressures they face and how healthcare organizations can build high performance work systems *that support* relational coordination, outlining an improvement process that can help them to move in the right direction. *High Performance Healthcare* concludes by exploring powerful barriers to high performance healthcare and suggesting key elements to include in the current overhaul of U.S. health policy.

Chapter 2

What Is Relational Coordination?

In a nutshell, relational coordination is the coordination of work through relationships of shared goals, shared knowledge, and mutual respect.

The basic coordination needs for a patient include getting information from those who cared for the patient previously; sharing that information among the care providers assigned to the patient; keeping one another informed as tests, diagnoses, and interventions are performed; bringing that information together to determine the discharge time and destination; and passing that information along to those who will care for the patient after discharge. These requirements seem fairly straightforward. But as we visited nine hospitals that were working to accomplish the same goals for the same kinds of patients, we observed that the coordination of patient care, like the coordination of other complex work processes such as airline departures, is very difficult to achieve. As a result of specialization, there are multiple parties involved in the care of each patient. As the vice president of human resources at Beth Israel Deaconess pointed out:

> *Handoffs in the hospital are even more complicated than in an airline. It's not just doctors, nurses, and technicians but all the distinctions among them. We have about 9,000 employees and 4,000 titles. It is an enormously complex place, but we want care to be seamless.*

In Exhibit 2-1, the lines connecting the providers indicate that the tasks performed by the different providers were often highly interdependent, meaning that physical or informational outputs from one task were needed for the successful completion of another task. These task interdependencies resulted from the division of labor, the interdependencies among subsystems of the body, and the interdependencies between clinical interventions and the resources used to carry out those interventions.

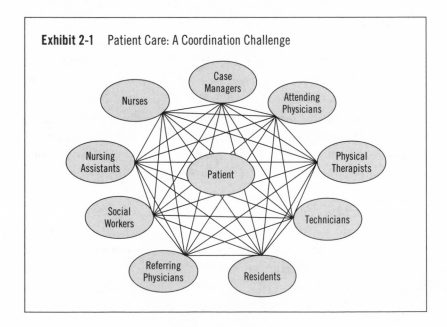

Exhibit 2-1   Patient Care: A Coordination Challenge

In addition to task interdependencies, there is often a great deal of uncertainty about how and whether a particular clinical intervention will produce a particular outcome. As a result, a patient's reaction to one intervention may give rise to the need for other interventions in a way that is difficult to predict. This uncertainty increases the challenge of delivering patient care. Moreover, the clinical information to be transmitted about patients is often complex as a result of the growth and specialization of clinical knowledge and the multitude of conditions that patients may have in combination. In addition to clinical and administrative information, patients' social information such as their family situation, values, and preferences is potentially critical to their healing. Time constraints further increase the challenge of patient care delivery. A social worker explained:

> There's a moment in time when the patient is identified as maybe needing extended care on through discharge. It's time-sensitive because you can't be too late or too early for the window. The window is determined by their functioning, based on lab tests, their temperature, whether they are ambulatory, and so on. This is a time when people are stepping over each other with overlapping responsibilities.

In light of these task interdependencies, uncertainties, and time constraints, it is all too likely that a critical insight or piece of information will fall through the cracks, resulting in a delay that creates unnecessary costs or, worse, resulting in an error that jeopardizes patient well-being.

❖ WHAT IS RELATIONAL COORDINATION?

Coordination is not just a technical process; it is also a relational process. While coordination is the management of interdependencies between *tasks*, relational coordination is the management of interdependencies between *the people* who perform those tasks.[12] Which dimensions of relational coordination deserve our attention? Should we be concerned with how frequently physicians, nurses, physical therapists, and case managers communicate with one another about patients under their common care? Should we be concerned about whether their communication is accurate, timely, and characterized by problem solving rather than blaming? Or should we be concerned about the quality of their relationships: the strength of shared goals, shared knowledge, and mutual respect?

The frequency of communication among care providers cannot be discounted, but neither can the quality of that communication. Patient care will be poorly coordinated if communication, no matter how frequent, is delayed, inaccurate or is focused on blaming. The quality of the relationships may also determine the effectiveness of the communication. Even timely, accurate information may not be heard or acted on if the recipient does not respect the source. That information also may not be heard or acted on if the recipient lacks shared knowledge or shared goals with the source and therefore misunderstands or is not motivated to act on the information. Relationships are therefore a key component of relational coordination.

In healthcare, however, as in many other industries, relationships between functions are highly fragmented. Functional boundaries are reinforced by professional identities, specialized knowledge, and status differentials. Each of these factors can pose serious obstacles to communication. Often the specialized knowledge of providers appears to divide them, acting as a barrier to communication. According to a hospital administrator:

> *Internally, there has always been a rift between the parties. Sometimes it's people's preconceived notions— this person does this and this but doesn't do this. Not everyone has the same skills, but they are still integral partners.*

In addition to being divided by their specialized knowledge and training, care providers are also divided by status differences. Though some professional organizations have fought to equalize status between providers, differences in status continue to divide the parties who care for patients. In the pecking order among physicians, specialists are considered superior to primary care physicians, cardiologists are considered superior to cardiac surgeons, and cardiac surgeons are considered superior to orthopedic surgeons. These differences are even stronger between physicians and nonphysicians. Physicians are considered superior to therapists, who are superior to nurses, who are superior to social workers, who are superior to housekeeping personnel. One administrator described how these status differences play out in her hospital:

> *Medicine has a hierarchical structure. We will break it down somewhat but never completely. [The chief of orthopedics here] may respect his physical therapists, because they measure outcomes. But physical therapists are on a higher plateau to him than the nurses are.*

According to a nurse at Massachusetts General Hospital:

> *Our culture attracts physicians with big reputations and big egos. This is very much a physician-run institution ... You really have to be a strong person and provide a role model for the younger ones ... to get the newest members of our staff to stand up and tell the doctors what they need to hear.*

Exhibit 2-2 illustrates how these dimensions of relational coordination influence one another for better or for worse.

❖ THE POWER OF RELATIONSHIPS

The concept of relational coordination provides new insights into the importance of relationships for coordinating work.[13] Scholars such as Karl Weick, Karlene Roberts, Samer Faraj, and

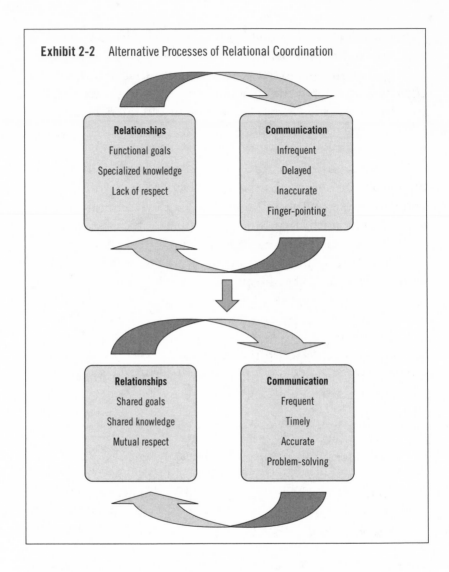

Exhibit 2-2   Alternative Processes of Relational Coordination

Relationships
Functional goals
Specialized knowledge
Lack of respect

Communication
Infrequent
Delayed
Inaccurate
Finger-pointing

Relationships
Shared goals
Shared knowledge
Mutual respect

Communication
Frequent
Timely
Accurate
Problem-solving

Beth Bechky have also provided important insights into the central role that relationships play in coordinating work.[14] However, relationships do more than facilitate the coordination of work. The Positive Organizational Scholarship movement envisions positive relationships as being central to individual and organizational well-being. One of founders of that movement, Jane Dutton, has written that:

High quality connections are marked by mutual positive regard, trust and active engagement on both sides. In a high quality connection, people feel more engaged, more open, more competent. They feel more alive. High quality connections can have a profound impact on both individuals and entire organizations.[15]

Feminist scholars such as Jean Baker Miller and Joyce Fletcher have argued that people's identities are socially constructed through their relationships with others and therefore neither individual identity nor the way people work together can be understood fully without understanding these relationships.[16] Applying these concepts to healthcare, Dana Safran, Thomas Inui and other members of the Relationship-Centered Care Network have proposed four principles: (1) Relationships in healthcare should include the personhood of the participants, (2) affect and emotion are important components of those relationships, (3) all healthcare relationships occur in the context of reciprocal influence, and (4) the formation and maintenance of genuine relationships in healthcare are morally valuable.[17]

There are clearly some common threads between relational coordination and these other perspectives. Like the other perspectives, relational coordination recognizes that relationships are central to our identities: They shape who we are. Relationships are therefore central for creating collective identity in an organization and for enabling work to be coordinated effectively. But relational coordination differs by focusing on relationships between roles rather than between specific individuals.[18] These relationships can extend beyond the roles to connect the individual participants and often they do so over time. The distinctiveness of role-based relationships, however, is that they are anchored in the roles rather than in the individual participants. This feature allows for the interchangeability of employees, allowing employees to come and go as needed to meet their obligations outside of work. In addition, role-based relationships help foster the systems thinking that organizational learning expert Peter Senge has described, enabling participants to carry out their own individual roles with an awareness of the larger process of which they are part.[19]

❖ DIFFERENCES IN RELATIONAL COORDINATION BETWEEN ORGANIZATIONS AND BETWEEN ROLES

Relational coordination varies greatly between organizations. Some organizations have a strong, robust process of relational coordination, whereas others have a weaker, more fragmented process of relational coordination. To uncover these differences, relational coordination can be measured by using the seven survey questions shown in Exhibit 2-3. We used these questions in a study of nine surgical units in nine different hospitals to survey physicians, nurses, physical therapists, case managers, and social workers about their ties with one another. This study and the methodology for measuring relational coordination will be described in Chapter 3. For now, note the differences

---

Exhibit 2-3 Relational Coordination Survey Items

Relationships

Shared Goals	Do people in these groups have the same work goals as you?
Shared Knowledge	How much do people in each of these groups know about your job?
Mutual Respect	How much respect do you get from the people in each of these groups?

Communication

Frequent Communication	How often do you communicate with people in each of these groups?
Timely Communication	Do the people in these groups communicate with you in a timely way?
Accurate Communication	Do the people in these groups communicate with you in an accurate way?
Problem-Solving Communication	When there is a problem, do the people in these groups try to solve the problem or try to determine whose fault it was?

in the strength of relational coordination in the nine different hospitals, as shown in Exhibit 2-4. Relational coordination at Hospital 6 is rated 4.22 on a five-point scale, and at Hospital 2 it is rated 3.84. As we will see in Chapter 3, these differences in relational coordination result in substantial differences in the quality and efficiency of patient care.

Ideally, relational coordination should include all participants in the key roles involved in patient care; otherwise, some critical insight or piece of information is likely to fall through the cracks, with negative effects on quality and efficiency. However, even organizations with high levels of relational coordination tend to have some weak links. Looking at surgical care at the same nine hospitals, we compared the strength of relational coordination between different care provider functions. Exhibit 2-5 shows the results for surgical care. Exhibit 2-6 shows similar results from a study of medical care.

Interestingly, physicians tend to be the weakest link in the coordination of both surgical care and medical care. Physicians' relational coordination with the rest of the care provider team tends to be systematically weaker than it is for any other care provider discipline despite the fact that physicians play a central role in delivering patient care. This is due in part to

Exhibit 2-4   Differences in Relational Coordination between Surgical Units*

	Hosp. 1	Hosp. 2	Hosp. 3	Hosp. 4	Hosp. 5	Hosp. 6	Hosp. 7	Hosp. 8	Hosp. 9
Relational Coordination	3.88	3.84	3.91	4.17	4.13	4.22	4.02	4.06	4.04
Shared Goals	4.15	4.11	4.14	4.29	4.21	4.34	4.13	4.22	4.16
Shared Knowledge	3.65	3.79	3.83	3.99	3.99	4.16	3.93	3.77	3.83
Mutual Respect	3.69	3.80	3.88	3.96	3.73	4.02	3.90	3.77	3.70
Frequent Communication	3.64	3.63	3.83	4.13	4.03	3.97	3.78	3.94	3.67
Timely Communication	3.92	3.74	3.85	4.22	4.45	4.35	4.06	4.14	4.09
Accurate Communication	4.19	3.96	3.99	4.41	4.41	4.37	4.24	4.33	4.26
Problem-Solving Communication	3.93	3.81	3.85	4.23	4.10	4.26	4.00	4.11	4.15

* This exhibit is discussed in the "Notes for Exhibits" chapter beginning on page 315.

Exhibit 2-5 Differences in Relational Coordination between Functions: Surgical Care

	Relational Coordination Reported With				
	Physicians	Nurses	Physical Therapists	Case Managers	Social Workers
Physicians	3.82	3.94	4.03	3.75	3.70
Nurses	3.81	4.48	4.27	4.03	3.92
Physical Therapists	3.85	4.25	4.71	4.06	3.94
Case Managers	3.83	4.36	4.43	4.45	4.37
Social Workers	3.93	4.01	4.03	4.17	4.36
All	3.85	4.21	4.29	4.09	4.06

Exhibit 2-6 Differences in Relational Coordination between Functions: Medical Care

	Relational Coordination Reported With				
	Physicians	Residents	Nurses	Therapists	Case Managers
Nurses	3.77	3.93	4.35	3.86	4.05
Therapists	2.36	2.46	3.97	4.28	3.74
Case Managers	3.65	3.25	4.23	3.17	4.52
All	3.26	3.21	4.18	3.77	4.10

physician job design. Physicians on surgical units spend much of their time in the operating room, away from the rest of the patient care team, and physicians on medical units spend much of their time in their private practices, coming to the hospital as needed to treat their patients. But there are other factors involved as well. This book will show how to design a high performance work system that strengthens relational coordination across all members of the care provider team, *including* the physician.

❖ BOTTOM LINE

Simply put, relational coordination is the coordination of work through relationships of shared goals, shared knowledge, and mutual respect. Part 2 of this book will explore how healthcare organizations can build high performance work systems that foster relational coordination among all members of the care provider team, including physicians. But first let us examine what's at stake. Why does it matter whether healthcare organizations succeed in creating high levels of relational coordination among their care providers?

Chapter 3

How Relational Coordination Drives Quality and Efficiency Performance

A fundamental process improvement such as relational coordination enables organizations to improve both cost and quality outcomes, allowing simultaneous excellence along both dimensions. When relational coordination is improved, organizations can shift out the quality-efficiency frontier, thereby achieving higher performance on both dimensions.

In a time of enormous stress for the healthcare system, with so many unmet or poorly met needs, why should we care about something as ephemeral as relational coordination? It would be nice to have positive working relationships, but perhaps that is a luxury we can't afford until we resolve the more urgent problems of poor quality and wasted resources that plague the system.

To the contrary, we propose that investments in relational coordination—coordination that occurs through high quality communication supported by relationships of shared goals, shared knowledge, and mutual respect—contribute substantially to overcoming these urgent problems. The process of relational coordination discussed in Chapter 2 results in fewer missed signals among colleagues who work in different areas of functional expertise. As a result, there is more consistent communication with the patient and thus fewer chances for errors to occur, driving quality performance in a positive direction. Relational coordination also reduces the time spent carrying out redundant communication, searching for missing information, and waiting to hear from colleagues, allowing healthcare organizations to utilize all their resources more productively and driving efficiency performance in an upward direction. Let's take a look at four very different studies that show how relational coordination matters for surgical performance, medical performance, long-term care performance, and—outside the healthcare context—airline performance.

❖ RELATIONAL COORDINATION AND SURGICAL PERFORMANCE

We measured relational coordination and performance in nine hospitals to find out whether relational coordination makes a difference for surgical performance.[20] Data were collected in the orthopedic department of each hospital, focusing specifically on the care of joint replacement surgical patients. Joint replacement is a relatively high-volume, high-revenue surgical procedure that has been one of the early targets for hospital-based process improvement efforts because of its attractiveness from a revenue standpoint and because it is relatively well understood from a clinical standpoint. Clearly, the coordination needs for this surgical procedure are more straightforward than they are for complex medical cases. Still, even for this fairly straightforward surgical procedure, relational coordination among physicians, nurses, physical therapists, social workers, and case managers was a significant and substantial driver of both quality and efficiency performance.

All nine hospitals were nonprofit. They were in three different urban areas—Boston, New York City, and Dallas—and were three different types of hospitals—general, specialty, and specialty institutes within general hospitals. In Boston, they included Massachusetts General Hospital, Brigham and Women's Hospital, Beth Israel Deaconess, and New England Baptist. In New York City, they were the Hospital for Special Surgery, the Hospital for Joint Diseases, and Beth Israel Medical Center. In the Dallas area, they were Baylor University Medical Center and Presbyterian Plano. Managed care penetration, measured at the state level, varied from 22 percent in Texas to 38 percent in New York to 55 percent in Massachusetts.[21]

In our interviews, we observed differences among hospitals in the frequency and quality of communication among physicians, nurses, social workers, therapists, case managers, and others regarding patients under their common care. In some hospitals, care providers reported that their communication with care providers in other disciplines was accurate, timely, and focused on problem solving when things went wrong. In others, the dominant theme was a lack of timely, accurate communication and a tendency toward blame seeking and blame avoidance when things went wrong. There also seemed to be differences in the quality of relationships between the care providers working with the same patients: the extent to which relationships were characterized by shared goals, shared knowledge, and mutual respect as opposed to strictly functional goals, specialized knowledge, and lack of respect.

Relational Coordination

To get a systematic measure of relational coordination, we conducted a survey in which we asked all physicians, nurses, physical therapists, social workers, and case managers in each hospital who were involved with joint replacement patients about their communication and relationships with one another regarding the care of those patients.[22] All were asked to answer questions about the frequency, timeliness, and problem-solving focus of communication and the strength of shared goals, shared knowledge, and mutual respect they experienced with each of the key disciplines involved in caring for joint replacement patients.[23]

Surgical Performance

We measured surgical performance along two dimensions: quality of care and efficiency of care. We surveyed patients six weeks after their discharge from the hospital about the quality of care they received.[24] Patient-perceived quality of care traditionally was not considered a relevant outcome in healthcare settings. However, "as the orientation to healthcare began shifting from scientific mandates and medical techniques to markets and the more human side of healthcare…, patient satisfaction has become an important dimension of the quality of care."[25] The importance of patient satisfaction became evident through clinical work on patient-centered care,[26] and patient satisfaction has continued to grow in importance as a dimension of healthcare quality.[27]

The clinical goals of joint replacement surgery are to reduce joint pain and increase the mobility of the patient. Thus, quality performance includes not only the patient's assessment of the quality of care but also the patient's assessment of his or her joint pain and mobility after surgery compared with before.[28] Efficiency performance was measured as the number of days a patient spent in acute care.[29] Control variables were included to factor out the effects of differences in patient age, health condition, type of surgery (hip versus knee), psychological well-being, race, gender, marital status, and the volume of joint replacements performed by the group in the last six months on these measures of performance.[30]

❖ JOB SATISFACTION

In addition to improving performance outcomes, relational coordination may improve job satisfaction for staff members. We know that having the necessary resources to accomplish one's work is an important source of job satisfaction. Relational coordination is a form of organizational social capital, an asset that makes it easier to access the resources needed to accomplish one's work.[31] As a result of this instrumental benefit of relational coordination, we expected that relational coordination would be positively associated with job satisfaction.

There is a second way in which relational coordination can be expected to increase job satisfaction. It is known from organizational psychology that high quality relationships are a source of well-being for people at work.[32] Jane Dutton and Emily Heaphy defined a high quality connection as one that is life-giving and a low quality connection as one that is life-depleting.[33] High quality connections take many forms, but they have in common a keen awareness of and attunement to the needs of the other and thus are energizing to the individuals involved in them. The energizing nature of high quality connections comes from the recognition and validation of one's self by others. These high quality connections tend to create a positive cycle that is generative of other high quality connections, just as low quality connections tend to create a negative cycle that is generative of other low quality connections. We expected that the positive relationships that underpin relational coordination (shared goals, shared knowledge, and mutual respect) would lead to higher levels of job satisfaction. Because of the instrumental and intrinsic benefits of connecting with others, we expected that relational coordination would contribute positively to job satisfaction and that its absence would diminish job satisfaction.

To measure job satisfaction of physicians, nurses, physical therapists, case managers and social workers, we used a one-item measure of job satisfaction on the same survey described above, asking "Overall, how satisfied are you with your job?" We expected that relational coordination would affect job satisfaction in a very broad sense, making the measure of overall job satisfaction the most appropriate one for this analysis.[34]

❖ WHAT WE FOUND

All of the communication and relationship components of relational coordination were strongly interrelated with each other.[35] In addition, there were significant differences between the hospitals on all aspects of relational coordination,[36] and on all aspects of patient care performance.[37]

Using statistical techniques to account for patient differences, [38] we found that relational coordination significantly improves surgical performance. Relational coordination among care providers enables shorter hospital stays, higher levels of patient-perceived quality of care, and improved clinical outcomes. To illustrate, doubling relational coordination among front line care providers enables a 33 percent reduction in the length of hospital stays and a 26 percent increase in the quality of service that patients receive. That same increase in relational coordination contributes to an 8 percent increase in postoperative freedom from pain and a 6 percent increase in postoperative mobility (the two key clinical outcomes of joint replacement surgery). Some of these performance effects of relational coordination are quite large and statistically significant. This means that healthcare organizations can be confident of achieving improved performance results if they achieve an increase in relational coordination.[39] Exhibit 3-1 shows these statistical results.

Exhibit 3-1   Impact of Relational Coordination on Surgical Performance†

	Surgical Performance				
	Length of Stay	Patient Satisfaction	Postoperative Freedom from Pain	Postoperative Mobility	Surgical Performance Index
Relational Coordination	−.33 ***	.26 ***	.08 *	.06+	.27 ***
Patient Age	−.02	.00	−.01	−.04	.01
Comorbidities	.09	.07 *	−.01	−.04	−.05
Preoperative Status	.03	−.01	.20 ***	.28 ***	.16 ***
Surgical Procedure	.01	.11 **	.22 ***	.10 **	.16 ***
Psychological Well-Being	−.08 *	.14 **	.41 ***	.41 ***	.40 ***
Surgical Volume	.11 **	.10 *	.06 +	.03	.05
R-squared	.82	.63	.50	.22	.83

† This exhibit is discussed in the "Notes for Exhibits" chapter beginning on page 315.

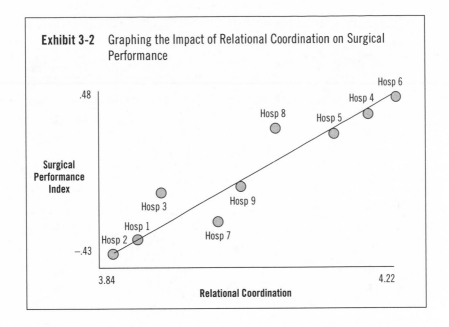

Exhibit 3-2 Graphing the Impact of Relational Coordination on Surgical Performance

There is a simpler, more graphic way to observe the overall effects of relational coordination on surgical performance. Efficiency and quality measures were adjusted for differences in patient characteristics then combined into a single measure of surgical performance. Overall surgical performance was plotted for each of the nine hospitals against relational coordination. Exhibit 3-2 illustrates the positive impact of relational coordination on surgical performance.

Consistent with our expectations, we also found that relational coordination is a significant predictor of care provider job satisfaction. Exhibit 3-3 shows that, other things equal, physicians and residents have a significantly higher baseline level of job satisfaction than nurses, but doubling relational coordination contributes to a 17 percent increase in care provider job satisfaction. Care provider job satisfaction further contributes to overall performance outcomes for surgical patients, with relational coordination increasing performance by 31 percent and job satisfaction increasing performance by an additional 9 percent. These results suggest that relational coordination is

Exhibit 3-3   Relational Coordination Increases Job Satisfaction, Further Enhancing Surgical Performance[†]

	Job Satisfaction		Surgical Performance Index	
Relational Coordination	.17 *	Relational Coordination	.27 ***	.31 ***
		Job Satisfaction		.09 *
Physician	.36 ***	Patient Age	.01	.01
Resident	.28 ***	Comorbidities	−.05	−.04
Physical Therapist	.09	Preoperative Status	.16 ***	.16 ***
Case Manager	.00	Surgical Procedure	.16 ***	.17 ***
Social Worker	.03	Psychological Well-Being	.40 ***	.41 ***
Surgical Volume	−.04	Surgical Volume	.05	.04
R-squared	.54	R-squared	.83	.90

† This exhibit is discussed in the "Notes for Exhibits" chapter beginning on page 315.

indeed a win-win solution—increasing both quality and efficiency outcomes for patients, and at the same time, improving job satisfaction for the care providers themselves. Exhibit 3-4 illustrates this dual impact of relational coordination on outcomes for patients and providers.

❖ RELATIONAL COORDINATION AND MEDICAL PERFORMANCE

The fact that relational coordination improves surgical performance does not mean that it will help improve performance in other areas, such as medical units. Medical units typically have patients with a greater variety of needs, and individual patients tend to be more complex, with a greater number of comorbid conditions compared with the relatively healthy patients who receive elective surgeries such as joint replacement. As a result of these challenges on medical units, relational coordination

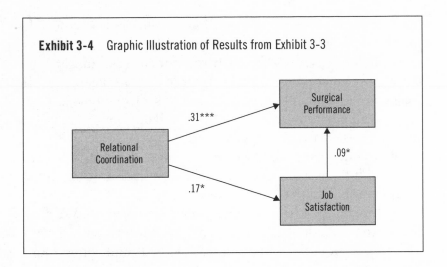

Exhibit 3-4   Graphic Illustration of Results from Exhibit 3-3

may be even more important than it is on surgical units for achieving desired outcomes.

To find out, we conducted a study at Newton-Wellesley Hospital in Boston, measuring relational coordination for each individual patient in our sample rather than for the unit as a whole.[40] We measured relational coordination for 335 patients, about half of all patients who were cared for on the medical unit over the three-month period from April 2003 to June 2003. We measured patient characteristics and outcomes for all 6,686 patients with complete data who were cared for on the medical unit from July 2001 to June 2003. A large sample of patients is useful for predicting patient outcomes, particularly when the patient population is as varied as it is on a medical unit, to distinguish the effects of organizational factors from the effects of individual patient characteristics.

Relational Coordination

For each patient in this sample, we surveyed each of the nurses, case managers, and therapists responsible for his or her care, asking detailed questions about coordination with other members of the care team, including the physician responsible for the patient (the attending physician).[41] Relational coordination was measured for each respondent regarding his or her work with each individual patient in the sample, including frequency of communication, timeliness of communication, accuracy of communication, problem-solving communication, shared goals, shared knowledge, and mutual respect with the other providers assigned to that team. The seven measures were averaged into an index of relational coordination.[42] Relational coordination for the patient care team varied significantly depending on the identity of the attending physician. We took the average relational coordination measure associated with each physician in this sample of 335 patients and applied it to all the patients that physician cared for in the larger sample of 6,686 patients to estimate the level of relational coordination for every patient in the larger sample.

Medical Performance

Medical performance included two efficiency outcomes and three quality outcomes. Efficiency outcomes were excess length of stay in the hospital and total costs of stay in the hospital.[43] Quality outcomes were patient readmission to the hospital within 7 days, patient readmission to the hospital within 30 days, and patient mortality while in the hospital. Patient readmissions are a common measure of quality performance on medical units, indicating the possibility that an error occurred during hospitalization or that a patient was discharged prematurely.[44] To serve as reliable measures, all quality and efficiency measures were risk-adjusted in our models.

Several control variables were used in this study to risk-adjust performance outcomes. Control variables included patient severity of illness, patient age, and patient gender, along with the number of days a patient stayed in the intensive care unit (ICU) during his or her stay. Severity of illness was expected to increase patient length of stay, total cost of stay, and likelihood of readmission and mortality.[45] Patient age and number of days in the ICU were expected to increase costs, length of stay, and likelihood of readmission and mortality.

What We Found

We found that higher levels of relational coordination produced more efficient medical care by significantly reducing both the patient's length of stay and the total cost of hospitalization per patient. For every one-point increase in relational coordination among the different providers caring for a patient, that patient's length of stay was reduced by two-thirds of a day and the cost of his or her hospital stay was reduced by about $670. Relational coordination also produced better-quality outcomes. For every one-point increase in relational coordination among the providers caring for a patient, that patient's likelihood of readmission within 7 days was reduced by 60 percent and his or her likelihood of readmission within 30 days was reduced by 69 percent. These performance effects of relational coordination are large and statistically significant. This means that healthcare organizations can be confident of achieving improved performance results if they achieve an increase in relational coordination.[46] The likelihood of mortality did not appear to be affected by relational coordination. Exhibit 3-5 shows statistical results from this study.

❖ RELATIONAL COORDINATION AND LONG-TERM CARE PERFORMANCE[47]

In recent years, Susan Eaton and other scholars who advocate for the elderly have called for a renewed focus on quality of life in addition to clinical outcomes. Specifically, they have asked nursing homes to deliver care that is more holistic and resident-centered and to become regenerative communities that nurture the capabilities of their residents rather than simply attend to their physical decline.[48] The concept of resident-centered care is based on the notion that all actions should respond to resident needs in a coordinated way, organized around horizontal,

Exhibit 3-5 Impact of Relational Coordination on Medical Performance†

	Length of Stay	Total Costs	Medical Performance		
			Readmit within 7 Days	Readmit within 30 Days	Mortality
Relational Coordination	−.66 ***	671 **	−.60 *	−.69 **	−.20
Patient Age	−.01 ***	−22 ***	.01 +	.01 **	.05 ***
Patient Risk Factors	.76 ***	1196 ***	.12 ***	.12 ***	8.49 ***
Patient Gender	.15	52	.01	−.13 +	.18
ICU Days	.66 ***	2502 ***	−.10 *	−.11 **	−.12
R-squared	.33	.55	NA	NA	NA
Chi-squared	NA	NA	.0000	.0000	.0000

† This exhibit is discussed in the "Notes for Exhibits" chapter beginning on page 315.

cross-cutting work processes rather than around the functions in which employees work. Relational coordination is therefore potentially of great importance for achieving this resident-centered vision of elder care.

Consider the following facts about long-term care. Although nursing aides deliver much of the direct care in nursing homes through one-on-one relationships with residents, they do not and cannot deliver all the care. There is *task interdependence* between them and the other staff members who work with the same residents, including other nursing aides, nurses, housekeeping staff, dietary staff, activities staff, social workers, physical therapists, and occupational and speech therapists. As in other service settings, these interdependencies are not the simple sequential handoffs found on production lines but are iterative, requiring feedback among staff as new information emerges regarding a specific resident. There is *uncertainty* about the physical and mental conditions of elderly residents, which can vary from day to day in unpredictable ways, requiring staff members to be highly attentive to the residents and to one another so that they can respond appropriately and collectively. Finally, there are *time constraints* caused by residents' need for assistance to eat, use the bathroom, get dressed, perform basic daily functions, cope with the emotional distress associated with aging and loss, and, ideally, experience growth through the final phase of human development. Failure to respond to resident needs in a timely way can be expected to lead to negative clinical outcomes such as urinary tract infections, pressure sores, dehydration, and depression as well as reduced quality of life. We therefore should expect relational coordination among nursing home staff to improve residents' quality outcomes by improving the exchange of information relevant to the care of a resident.

This rationale seems compelling. To find out whether relational coordination matters for long-term care performance, we studied 15 nursing homes in the state of Massachusetts, including 5 for-profits and 10 nonprofits.

Relational Coordination

To measure relational coordination, we adapted our previously validated survey to the long-term care setting by changing it in three ways. First, because of the time constraints nursing home staff members face, we reduced the number of relational coordination questions from seven to five, dropping questions about timely and accurate communication. By keeping two of the four communication dimensions and keeping all the relationship dimensions, we hoped to capture the heart of the relational coordination construct. In addition, we simplified the remaining questions because of the low educational levels of most respondents in our sample while retaining the meaning of the original questions to the greatest extent possible. Finally, the items were scored on a four-point rather than a five-point scale, again for the purpose of simplification because of the low educational levels of our respondents.

We attempted to survey all nursing aides working on the same two target units in each of the 15 facilities on the day the survey was administered. The survey was translated into Spanish and Haitian Creole because of the prevalence of those languages among the nursing home aides in participating facilities and was administered in paper and pencil form, with an optional accompanying audiotape of the survey in each of the three languages. Nursing aides were given a small monetary incentive for their participation. We received responses from 252 of the 255 nursing aides we attempted to survey, for a response rate of 99 percent. Using the survey responses, we created an index of relational coordination between nursing aides and each of the other job functions studied: nurses, housekeepers, and dietary staff.[49]

Long-Term Care Performance

We measured long-term care performance in two ways: the quality of life as perceived by the residents and the job satisfaction of the nursing aides, the care providers with the greatest amount of day-to-day contact with the residents. To measure resident quality of life, we approached five residents from each of the two target units in the 15 participating facilities to complete a verbal survey.[50] We surveyed those residents in person in the comfort of their rooms, asking them questions about their quality of life. We then chose 14 of the items that covered seven key areas identified by previous researchers as being of particular importance to nursing home residents: privacy, spiritual well-being, meaningful activity, food enjoyment, relationships, individuality, and global quality of life.[51] We received responses from 105 of 123 eligible residents approached, for a response rate of 85 percent.

Job Satisfaction

In addition to improving performance outcomes, relational coordination may improve job satisfaction for staff members due to its instrumental and psychological benefits, as explained above. To measure the job satisfaction of nursing aides, we used a one-item measure of job satisfaction from the same nursing aide survey described above, asking, "Overall, how satisfied are you with your job?" We expected that relational coordination would affect job satisfaction in a very broad sense, making the measure of overall job satisfaction the most appropriate one for this analysis.[52]

What We Found

Using statistical techniques to account for resident and employee differences,[53] we found that relational coordination significantly improves long-term care performance. Relational coordination between nursing aides and other functions improves the quality of life for residents. To illustrate, a doubling of relational coordination between nursing aides and other functions produced a 37 percent improvement in resident quality of life. Relational coordination between nursing aides and other functions also improved job satisfaction for nursing aides. To illustrate, a doubling of relational coordination between nursing aides and other functions was associated with a 30 percent increase in job satisfaction for nursing aides.

These performance effects of relational coordination are large and statistically significant. This means that healthcare organizations can be confident of achieving improved performance results if they achieve an increase in relational coordination.[54] Exhibit 3-6 shows these statistical results.

❖ RELATIONAL COORDINATION AND AIRLINE PERFORMANCE[55]

Looking beyond healthcare, we find that relational coordination is a more universal dynamic that also drives performance in other settings. In an earlier study of the airline industry that was focused on the flight departure process, I explored the impact of relational coordination on key outcomes of interest for struggling airlines. Like the healthcare industry, the airline industry is increasingly under pressure to achieve cost savings while delivering higher quality more reliable service. Airlines face consumers who are increasingly willing and able to shop for the cheapest available fare; even corporate travel departments have become increasingly price-sensitive since the recession of the early 1990s.

Exhibit 3-6   Impact of Relational Coordination on Long-Term Care Performance†

	Long-Term Care Performance		
	Resident Quality of Life		Nursing Aide Job Satisfaction
Relational Coordination	.37 **	Relational Coordination	.30 ***
Resident Age	−.13	Nursing Aide Age	.04
Resident Tenure	.16	Nursing Aide Tenure	−.04
Resident Gender (female = 1)	.19 +	Nursing Aide Gender (female = 1)	−.01
Nursing Aide Language (English = 1)	.23	Nursing Aide Language (English = 1)	−.07
Facility Size	.12	Facility Size	−.00
Facility Ownership (nonprofit = 1)	.21	Facility Ownership (nonprofit = 1)	−.02
R-squared	.24	R-squared	.31

† This exhibit is discussed in the "Notes for Exhibits" chapter beginning on page 315.

The airline study included two sites from Southwest Airlines, two from Continental, two from American, and two from United. The sites included some that were considered high performers and some that were considered troubled, particularly the second site at Southwest, which was situated in Los Angeles and was suffering greatly at the time from rapid rates of growth, high employee turnover, and managerial inexperience. A third site from United that was considered very promising was then included: the launch site for the United Shuttle, which was designed to counter Southwest's incursions into the California market.

Relational Coordination

At each of the nine sites, employees from five functional groups were surveyed—ticketing agents, gate agents, baggage transfer agents, ramp agents, and operations agents—about their communication and relationships with one another and with pilots, flight attendants, mechanics, caterers, cabin cleaners, fuelers, and cargo agents. The survey questions reflected the six original dimensions of relational coordination: the frequency, timeliness, and problem-solving focus of communication among participants and the degree to which their relationships were characterized by shared goals, shared knowledge, and mutual respect. Four hundred surveys were administered, with a response rate of 89 percent, yielding 354 surveys. From the responses, an index of relational coordination was created.[56]

Flight Departure Performance

Quality was measured in three ways: customer complaints, mishandled bags, and late arrivals. These are the same measures that are tracked on a monthly basis by the U.S. Department of Transportation. In addition, efficiency was measured in two ways: gate time per departure and staff time per passenger.[57] Of course, there are other factors besides coordination that affect quality and efficiency performance. To capture those product characteristics, average length of flight, number of passengers per flight, tons of cargo per flight, and percentage of passengers connecting were measured.[58] Number of flights per day at a site was included to capture the potential effects of operational scale.

What We Found

There were substantial differences in overall levels of relational coordination from one site to another, even within the same airline. Among the nine sites in the study, Southwest's Chicago site had the highest overall level of relational coordination. The next highest level of relational coordination was found at the United Shuttle's Los Angeles site. Southwest's Los Angeles site ranked third. Because that site deliberately was chosen as one that was struggling with growth issues at the time, this was not surprising. Continental, United, and American Airlines each had one site with moderately high levels of relational coordination, and each also had one site with low levels of relational coordination.[59] In addition to significant differences in relational coordination across the nine sites, there were significant differences in product characteristics and performance.[60]

Using statistical techniques to account for the effects of product differences,[61] relational coordination was found to have a significant impact on the performance of the flight departure process. Relational coordination enabled shorter turnaround times, greater employee productivity, fewer customer complaints, fewer lost bags, and fewer flight delays. A doubling of relational coordination enabled a 21 percent reduction in turnaround time and a 42 percent increase in employee productivity. The same increase in relational coordination contributed to a 64 percent decrease in customer complaints, a 31 percent decrease in lost baggage, and a 50 percent decrease in flight delays. These performance effects of relational coordination are large and statistically significant. This means that healthcare organizations can be confident of achieving improved performance results if they achieve an increase in relational coordination.[62] Exhibit 3-7 shows these statistical results.

There is a simpler, more graphic way to observe the overall performance effects of relational coordination. After efficiency and quality measures were adjusted for product differences, they were combined into a single measure of performance. Overall performance for each of the nine sites then was plotted against relational coordination. Exhibit 3-8 shows a positive impact of relational coordination on flight departure performance.

Exhibit 3-7   Impact of Relational Coordination on Airline Performance†

| | Airline Performance | | | | |
	Turnaround Time	Staff Time per Passenger	Customer Complaints	Lost Bags	Late Arrivals
Relational Coordination	−.22 ***	−.46 ***	−.49 ***	−.29 *	−.48 **
Flights/Day	−.19 ***	−.37 ***	−.30 ***	0.13	−.22 +
Flight Length, Passengers, and Cargo	.79 ***	.45 ***	.13	0.12	−.54 **
Passenger Connections	.12 **	.19 **	.09	.13	.00
R-squared	.94	.79	.63	.18	.19

† This exhibit is discussed in the "Notes for Exhibits" chapter beginning on page 315.

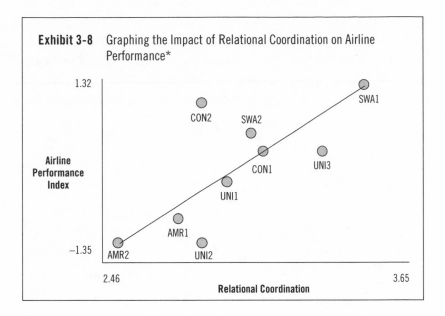

Exhibit 3-8   Graphing the Impact of Relational Coordination on Airline Performance*

❖ BOTTOM LINE

What do these results tell us? Although every organization faces trade-offs between quality and efficiency, a fundamental process improvement such as relational coordination enables organizations to improve quality *and* efficiency outcomes, allowing simultaneous excellence along both dimensions. When relational coordination is improved, organizations can shift out the quality-efficiency frontier, achieving higher performance on both dimensions. Consider the notion of service breakthroughs introduced by James Heskett, Earl Sasser, and Christopher Hart.[63] Breakthrough services are services that better meet the customer's need at a lower cost. They have the potential to transform an entire industry, as has been seen in the case of Southwest Airlines and the airline industry. There are multiple paths for achieving service breakthroughs, but often they involve a fundamental process improvement such as relational coordination. What is more, we have found evidence that relational coordination increases job satisfaction for care providers

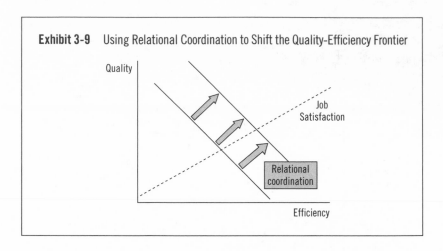

Exhibit 3-9 Using Relational Coordination to Shift the Quality-Efficiency Frontier

themselves. See Exhibit 3-9 for an illustration of how relational coordination shifts out the quality–efficiency–job satisfaction frontier.

Although coordination is a technical activity that benefits from process mapping, it is not only a technical activity. It is also a relational activity that requires shared goals, shared knowledge, and mutual respect among key participants in order to be carried out reliably. Moreover, relationships are not just personally gratifying. Because they provide one of the greatest sources of information-processing capacity ever discovered, relationships are immensely practical in settings, such as healthcare, that are characterized by high information-processing demands. It is therefore no surprise that we have found relational coordination to be such a powerful driver of high quality, efficient patient care as well as providing a source of job satisfaction for care providers themselves.

More generally, under what conditions does relational coordination matter for performance? Relational coordination is particularly important for achieving performance in any setting with high information-processing demands driven by characteristics such as task interdependence, uncertainty, and time constraints.[64] Why? When task interdependence is low, participants can carry out their work in a relatively autonomous way with little regard for other participants in the work process. However, when task interdependence is high, participants must be aware of and responsive to the actions that are taken by other participants. When uncertainty is low, responses and handoffs can be preplanned, requiring little need for coordinated responses to changing conditions. However, when uncertainty is high, participants must be sensitive not only to changes that affect their own tasks but also to changes that affect the tasks of others with whom they are interdependent. Time constraints exacerbate the effects of both interdependence and uncertainty, leaving little slack in the system and placing a premium on responsiveness. Many industries are increasingly characterized by task interdependence, uncertainty, and time constraints, suggesting that relational coordination may be increasingly relevant for achieving high performance in a wide array of industry settings.

Now we face a question that is daunting indeed: In light of the powerful obstacles that exist in the healthcare industry, how can healthcare organizations achieve higher levels of relational coordination? The answer to this question can be found in Part II.

Part II

Building a High Performance Work System

Chapter 4

A Different Kind of High Performance Work System

The high performance work system discussed in this book is different because it fosters the critical missing ingredient that other high performance work systems tend to neglect: the social capital or relationships among employees that enable them to coordinate their work with one another.[65]

We now understand the challenges of coordinating patient care and realize that relational coordination among care providers is a powerful tool for shifting out the quality–efficiency–job satisfaction frontier, enabling healthcare organizations to in all three dimensions. But how can healthcare organizations increase relational coordination in light of the differences in goals, knowledge, and status that divide care providers from one another?

In Part II, we identify 12 work practices that foster relational coordination in healthcare organizations. It is well known that certain kinds of work practices enable employees to achieve higher levels of performance across a broad range of outcomes, including quality, efficiency, and financial outcomes,[66] and across a broad range of industries, including steel, telecommunications, airlines, banking, and high technology.[67] When implemented in mutually reinforcing systems or bundles, these practices can shape employee behavior consistently in a positive direction. We call these bundles of work practices *high performance work systems* to indicate that they are systems of mutually reinforcing practices that work together in a cumulative way to foster employee behaviors that lead to high levels of performance.[68]

High performance work systems can function in several different ways. They can foster the development of human capital in the form of firm-specific skills, creating a performance advantage for organizations through increased employee problem solving or improved customization.[69] High performance work systems also can function by enhancing employee commitment.[70] Commitment-based practices create an organizational climate that motivates employees to act in the best interest of the organization, thus enhancing performance.[71] Most high performance work systems focus on building human capital—individual employee expertise and skill, or building commitment—the commitment of individual employees to the organization.

❖ A HIGH PERFORMANCE WORK SYSTEM THAT SUPPORTS RELATIONAL COORDINATION

But the high performance work system described in this book is different because it fosters a critical ingredient that other high performance work systems tend to neglect: the social capital or relationships among employees that enable them to coordinate their work with one another.[72] Although it sounds simple, most work practices do not foster employee relationships in a systematic way. Instead of bringing employees together, many traditional work practices tend to foster and solidify divisions among them. According to Michael Piore, the bureaucratic work practices that first became widespread during early industrialization "have pushed us to restrict communication among the people responsible for the way in which the different parts are performed."[73] Charles Heckscher and colleagues envisioned an alternative: a postbureaucratic, interactive organizational form in which "everyone takes responsibility for the success of the whole" and in which "workers need to understand the key objectives in depth in order to coordinate their actions intelligently 'on the fly.'"[74] It is not enough for healthcare organizations to have highly skilled, committed employees; the employees must also be able to coordinate their actions with one another intelligently and on the fly. What kinds of work practices enable healthcare organizations to achieve that ideal?

Others have taken steps toward identifying work practices that foster the development of employee-employee relationships. Carrie Leana and Harry Van Buren argued that stable employment relationships and reciprocity norms facilitate the formation of social capital among employees.[75] Randy Evans and Walter Davis argued that work practices such as selective staffing, self-managed teams, decentralized decision making, extensive training, flexible job assignments, open communication, and performance-contingent compensation influence the formation of ties among frontline employees.[76]

Similarly, Jon Gant and colleagues showed that on steel finishing lines with high performance work systems—defined as selection, training, incentive pay, job design, problem-solving teams, and extensive labor-management communication—production networks have denser communication networks with one another and that those finishing lines also have higher performance in the form of fewer delays and higher yields.[77] Christopher Collins and Kevin Clark showed that the social networks of top management teams provide a source of competitive advantage because they enhance a firm's information-processing capability and that work practices such as mentoring, incentives, and performance appraisals can be designed to encourage the development of those networks.[78] More recently, Tim Vogus showed that high performance work practices such as selection, training, performance appraisal, performance-based rewards, and job security contribute to high quality interactions among the nurses on hospital units and that those high quality interactions contribute to higher quality outcomes for patients, particularly in the area of patient safety.[79]

Each of these researchers has identified work practices that overcome the divisions typically found in organizations by strengthening relationships among employees. These work practices are distinct from traditional bureaucratic practices because they serve to overcome rather than reinforce the silos by connecting workers directly with one another, enabling them to coordinate their work intelligently and on the fly. The ability of a high performance work system to foster relational coordination is expected to vary with the number of work practices adopted, the intensity of their adoption, and the degree to which they reach across all the relevant employee functions; in other words, it depends on both the strength and the inclusiveness of the organization's high performance work practices.

Exhibit 4-1 presents an overview of the high performance work system that is discussed in this study and the 12 work practices that constitute it. The exhibit illustrates how this high performance work system drives quality and efficiency performance through its impact on relational coordination among care providers.

Readers who are already familiar with the high performance work system presented in *The Southwest Airlines Way* will notice some differences. There are no specific work practices for Leading with Credibility and Caring; Balancing Work and Family; or Partnering with Unions, not because these work practices do not matter in healthcare, but because the data I collected with my colleagues were less informative regarding these important issues. Nevertheless, leading change is addressed in Chapter 19, and partnering with unions is addressed in Chapter 20. On the positive side, our data did allow us to explore five new high performance work practices—reward for teamwork, design jobs

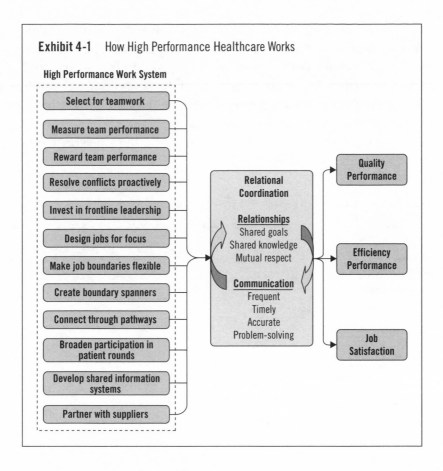

Exhibit 4-1   How High Performance Healthcare Works

High Performance Work System

- Select for teamwork
- Measure team performance
- Reward team performance
- Resolve conflicts proactively
- Invest in frontline leadership
- Design jobs for focus
- Make job boundaries flexible
- Create boundary spanners
- Connect through pathways
- Broaden participation in patient rounds
- Develop shared information systems
- Partner with suppliers

Relational Coordination

Relationships
Shared goals
Shared knowledge
Mutual respect

Communication
Frequent
Timely
Accurate
Problem-solving

- Quality Performance
- Efficiency Performance
- Job Satisfaction

for focus, connect through pathways, broaden participation in meetings, and develop shared information systems.

To understand how these practices work in healthcare organizations, my colleagues and I interviewed administrators and direct care providers in nine hospitals, including at least one physician leader, one nurse leader, one physical therapist leader, and one case manager leader. In our initial visits, we conducted unstructured interviews and observations in person and followed up with more systematic, structured interviews carried out by phone. When we heard conflicting reports from different informants in the same hospital about the same work practice, we went back to each informant until we were confident that we understood the work practices in place in that hospital. These work practices often included some disciplines but not others; for example, nurses and therapists might be selected for relational competence, whereas physicians often were not. Exhibit 4-2 provides a preview of how we measured these work practices at each of the nine participating hospitals before combining them into an overall measure of the high performance work system.[80]

Exhibit 4-2   Measuring High Performance Work Systems*

	Range	Mean	Standard Deviation	Observations
High Performance Work System Index				
Selection for Cross-Functional Teamwork Index				
Physician selection for cross-functional teamwork	0–2	0.44	.88	9
Nurse selection for cross-functional teamwork	0–2	1.44	.73	9
Physical therapist selection for cross-functional teamwork	0–2	1.67	.88	9
Cross-Functional Performance Measurement Index				
Cross-functional approach to quality measurement	1–5	3.33	1.41	9
Problem-solving approach to quality measurement	1–5	2.78	1.39	9
Cross-functional approach to efficiency measurement	1–5	2.56	1.88	9
Problem-solving approach to efficiency measurement	1–5	3.00	1.58	9
Cross-Functional Rewards Index				
Physician rewards for cross-functional teamwork	0–2	.22	.67	9
Nurse rewards for cross-functional teamwork	0–2	.56	.88	9
Physical therapist rewards for cross-functional teamwork	0–2	1.11	1.05	9
Cross-Functional Conflict Resolution Index				
Physician access to cross-functional process	0–1	.44	.53	9
Nurse access to cross-functional process	0–1	.22	.44	9
Physical therapist access to cross-functional process	0–1	.33	.50	9
Supervisory Staffing Index				
Physician supervisory staffing	.02–.25	.09	.07	9
Nurse supervisory staffing	.02–.20	.06	.06	9
Physical therapist supervisory staffing	.06–.33	.15	.09	9

(Cont'd)

	Range	Mean	Standard Deviation	Observations
Focused Job Design Index				
Physician-focused job design	.44–.88	.63	.19	9
Nurse-focused job design	.54–.88	.71	.13	9
Physical therapist–focused job design	.31–.88	.66	.18	9
Case manager–focused job design	.38–.88	.57	.17	9
Cross-Functional Boundary Spanner Index				
Case manager caseload	6.7–40	26.3	10.8	9
Case manager discharge planning role	0–1	.89	.33	9
Case manager coordination role	0–1	.44	.53	9
Primary nursing model	0–1	.56	.53	9
Cross-Functional Pathways Index				
Physician tasks included	0–1	.22	.44	9
Nurse tasks included	0–1	1	0	9
Physical therapist tasks included	0–1	1	0	9
Case manager tasks included	0–1	.56	.53	9
Percentage of patient who were kept on pathway	.70–1	.93	.10	9
Cross-Functional Team Meetings Index				
Nurses included in physician rounds	0–2	1.33	.87	9
Physical therapists included in physician rounds	0–2	.56	.88	9
Case managers included in physician rounds	0–2	.67	.87	9
Physicians included in nursing rounds	0–2	.78	.44	9
Physical therapists included in nursing rounds	0–2	1.44	.73	9
Case managers included in nursing rounds	0–2	1.33	1	9
Cross-Functional Information Systems Index				
Laboratory results included	0–1	.89	.33	9
Insurance information included	0–1	.67	.50	9
Financial data included	0–1	.44	.53	9
Medical history included	0–1	.44	.53	9
Inpatient procedures included	0–1	.44	.53	9
Provider order entry included	0–1	.44	.53	9
Inpatient consult history included	0–1	.33	.50	9
Discharge summary included	0–1	.33	.50	9
Current condition/functioning included	0–1	.11	.33	9

* This exhibit is discussed in the "Notes for Exhibits" chapter beginning on page 315.

❖ BOTTOM LINE

In the following chapters we will explore each of these work practices one by one to understand how each one in its traditional form serves to divide care providers from one another, creating fragmented care and dysfunctional outcomes, and how each one can be transformed to foster high levels of relational coordination among care providers, driving the quality and efficiency of patient care in a positive direction.

Chapter 5

Select for Teamwork

*Technical expertise exceeds teamwork ability as a criterion; doc-
tors are able to expect teamwork of others simply by virtue of
the fact that they are doctors, after all.*

Organizational theorists have long argued that employee selection is one of the most important ways to achieve a fit between an
employee and a job.[81] Depending on the job, the relevant skills
may go beyond the technical realm to include personality traits,
emotional intelligence, organizational fit, and attitudes conducive to teamwork.[82] As I showed in an earlier study of the airline
industry, selection for teamwork or "relational competence"
has the potential to affect the coordination of work across functional boundaries, in two ways.[83] First, it affects who is selected:
the so-called selection effect. Second, incoming employees have
already begun to learn what the organization values through
their experience of being selected: this is the enculturation
effect. In other words, people who are hired explicitly on the
basis of their teamwork skills have already begun to be influ-
enced by the hiring process itself. A psychological contract has

been established between the organization and the employee regarding the importance and expectation of teamwork.

The coordination of patient care requires a great deal of teamwork across functional groups. Increasingly, nurses, case managers, social workers, and therapists are hired with some consideration of their teamwork skills in addition to their clinical skills and ability to interact well with the patient. Even for physicians, teamwork slowly but surely is gaining recognition as an important skill. But the extent to which these qualities were actively sought varied greatly among the hospitals we studied. Across the nine hospitals, we observed variation in the importance attached to teamwork skills in the selection of nurses, social workers, therapists, and physicians. Some departmental administrators were vague about the ways in which teamwork skills were evaluated in the selection process or stated outright that those characteristics were not considered, whereas others had specific processes in place for identifying teamwork skills. Sometimes teamwork was not given importance as a hiring criterion either because it was considered difficult to assess or because it was considered far less important than clinical skills.

Teamwork skills were considered to be particularly relevant for physical therapists. When hiring physical therapists, eight of the nine hospitals looked for teamwork with other functions. A physical therapy administrator at New England Baptist explained:

> *Teamwork with nurses is always important—we're always dealing with them. So is teamwork with physicians. We need to know if the physical therapist has an attitude toward physicians because it is so important to communicate with the doctors.*

Some hospitals had specific procedures for determining whether a physical therapist candidate had the required cross-functional teamwork skills:

Although we usually call the former employer, references are not as helpful as actually interviewing the prospective physical therapist. I use different scenarios during an interview, for example, what would you do in a situation where the doctor disagrees with you? Also, we have the candidate shadow two staff members for as long as he or she is able, ideally four hours. You really learn a lot about the candidate in this kind of scenario.

For social workers as well, cross-functional teamwork was considered an essential attribute in many of the hospitals we studied. A director of social work at Massachusetts General Hospital explained:

We look for a master's in social work, for healthcare experience, or for some kind of multidisciplinary practice. And strong team skills. You can be the best social worker in the world, but if you can't work with other disciplines, then you can't work here. Some are very good diagnostically. But it's the communication skills. If they come out of an agency that's only social work, the learning curve is too steep. They're not used to being challenged by other disciplines, practicing in a fishbowl.

When hiring nurses, teamwork with other functions was considered somewhat less often and less systematically. Six of the nine hospitals placed at least some importance on teamwork skills and attitudes for nurses, though only four of those hospitals had screening methods in place for that purpose. At Beth Israel Deaconess, where nurses were hired with a great deal of attention to teamwork, the director of human resources described the process:

We do value-based interviewing to ensure that any individual coming into the organization, whether a nurse or a housekeeper, believes in teamwork and collaboration. Also, we want to see that they have the goal orientation, the spirit, to do that work. We don't want people so highly competitive that they wouldn't function well as a team member.

Baylor University Medical Center also selected nurses for teamwork. The director of human resources explained:

First, of course, we consider competency. And second is the person's team spirit. Teamwork in general is assessed. Prospective candidates interview with the clinical manager and then with other nurses in a group interview.

At Massachusetts General, where social workers were assessed for teamwork skills, a clinical nurse specialist argued that it was less important to assess nurses for teamwork because of the greater importance of clinical skills:

We ask about clinical skills and team spirit in every interview. How do they see themselves as a team member, with the physician, the therapists, the case manager, and social services? But it's harder to do when you're hiring for clinical skills. Teamwork would be great, but it's not worth a nickel if you're not skilled. Besides, it's hard to know if someone really will be good at teamwork.

This comment reflected the belief, often found in highly technical occupations, that it is often necessary to sacrifice relational skills in favor of technical skills, overlooking the fact that technical skills deliver less value when an employee's relational skills prevent him or her from effectively coordinating his or her work with other functions.

The tendency to overlook teamwork skills was most pronounced in physician selection. Although physicians are less likely to be hired by hospitals relative to the other disciplines, they are granted admitting privileges and therefore are selected in that sense. Only four of the nine hospitals in this study used any cross-functional teamwork criteria in the selection of physicians. When asked whether physicians were selected for teamwork, a director of human resources responded:

> *Probably not so much. The physicians hired here are hired jointly as appointees of the medical school. While they look beyond academic credentials, still there is more emphasis on a person's achievements as a scholar and as a clinician. The chiefs of services here expect a lot of collaboration, but they don't select for it.*

Indeed, when applied to physicians, the word teamwork often was taken to mean cooperation from others that physicians were not expected to reciprocate. An administrator for the Hospital for Joint Diseases explained:

> *Technical expertise exceeds teamwork ability as a criterion; doctors are able to expect teamwork of others simply by virtue of the fact that they are doctors, after all.*

At Beth Israel Deaconess, the director of human resources argued forcefully that physicians should be selected for teamwork:

> *In the OR [operating room] you don't have the time to garner everyone's opinion on what has to be done. But the OR is only one step in a very comprehensive process. The surgeon needs to be integrated into the overall process. It is just as critical as for anyone else. They need to see the overall process and not to see everything as flowing around them.*

In another hospital, teamwork with other functions was thought to be an essential hiring criterion for nurses, social workers, and therapists. However, teamwork ability for physicians was considered only vis-à-vis fellow physicians and even then was considered only somewhat important for physician selection. One administrator explained: "Teamwork ability for physicians is essential, but it's not really considered in our selection process." At another hospital, a case manager noted that physician selection seemed to favor a "command" personality and argued that this selection criterion was based on an outmoded understanding of the job of a physician, even among physicians themselves:

> *People may self-select to be physicians because they are independent and don't want to take advice from anyone. That seems like a personality type that would do well in this kind of occupation. But the occupation has changed over time to one that involves a lot more teamwork.*

By contrast, one of the highest-performing hospitals in the study—New England Baptist—placed a high priority on selecting physicians for teamwork. Hospital leaders used formal methods such as written references as well as informal methods such as their own personal networks to identify physicians who would be a good fit from a teamwork perspective. The chief of orthopedics explained:

> *We pick it up through their references. The doctors here are also sure to know someone who knows that doctor. You've got to be a nice person to work here. ... Nurses like it here because physicians respect their input.*

❖ ASSESSING THE IMPACT OF SELECTING FOR TEAMWORK

To assess the impact of selection for teamwork, we measured the number of functions for which teamwork was an important selection criterion in each of the nine hospitals, considering nurses, physical therapists, and physicians.[84] The results suggest that selection for teamwork significantly strengthens relational coordination among care providers. Exhibit 5-1 suggests that doubling the number of functions that are selected

Exhibit 5-1   Impact of Selection for Teamwork on Relational Coordination†

	Relational Coordination
Selection for Teamwork	.12 **
Physicians	−.17 ***
Residents	−.05
Physical therapists	.07
Case managers	.04
Social workers	−.07
Surgical volume	−.05
R-squared	.55

† This exhibit is discussed in the "Notes for Exhibits" chapter beginning on page 315.

for teamwork produces a 12 percent increase in relational coordination among nurses, physicians, residents, therapists, case managers, and social workers. There is a simpler, more graphic way to observe the impact of selection for teamwork on relational coordination. Selection for teamwork was plotted for each of the nine hospitals against relational coordination. Exhibit 5-2 illustrates a positive impact of this work practice on relational coordination among care providers.

Using statistical techniques to account for patient differences,[85] we also found that selection for teamwork significantly improved patient care outcomes. Specifically, this work practice produced shorter hospital stays, higher levels of patient-perceived quality of care, and improved clinical outcomes. To illustrate, doubling the intensity of this work practice enabled a 15 percent reduction in the length of hospital stays and a 20 percent increase in patient satisfaction. The same change in selection for teamwork contributed to a 7 percent increase in postoperative freedom from joint pain. Combining these four performance metrics into a single measure of surgical performance, we found that selection for teamwork increased overall

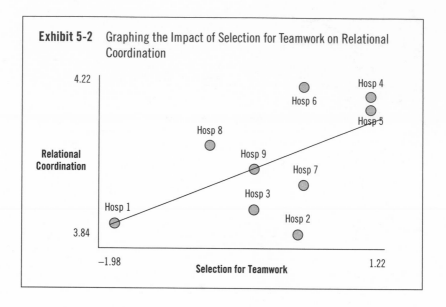

Exhibit 5-2   Graphing the Impact of Selection for Teamwork on Relational Coordination

surgical performance by 17 percent. Furthermore, our analysis showed that selection for teamwork achieves its performance effects *through* its effect on relational coordination.[86]

Exhibit 5-3 summarizes these results. These results suggest that healthcare organizations can achieve improved performance by increasing the number of functions for which teamwork is an important selection criterion. Selection for teamwork is only one component of a larger system, however. We have measured it in the context of a high performance work system whose overall effects will be explored in Chapter 17.

❖ BOTTOM LINE

Reluctance to select highly skilled professionals for teamwork is not unique to physicians or the healthcare industry. My study of the airline industry uncovered a similar phenomenon. Like doctors, pilots tended to be selected for their "command" personality, partly as a result of an outmoded understanding of the pilot's job. We have seen however that selection of care providers with

Exhibit 5-3 Impact of Selection for Teamwork on Surgical Performance†

	Length of Stay	Patient Satisfaction	Postoperative Freedom from Pain	Postoperative Mobility	Surgical Performance Index	Surgical Performance Index
Selection for Teamwork	−.15 ***	.20 ***	.07 *	.05	.17 ***	.01
Relational Coordination						.26 ***
Patient Age	−.02	.01	−.01	−.05	.00	.01
Comorbidities	.09 *	.06	−.01	−.04	−.05	−.05
Preoperative Status	.03	−.01	.20 ***	.28 ***	.17 ***	.16 ***
Surgical Procedure	.01	.10 *	.21 ***	.10 **	.15 ***	.16 ***
Psychological Well-being	−.08 +	.14 **	.41 ***	.41 ***	.41 ***	.40 ***
Surgical Volume	.20 ***	.09 +	.04	.01	−.02	.04
R-squared	.36	.37	.42	.10	.37	.83

† This exhibit is discussed in the "Notes for Exhibits" chapter beginning on page 315.

an eye to their teamwork helps to foster relational coordination, producing improvements in both the quality and the efficiency of care. On the basis of both our fieldwork and our quantitative analysis, it appears that the selection of physicians for teamwork represents a promising new frontier.

Chapter 6

Measure Team Performance

> *QA [quality assurance] used to be completely reactive, with incident reports. There would be a review to determine injury or no injury. QA is more real-time now, not so reactive. But we don't have a full system in place. It's evolving. ... It's not cross-functional yet. Usually, I take the nurses and the chief of the service takes the physicians. There is finger-pointing.*

Even when problems are systemic and collective in nature, performance measurement systems often assign accountability to individual functions. Classical organizational theorists James March and Herbert Simon found that this kind of functional accountability encourages people to "subgoal optimize"—to focus on optimizing the outcomes of their own jobs, even at the expense of the larger goal. Indeed, this is a common flaw of bureaucratic organizations. But there are better ways to measure performance. In particular, shared forms of accountability encourage people to adopt a broader systems perspective and to focus on achieving goals that transcend their own individual function.[87]

The purpose of quality improvement programs is to identify the faulty systems and processes that underlie errors and to set up cross-functional teams to recommend process improvements that can prevent the occurrence of errors in the first place. These changes in performance measurement are expected to improve coordination among workers by creating a sense of shared accountability for outcomes, thereby encouraging a move away from finger-pointing toward problem solving.[88] Approaches to performance measurement that focus on problem solving have been found to preserve and strengthen working relationships, whereas the reactive assignment of blame has been found to promote silo mentalities.[89] A shared approach to performance measurement is particularly important when tasks are part of a highly interdependent work process, as they are in healthcare.[90]

Healthcare organizations typically use two different kinds of performance measurement systems: quality assurance for monitoring the quality of care and utilization review for monitoring the efficiency of resource utilization. The central task of quality assurance and utilization review is to identify errors after the fact and assign accountability for those errors. Quality assurance often is tied organizationally to the legal department, or risk management, where malpractice issues are addressed. Quality assurance committees typically are established separately for the physicians and for other hospital personnel and conducted along the lines of professional peer review. Incident reports are reviewed by the quality assurance committee, which hears the evidence and determines whether an injury has occurred and then determines which party was responsible for the injury.

Utilization review departments are staffed with nurses specially trained to review medical records for unnecessary admissions, excessive lengths of stay, and unnecessary tests or procedures. Excess utilization typically is defined through comparison to clinical protocols developed internally by clinicians or externally by clinicians working for payers and consultants, which are intended to represent an acceptable standard of care, adjusted for the severity of a patient's condition. Utilization review nurses make this information available to the payer, patient by patient, to justify admission, length of stay, and the tests and procedures administered during hospitalization. Often these reviews are conducted with a time lag of several weeks, frequently after the patient has been discharged. The primary purpose of traditional utilization review, much like traditional quality assurance, is not to correct errors but to identify them after the fact and assign responsibility for them to an individual or department.

There are thus two primary weaknesses in these performance measurement systems. First, they are reactive, assigning responsibility after the fact without putting in place a process for preventing the problems from occurring. Second, they assign accountability to individuals or functions despite the interdependencies among individuals and functions that often make errors the responsibility of a larger team. Overall, traditional quality assurance and utilization review tend to focus on individuals or functions even when the problems are systemic or collective in nature.

The movement toward continuous quality improvement (CQI) represents an attempt to address the shortcomings of quality assurance. CQI is informed by the total quality movement, which was inspired by the work of J. Edward Deming. Although this movement began in manufacturing, it was embraced enthusiastically in healthcare organizations in the 1990s due in part to the leadership in this area by a key healthcare accrediting agency and also due to a national demonstration project conducted by the Institute for Healthcare Improvement in the early 1990s.[91] The purpose of CQI programs is to identify the faulty systems and processes underlying errors and set up cross-functional task teams to recommend process improvements to prevent the occurrence of errors. The governing assumption of CQI is that faulty systems and processes create many of the errors that occur and that often the responsibility is collective and cross-functional rather than individual or functional. However, many CQI programs have been developed alongside traditional quality assurance (QA) programs, leaving the basic approach to quality performance measurement unchanged in those hospitals.

Some quality programs have been transformed from a reactive process to a proactive process through the incorporation of CQI principles into the traditional QA process but have not evolved toward a cross-disciplinary assignment of responsibility. In the absence of an alternative way to assign responsibility, administrators tended to fall back on the traditional QA approach. In addition, even when hospitals developed a way of sharing responsibility for quality problems across disciplines, they still were bound by external reporting requirements to assign responsibility for so-called sentinel events to individual care providers. As we heard from an administrator at the Hospital for Joint Diseases:

> *The QA committee is not cross-functional. It is strictly departmental, and it's strictly reactive. Everybody is giving reports to QA, but nobody is listening or learning. The QA committee satisfies hospital-wide reporting requirements. But it's not effective. We have board members on that committee, but we still can't get it to work. People have a bad attitude when they go. It's a lengthy, cumbersome meeting. My job is as a mechanic, to have nice tracking and reporting mechanisms and to make our reports look good. Our CEO wants to get [JCAHO] accreditation with commendatio.*

This experience with quality assurance was shared by other hospitals in the study. According to one chief of orthopedics:

Traditionally we've looked at morbidity and mortality. This was the traditional function of the quality assurance committee. These meetings were punitive, a slap on the wrist. There was a tendency to underreport. ... The tenor of these committees varied from one service to another. In some, it was very unpleasant to present a complication. If you had a chief who was an ogre ... it was just not a good way to assure quality. Mainly it caused underreporting. People forgot to submit complications. ... Also, it didn't create a database. There was no long-term picture about particular problems.

Massachusetts General Hospital had begun to change toward a more problem-solving approach to quality measurement at the time of the study but had not completed the transformation. A nurse manager of orthopedics explained:

QA used to be completely reactive, with incident reports. There would be a review to determine injury or no injury. QA is more real-time now, not so reactive. But we don't have a full system in place. It's evolving. ... It's not cross-functional yet. Usually, I take the nurses and the chief of the service takes the physicians. There is finger-pointing.

A physician at Massachusetts General Hospital concurred:

There's a tendency in healthcare to find the bad person. You see it everywhere. But most health professionals want to do right by the patient. We have a calling to help people. Much of what happens is not inattention, negligence, or ignorance. The vast majority of errors are due to system breakdowns. There isn't a good system in place. That's why the whole area of individual report cards is a very tough area.

A director of regulatory affairs at the Hospital for Joint Diseases explained the dysfunctional nature of quality assurance at her hospital:

> *Quality assurance, if people were to be real honest, never worked. Good intentions, good hearts, people trying to see what's going on—it never really worked. It's the doctor's fault, it's the stupid nurse's fault, it's the lab—sometimes it's not a people thing. And I think over the years, we've kind of come to accept that it's a process. It's communication, and we don't know how to communicate, or I don't really know what you're asking me, or I don't like your attitude, so I may not tell you. We were all trying to learn, but what we were doing—and I think it's pretty human—was saying, "It's his fault." The patient didn't get to the OR on time. I did my job, but the lab person didn't get that done—it's probably sitting somewhere. What we never really looked at in terms of process was, Did he get notified? Did he know? Did anyone tell him what's going on?*

Although some leaders at Hospital for Joint Diseases were working hard to move away from this dysfunctional approach, it was difficult:

> *I feel that our approach is still kind of punitive in a way. In terms of performance evaluation, sometimes we're too quick to judge a doctor or a nurse or even our housekeeping people. And we never really know what the process is or what's going on, or how did this job not get done?*

Other hospitals were further along in implementing new approaches to performance measurement. The purpose of the new approaches was to identify the faulty systems and processes underlying errors and set up cross-functional task teams to recommend process improvements to prevent the occurrence of those errors. An administrator at Brigham and Women's Hospital explained:

We have a history of using punitive measures. Now it's "What makes competent people fail? What in the system failed? What piece of information was missing?" We are looking at a learning perspective now. It's still a QA function. But now it's more like quality improvement."

A case manager at Baylor University Medical Center explained the changes she had observed:

In the 1980s when we were involved in quality assurance, it was mostly looking at people. Instead of looking at what could be improved in the process or considering what was wrong with it, we were really focusing on the person. And we had a lot of monitors at the time that focused on staff and things that staff did. Where the problems lay in terms of staff. Slowly we've evolved into looking at processes and where we can improve those processes of care. That's where I see the evolution of the QA that we had to the CQI that we now have. I think now the processes are much more multidisciplinary.

At Beth Israel Deaconess, the chief of orthopedics described a similar transition at his hospital:

Quality assurance was the traditional departmental thing to do. We had monthly meetings about complications. It was based on information that was idiosyncratic, anecdotal. There are guys in my department who are full of themselves. I do it this way, they assert. We tried to change the tone of the meetings. Now it's more peer review. We include nurses, OR, technicians. It's meant to correct things, not just blame someone. In the past, it had to be someone's fault. But it might just be a structural dysfunction. Often we would hear, "It's not my job." But that's not satisfactory. Often something that fed them was dysfunctional, but then we have to explore it.

Parallel with the shift from quality assurance to quality improvement, hospitals moved toward utilization management to correct the weaknesses of utilization review. As payers became more aggressive about cost cutting, hospital utilization review departments were forced to justify decisions to admit and treat patients either simultaneously or before the fact rather than afterward. The process evolved from retrospective review to prospective or concurrent review. Utilization review nurses began to interact with payers on a more continuous basis as part of the decision-making process for admission, tests, treatments, and lengths of stay.

Some hospitals also implemented new approaches to measuring resource utilization. The new approaches focused on proactive problem solving and on looking for ways to reduce resource utilization. The focus on problem solving also tended to shift accountability from individuals to the collective. In addition, the newer approaches often combined quality and resource utilization issues into a common problem-solving process. According to the senior orthopedic case manager at New England Baptist:

> We have a Bone Team which includes the service line director, the case management supervisor, the head of rehab, the VP for nursing, the nurse manager in ortho, the clinical specialist in ortho, three social workers, and three case managers. We generally look at system problems. ... For example, we did a review of 20 records to see if they met the criteria to see a physical therapist two times a day, then we did a report to the Bone Team and discussed who within the group should pursue what."

A senior administrator at New England Baptist gave another example of how this systems approach worked:

> We report on quality. We write a monthly summary of events that have been discussed in case review. The

summary is reviewed by the ortho staff group, which is made up of physicians, nurses, and therapists. The goal of this reporting is to improve processes and systems. If there is a pattern, we send the issue to a subcommittee for examination. We have a Bone Team Meeting for this purpose. It is like a QI team. ... In one case, we discovered that we were receiving patients late, that somewhere things were getting delayed. We also noticed that this tended to happen especially for patients receiving blood transfusions. It turned out that the transfusions were holding things up, and so we adjusted our scheduling accordingly. We also use patient satisfaction surveys to track issues that patients have had with the doctor and the healthcare team, and we have the case managers track things like the percentage of patients who got pre-op teaching classes so we can work to get that number up.

Another hospital had moved from the old compliance approach to a more proactive problem-solving approach to both quality and utilization:

In the sense of us looking through charts and seeing if everything is compliant, we've gotten away from filling out forms when something happens. That would be the old approach. Now we're looking for an underlying variance in problems that occur. You have a trend that you have most of your falls every night at one o'clock, so you try to see where things are happening. We call it a quality improvement group. Each area is looking at data to discover ways and areas that it needs to improve. If all of a sudden our infection rate goes up to 10 percent, then we look to see if there is just one clinician or one group of operating rooms that all these patients went through. We try to look for common denominators, and then we correct it. It's usually an educational problem.

Yet another hospital—Brigham and Women's—established an Orthopedics Care Improvement Team led by the chief of orthopedics. He explained:

> *We got together a team that involved everyone in inpatient care. From preadmission testing and lab testing on down the line. We tracked patients from there to discharge. We included only the part that we control because that's where we have to reduce costs. Our goal was care improvement, but in some ways that's a euphemism. Cost-effectiveness is what is meant, and doctors don't like it. But whatever you call it, you want to make sure [that] as you decrease costs, you don't impair quality. You might actually improve it.*

Costs could be controlled not only by denying unnecessary care but also by increasing the efficiency of care delivery. Increased efficiencies were achieved through better coordination of care, particularly by communicating in a timely way across disciplines to allow decisions to be made with full and accurate information. With better coordination, less repetition was required and fewer days were wasted waiting for delayed test results or delayed physician orders.

Another problem with traditional utilization review, in addition to its reactive nature, was the assignment of responsibility for problems such as delays and unnecessary tests or procedures to functions or individuals rather than to multiple parties across functional boundaries. This functionally specific assignment of responsibility, in the face of a highly cross-functional process of patient care, tended to deteriorate into unproductive finger-pointing rather than supporting problem solving. The issue of cross-functional accountability was not addressed fully by the move toward utilization management in much the same way that it was not addressed fully by the move toward quality improvement.

Some hospitals had moved deliberately toward a cross-functional approach. The director of care coordination at Baylor

University Medical Center explained how this cross-functional approach worked:

> *It's basically our whole healthcare system that's has taken on a CQI approach. We use data to define an area that you want and need to improve. It's not departmentally focused. It's every discipline that is involved in taking care of that patient. You bring in all the players instead of one department looking at it and passing it on to another department at a separate time. It's become much more collaborative— it's a group of people working together. That's also a way to promote operational efficiencies. You might find out that pharmacies are doing this, nursing is doing this, and the physician is doing it again. As soon as they start looking at the process, they can be more efficient in delivering the care.*

In hospitals with a cross-functional proactive approach to performance measurement, the staff argued that quality and efficiency could be improved together and at the same time:

> *Quality and efficiency really do go together, we're finding. If you reduce infections, you also reduce the costs of antibiotics. If you reduce readmissions back into the hospital, you reduce the cost of that condition. So that thought that overutilization is as much a quality issue as underutilization—there's now data to support that. As you reduce the costs, some of the quality indicators in fact improve, because you are not doing things to patients that you shouldn't have been doing.*

❖ ASSESSING THE IMPACT OF CROSS-FUNCTIONAL PERFORMANCE MEASUREMENT

To assess the impact of cross-functional performance measurement, we measured both quality and efficiency performance measurement, assessing each on two dimensions that reflected a functional versus cross-functional approach and a reactive/blaming versus a proactive/problem-solving approach. These four measures were combined into a single index of cross-functional performance measurement.[92] The results suggest that cross-functional performance measurement significantly strengthens relational coordination among care providers. Exhibit 6-1 suggests that doubling the strength of this work practice produced a 17 percent increase in relational coordination among nurses, physicians, residents, therapists, case managers, and social workers. There is a simpler, more graphic way to observe the impact of cross-functional performance measurement on relational coordination. Cross-functional performance measurement was plotted for each of the nine hospitals against relational coordination. Exhibit 6-2 illustrates a positive impact of this work practice on relational coordination among care providers.

Using statistical techniques to account for patient differences, [93] we also found that cross-functional performance measurement significantly improved patient care outcomes. Specifically, this work practice produced shorter hospital stays

---

Exhibit 6-1   Impact of Cross-Functional Performance Measurement on Relational Coordination†

	Relational Coordination
Cross-Functional Performance Measurement	.17 **
Physicians	−.17 ***
Residents	−.03
Physical Therapists	.04
Case Managers	.04
Social Workers	−.07 +
Surgical Volume	−.02
R-squared	.72

† This exhibit is discussed in the "Notes for Exhibits" chapter beginning on page 315.

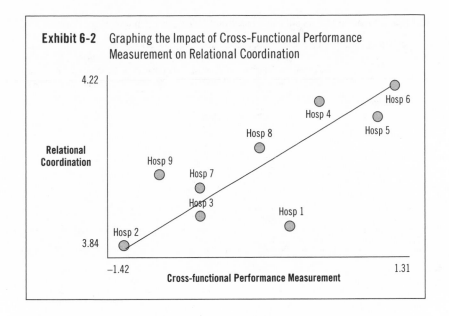

Exhibit 6-2 Graphing the Impact of Cross-Functional Performance Measurement on Relational Coordination

and higher levels of patient-perceived quality of care. To illustrate, doubling the strength of this work practice enabled a 36 percent reduction in the length of hospital stays and a 21 percent increase in patient satisfaction. Though performance measurement produces the largest decrease in length of stay of any work practice in our high performance work system and a considerable increase in patient satisfaction, it does not produce significant changes in clinical outcomes. Combining these four performance metrics into a single measure of surgical performance, we found that cross-functional performance measurement increased overall performance by 20 percent. Furthermore, our analysis shows that this work practice achieves its performance effects *through* its positive effect on relational coordination.[94]

Exhibit 6-3 summarizes these results, suggesting that healthcare organizations can improve outcomes by transforming performance measurement from being reactive and function-specific to being proactive and cross-functional. But performance measurement is just one component of a high performance work system, whose overall effects will be explored in Chapter 17.

Exhibit 6-3   Impact of Cross-Functional Performance Measurement on Surgical Performance†

	Length of Stay	Patient Satisfaction	Postoperative Freedom from Pain	Postoperative Mobility	Surgical Performance Index	Surgical Performance Index
Cross-Functional Performance Measurement	−.36 ***	.21 ***	.01	.00	.20 ***	−.01
Relational Coordination						.28 ***
Patient Age	−.02	.00	−.01	−.05	.00	.01
Comorbidities	.07ᵃ +	.07ᵃ +	−.02	−.04	−.04	−.05
Preoperative Status	.04	−.02	.20 ***	.28 ***	.16 ***	.16 ***
Surgical Procedure	−.01	.12 *	.22 ***	.11 **	.17 ***	.16 ***
Psychological Well-being	−.08 *	.14 ***	.40 ***	.41 ***	.40 ***	.40 ***
Surgical Volume	.12 **	.09 *	.04	.01	.02	.04
R-Squared	.82	.52	.37	.09	.54	.83

† This exhibit is discussed in the "Notes for Exhibits" chapter beginning on page 315.

❖ BOTTOM LINE

A proactive, cross-functional approach to performance measurement helps to create a sense of shared goals, shared knowledge, and mutual respect among care providers who are working together to provide care to patients. These positive relationships support frequent, timely, problem-solving communication, helping to further develop positive relationships. An approach to performance measurement that is both proactive and cross-functional helps to develop high levels of relational coordination, ultimately improving the quality and efficiency of patient care.

Chapter 7

Reward Team Performance

Unreimbursed days are a big issue for the hospital. But not as much for the physician. Right now, a physician is held responsible for unreimbursed days, technically. But he doesn't hear about them. I try to educate him. The doctor might not even care. It affects the hospital if it's not reimbursed. But whether it ever affects the physician, I don't know.

Rewards are another means for supporting—or undermining—the coordination of work. Rewards traditionally have been tied to individual or functional outcomes, which tends to focus attention on subgoal optimization at the expense of outcomes that are important to the organization.[95] Ruth Wageman and George Baker showed that parties engaged in interdependent tasks are most likely to coordinate their tasks effectively if their rewards are also interdependent.[96] However, because rewards often are put in place without a clear understanding of how they are expected to work, misalignment is common.[97] Research indicates that more individualized rewards are associated with lower levels of coordination, whereas shared rewards

have been found to support coordination and goal commitment.[98] The bottom line of this research is clear: Participants
with shared rewards are more likely to work in a coordinated
way with one another.

Some of the hospitals in our study had adopted rewards as
another means for aligning the behavior of participants with
the goals of the hospital. In five of the nine hospitals, nurses
or physical therapists or both were rewarded for contributing
to team performance. At Presbyterian Plano Hospital, a high
performing hospital in our study, employees were rewarded
for both team performance and individual performance. The
administrative director of patient services explained:

> *There is a system of "success sharing." The hospital has
> three targets, relating to cost, service, and quality. If they
> are met, there are payments to all employees. In addition,
> each employee is given an individual bonus depending on
> (1) service, (2) whether she or he has received any disci-
> plinary complaints, and (3) whether the employee has met
> or exceeded the standards of care delivery.*

The Hospital for Special Surgery instituted merit pay for its
physical therapists and social workers, but the system was considered unfair and was dropped after one year. The director of
rehab services explained:

> *There was a merit compensation program at the hospital
> last year. Bonuses were available according to performance,
> but the performance appraisal wasn't done right. I was
> told by the administration to give bonuses to 20 percent of
> my staff. This year the bonus system was eliminated. Now
> there will be an across-the-board increase for all who meet
> a certain standard.*

New England Baptist had a merit pay system in place for its
physical therapists: a 0 to 4 percent annual pay increase that

was based on therapists' self-evaluation. The problem with the system, according to the supervisor, was that it added stress and made the work environment less congenial. It also focused care providers' attention on how they were doing individually relative to others. By contrast, rewards for teamwork among those who worked together on a specific group of patients appeared to focus attention more productively.

Rewards were structured very differently for the physicians. Nearly all the physicians maintained private practices and thus had built-in financial rewards associated with those practices. Their incomes were tied to their individual surgical volumes, and their surgical volumes were tied to their reputations. However, the financial rewards associated with their private practices were not necessarily aligned with the interests of the hospital and its staff. Physicians typically billed the payer directly for the care they provided to their hospitalized patients, separately from the hospital's billing for patient care. If the payer denied reimbursement to the hospital for an admission or for part of an admission, the hospital suffered the financial consequences even if a physician's initial decision to admit or delayed decision to discharge was the cause of the unreimbursed charges. An administrator at the Hospital for Special Surgery explained:

> The key element in any discharge planning is the physician—we can come up with many different plans for getting people out of the hospital sooner, and I think we've been very creative. But unless the physician is on board and supports our plan, then it's going to fail. Some of it is based on profit, on financial motives. It's the physician's private patient. They don't want to antagonize this person. So there's a conflict between their need to attract patients and doing what the patients want and for the institution to set some limits for these patients based on what the payer is willing to pay. They're not necessarily mutually exclusive, but it creates a conflict. People are looking at these things from different perspectives.

The problem of unreimbursed hospital charges grew with the rise of managed care and the increased willingness of managed care payers to deny payment for hospitalization and related care they judged to be medically unnecessary. A case manager from Massachusetts General Hospital explained:

> *Unreimbursed days are a big issue for the hospital. But not as much for the physician. Right now, a physician is held responsible for unreimbursed days, technically. But he doesn't hear about them. I try to educate him. The doctor might not even care. It affects the hospital if it's not reimbursed. But whether it ever affects the physician, I don't know.*

When asked whether minimizing unreimbursed days was a big deal for him, a physician at Brigham and Women's Hospital replied:

> *We don't measure unreimbursed days. A managed care company might call up and say, "You're not getting the patient out." But this is very rare.*

A director of patient care at Massachusetts General Hospital explained this gap between hospital and physician interests:

> *Until we are fully capitated, physicians will keep the patient as long as Medicare pays. Some physicians put our variances way off because they'll keep the patient in as long as insurance pays them for it. It's because the hospital is being charged, not the physician. But it would be very difficult for a nurse to say it was your issue that caused the variance. The chief of the service might disagree with her even if the patient was in for four days extra. This culture is physician to physician. But even peer review [between physicians] doesn't work because it comes down to the physician's judgment.*

To solve the problem of misaligned financial rewards between physicians and hospital staffs, some hospitals sought to join with their physicians through a joint physician-hospital governing body called a physician-hospital organization (PHO) to negotiate contracts with payers. Those contracts often took the form of capitation, in which physicians and hospitals shared the financial risk for a patient population. The PHO received a "per member per month" payment and in return provided the specified range of care for the group of patients. Those contracts were intended to align the rewards of physicians and the hospital staff to provide quality care in a cost-effective way. PHOs were present in four of the nine hospitals studied here. Under risk sharing or capitation, unreimbursed hospital days are paid out of the physicians' pool, potentially increasing their interest in coordinating care for timely discharge. An administrator at Brigham and Women's Hospital described the impact of the new arrangements on the physicians in her department:

> *I knew [the chief of orthopedics] in 1972, and we were not on an equal playing field. It was more like "I'm the king." It still happens. … They want to be number one, the top. They are Harvard. They don't want to be number two to Tufts or Boston University. But they can't do it themselves. They are realizing with the physician-hospital organization and with managed care that they need a lot of other entities in order to succeed.*

According to the chief medical officer at Massachusetts General Hospital, however:

> *Managed care itself has not been sufficient to create incentives for providers to integrate. Managed care providers tried to build links with each player, to be the convener with individual links to all players. But it is difficult for them to be the convener. … It works better when physicians and*

> *hospitals coordinate their relationship directly. There is still a role for insurers to do the marketing, enrollment, and actuarial tasks. But the providers need to bear the risk together.*

Only one hospital in our study, the Hospital for Joint Diseases, had introduced surplus sharing with its physicians. The director of case management explained:

> *The hospital has negotiated global contracts that include surgeons' fees. About 10 percent of our contracts place us at risk, like Oxford. There is some degree of egalitarian profit sharing among the surgeons—as long as the docs meet their billing requirements, they all get a small bonus at the end of the year, providing there's a profit to be shared.*

In four other hospitals, physicians belonged to an independent practice association (IPA) or physicians organization (PO) that negotiated risk contracts with payers such as managed care companies, employers, and the government but did not negotiate those contracts jointly with the hospital. By leaving hospitals out, these contracts had the potential to increase misalignment between physicians and hospitals. Even when risk sharing was introduced between physicians and the hospital, those arrangements applied only to a small minority of patients: less than 5 percent.

The bottom line was that physicians—key participants in the delivery of patient care—often had rewards that were severely misaligned with the other care providers on the team.

❖ ASSESSING THE IMPACT OF CROSS-FUNCTIONAL REWARDS

To assess the impact of cross-functional rewards, we measured rewards in each of the nine hospitals by asking about the criteria for rewards for nurses, physical therapists, and physicians, probing whether rewards were based purely on individual performance or were based on some cross-functional performance criteria as well. This variable was coded from 0 to 2. For nurses and physical therapists, 0 indicated no rewards, 1 indicated individual rewards only, and 2 indicated some cross-functional rewards. For physicians, 0 indicated individual rewards only, 1 indicated surplus sharing with the hospital, and 2 indicated risk sharing with the hospital. When surplus or risk was shared with the hospital, physicians' rewards were more closely aligned with those of their colleagues in other functions who were employed by the hospital.[99] The results suggest that cross-functional rewards significantly strengthen relational coordination among care providers. Exhibit 7-1 suggests that doubling the use of this work practice produced an 18 percent increase in relational coordination among nurses, physicians, residents, therapists, case managers, and social workers. There is a simpler, more graphic way to observe the impact of cross-functional rewards on relational coordination. Cross-functional rewards were plotted against relational coordination for each of the nine hospitals. Exhibit 7-2 illustrates a positive impact of this work practice on relational coordination among care providers.

Using statistical techniques to account for patient differences, we also found that cross-functional rewards significantly

---

Exhibit 7-1 Impact of Cross-Functional Rewards on Relational Coordination†

	Relational Coordination
Cross-Functional Rewards	.18 ***
Physicians	−.16 ***
Residents	−.02
Physical Therapists	.06
Case Managers	.04
Social Workers	−.07
Surgical Volume	−.01
R-squared	.64

† This exhibit is discussed in the "Notes for Exhibits" chapter beginning on page 315.

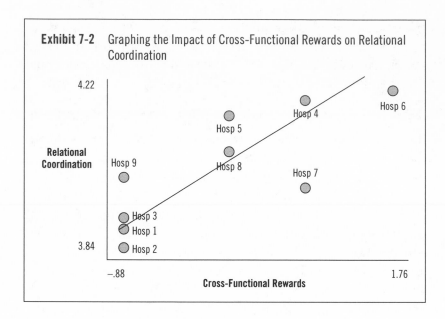

Exhibit 7-2   Graphing the Impact of Cross-Functional Rewards on Relational Coordination

improved patient care outcomes.[100] This work practice produced shorter hospital stays, higher levels of patient-perceived quality of care, and improved clinical outcomes. To illustrate, doubling the strength of this work practice enabled a 24 percent reduction in the length of hospital stays and a 25 percent increase in patient satisfaction. This work practice also improved clinical outcomes, producing a 7 percent increase in postoperative freedom from joint pain and a 5 percent increase in postoperative joint mobility. Combining these four performance metrics into a single measure of surgical performance, we found that cross-functional rewards increased overall performance by 23 percent. Furthermore, our analysis showed that cross-functional rewards achieve their performance effects *through* their effect on relational coordination.[101]

Exhibit 7-3 summarizes these results, which suggest that healthcare organizations can improve performance by transforming rewards from being function-specific to being cross-functional. Physicians often represent the last frontier in this change process: Otherwise well-managed hospitals often neglect

Exhibit 7-3   Impact of Cross-Functional Rewards on Surgical Performance†

	Length of Stay	Patient Satisfaction	Postoperative Freedom from Pain	Postoperative Mobility	Surgical Performance Index	Surgical Performance Index
Cross-Functional Rewards	−.24 ***	.25 ***	.08 *	.07 +	.23 ***	−.02
Relational Coordination						.28
Patient Age	−.03	.01	−.01	−.05	.01	.01
Comorbidities	.09 *	.07	−.01	−.04	−.05	−.05
Preoperative Status	.02	−.01	.20 ***	.28***	.17 ***	.16 ***
Surgical Procedure	.00	.11 **	.22 ***	.11 **	.16 ***	.16 ***
Psychological Well-being	−.08 +	.14 **	.40 ***	.40 ***	.40 ***	.40 ***
Surgical Volume	.14 ***	.08 +	.06 +	.03	.03	.04
R-squared	.51	.57	.49	.24	.62	.82

† This exhibit is discussed in the "Notes for Exhibits" chapter beginning on page 315.

to tie physician rewards to the hospital, undermining relational coordination and thereby reducing both the quality and the efficiency of patient care. Remember however that rewards are only one component of a larger system. We have measured rewards in the context of a high performance work system whose overall effects will be explored in Chapter 17.

❖ BOTTOM LINE

Shared rewards strengthen relational coordination when they include all care providers who are working with the same patients and whose work is highly interdependent. Rewards that are designed according to these principles help increase levels of relational coordination. However, shared rewards are just one piece of the puzzle. Even though financial alignment sometimes is viewed as the silver bullet that will solve the problems of our healthcare system, in reality it is just one piece of the puzzle, one element of the high performance work system that, together with the other elements, helps to build relational coordination between the physician and other care providers working with the same patient population. Indeed, David Dranove and colleagues found that high-powered incentives for physicians by themselves can lead to "cream skimming" and other undesirable provider behaviors.[102]

As a leader at Beth Israel Deaconess, one of our highest-performing hospitals, explained: "We are seeking integration with the physicians not only from an economic standpoint but from a heart and soul standpoint." This deeper form of integration requires all the elements in our high performance work system, including selection, performance measurement, and conflict resolution. Chapter 8 sheds light on the potentially powerful role of conflict resolution.

Chapter 8

Resolve Conflicts Proactively

I would say that for any nonphysician to challenge a physician has the whole episode laced with pitfalls. For a nurse, a therapist, a pharmacist, a social worker, a nutritionist, an occupational therapist to challenge a physician is up there with losing a job or getting a divorce—very stressful. And I can say personally as a nurse that in my more formative years that was something that you would try to avoid at all costs.

Because of the intensity of interaction among groups involved in highly interdependent work processes, conflicts tend to be common. Organizational theorists have shown that conflicts are more likely to occur in the presence of high levels of task interdependence or high levels of diversity among participants.[103] However, conflict is not all bad. Conflicts can provide a way to articulate and accommodate multiple points of view, each of which has the potential to add value to the work process. For example, Karen Jehn demonstrated that conflict can improve performance when it takes place in a group that values task-related conflict but that unresolved conflicts cause relationships to deteriorate and hinder performance over time.[104] In addition, efforts to resolve conflicts provide opportunities for building a shared understanding of the work process among participants who may not understand one another's perspectives, thus strengthening the relationships through which coordination occurs.[105]

There are substantial differences between individuals and their abilities to engage in conflict resolution: Some have the capabilities and resources that enable them to resolve conflicts effectively, whereas others do not.[106] However, organizations should not accept these disparities as a given. They can act to increase their employees' ability to resolve conflicts by designing conflict resolution processes for that purpose. Those processes can take many different forms, but they have the common characteristic of providing opportunities for building a shared understanding of the work process among participants who may not understand one another's perspectives.[107] Because conflicts often span functional boundaries, these conflict resolution processes must do the same.

Conflict resolution is especially important in healthcare settings. Conflicts among care providers are common, driven by the intensity of interactions among the care provider functions involved in patient care, the critical nature of the outcomes, differences in training and perspectives, and increasing awareness of time and cost pressures. Some conflicts were seen as desirable because they provided a way to articulate and accommodate multiple points of view, each with the potential to add value to the work process. Case managers typically were expected to take a hard line on resource utilization, for example, whereas doctors and nurses were expected to push back to assure high quality care for their patients. Unresolved conflicts, however, had the effect of hindering communication and weakening relationships over time.

Each of the nine hospitals we studied had some kind of grievance process to resolve conflicts between workers and their supervisors. According to an administrator at the Hospital for Joint Diseases:

> *There is, of course, a grievance process that goes into effect in cases of termination or contract violation. It first goes up to the immediate supervisor, then the director of the department, then to the director of human resources, and if that doesn't work, we bring in an arbitrator from the American Arbitration Association.*

This grievance process was also used for performance issues between workers and their supervisors.

> *In HR, there is a grievance process around performance issues. More for resolving conflicts with managers—for example, for a social worker to challenge a performance review.*

But mechanisms for resolving cross-functional conflict were much less common. Often there was some degree of direct supervisory involvement in mediating conflicts with supervisors who were actively engaged in bringing the parties together to work out the conflict, although in other hospitals supervisors either did nothing or encouraged the parties to resolve conflicts on their own. Effective supervisory involvement clearly would required time and attention, which was limited in many of our hospitals due to reductions in supervisory staffing, as we will see in Chapter 9.

In many hospitals, conflict resolution was formally considered part of a supervisor's job, but supervisory spans of control were often so large that it was not feasible for supervisors to play a meaningful role in conflict resolution. As the director of physical therapy at Massachusetts General Hospital explained, "I encourage people to resolve conflicts directly with each other. We don't have the staffing to deal with that kind of stuff."

Often supervisors lacked not only the time but also the training or inclination to engage in conflict resolution. At Beth Israel New York, managers and administrators had the option of participating in a one-day program on conflict resolution. However, a nurse manager in that hospital explained, "It's the nurse manager's job, but I don't feel I should be a court of law." For interdisciplinary cases, sometimes supervisors would get together, but this was less likely if one party to the dispute was a physician. The director of physical therapy at Beth Israel New York explained:

> *I sit down with the involved parties first individually, then together. I keep documentation of any conflict in the employee's file. For an interdisciplinary case, I go to that person's supervisor and discuss things. But a doctor and a PT wouldn't sit down with each other. I would have to arrange something.*

She didn't explain what kind of arrangement that might be. Clearly, it was not something she would do on a regular basis or perhaps ever.

Although it may sound harmless or even empowering to ask care providers to work it out themselves, there were power differentials that made this solution potentially hazardous, laden with risk, and therefore not likely to occur. An administrator at the Hospital for Joint Diseases explained:

> *We don't have a formal procedure for a difference of opinion about the treatment plan. Basically it would depend on what it is and what the disagreement is and how forcefully the individual who had the opposing opinion felt about that. And there are varying degrees of comfort. There is one nurse on the eighth floor who will challenge the physician: "What the hell have you got the patient in for? He's walking a mile every day." Her personality allows her to do that, and her knowledge base allows her to back up what she's saying with significant experience.*

The administrator went on to explain:

> *The vast majority of nurses are female. The vast majority of doctors are male. And they're big men, orthopedists.*

You don't see small orthopedists; they're physically power-
ful men. And a lot of the nurses are petite or certainly not,
you know, linebackers.

So there is a great deal of everything else floating
around plus what happens then if the dispute is taken to
the next level. That person needs to have a backup like
the director of case management, again someone with a
great deal of experience clinically, somebody whose title
demonstrates a little bit more authority, and eventually if
that doesn't sway, you have a physician, and in our situ-
ation that would be our medical director. And that's very
important because then you have the physician talking to
a physician.

Further commentary from this administrator illustrated
the hazards of having no formal mechanisms for conflict resolution in a setting with intense power differentials and with
potentially dire consequences of miscommunication for the
patient:

I think in any industry there is one individual who is usu-
ally the quarterback. When the others start to—or wish
to—bring up a suggestion, it's fraught with a great deal
of concern by the individual who wants to make that sug-
gestion. Quite frankly, oftentimes those suggestions are
never made, so their reputations are never at risk.

The Hospital for Joint Diseases was not unique in this regard.
Other hospitals, such as Massachusetts General Hospital, also
lacked formal mechanisms for resolving conflicts between disciplines, particularly when the conflict involved a physician:

The kinds of conflicts we often have are disagreements
about the patient's treatment plan: what it should be.
It can go across all of the groups. The other big thing is
getting a physician to come up to the unit, to be available.

... We have a formal grievance process if you're fired, but not for conflicts among clinicians. ... There are no particular processes. We just hope people use common sense and talk to each other.

Some of the hospitals in our study did have formal processes for resolving conflicts that were horizontal across care providers. The vice president of human resources at Beth Israel Deaconess explained:

We try to develop conflict resolution skills in managers. We also have a formal process based in the employee relations department that includes horizontal as well as vertical conflicts. Physician conflict resolution happens differently. But either way, we work hard to have conflicts resolved at the local level so that they don't go on and on.

At Massachusetts General Hospital, administrators discovered the limitations of referring conflicts high in the organization's chain of command and experienced better outcomes when immediate supervisors or others close to the front line sat the parties down together to work it out face to face:

Our formal process was just a chain of command. When there was a conflict between people in different departments, we would give advice to our social workers and presumably the other department would give advice to their person. Often it couldn't be resolved that way, so it moved up to associate directors, then directors, then to the head of operations. It seldom worked to bring it to the top—it just resulted in a fiat. We got better resolutions when we could get the parties together in a room and work things out. As we got clearer on roles, that enabled people to work together better.

Other hospitals had developed cross-functional councils or protocols dedicated specifically to the resolution of cross-functional conflict. At Beth Israel New York, there was an Office of

Intercultural Communication that helped to resolve conflicts. The director of social work explained:

> *They don't just deal with the cultures of color and gender but also take into account the fact that nursing, social work, physical therapy—these are cultures too.*

As in many of the other interdisciplinary processes we observed, however, that office did not address conflicts between physicians and nonphysicians. Still, this hospital was about to adopt a physician liaison for that purpose. An administrator explained: "Dr. Scott [the chief of orthopedic surgery] deals with conflict resolution issues among physicians right now. But soon, for cross-functional issues, the physician liaison will be the person to turn to."

A common source of conflict was the integration of social workers into the case management department. Social workers traditionally had been responsible for coordinating patient discharge, with a focus on providing psychosocial support to the patient and his or her family and connecting the patient to services in the community. Case managers were taking over the coordination of discharge and were expected to oversee clinical issues and proactively manage the patient's stay up through and including discharge. After the social workers were merged into the case management department, New England Baptist attempted to address the potential conflicts proactively by bringing the parties together over an extended period. A senior case manager explained:

> *So the social workers wouldn't feel dispossessed, we spent the first month together just doing team-building exercises. During that orientation, we had the social workers and the new case managers (who were formerly all nurses) together. We had several sessions where we met from 5 to 7 p.m. with dinner afterward. We reviewed our job descriptions and discussed areas of potential conflict. We even had a few speakers come in.*

From a nurse manager's perspective, that investment paid off: "When case management first started, there were some issues of role clarification. It took a little time, but with frequent meetings and training we quickly established a sense of work roles."

The Hospital for Special Surgery had multiple mechanisms for working out conflicts among nonphysician care providers:

> *You gotta talk to the person you're having a problem with. Even across functions, we encourage the person-to-person method of conflict resolution. If it's a system problem, a team is assigned to solve it. Then we have "bitch" meetings twice a year where employees are encouraged to bring up any concerns, issues, or suggestions for change. It's a constructive meeting. Staff tell other staff how to resolve their problems.*

As in most other hospitals, however, the options for resolving conflicts between physicians and nonphysicians were not well defined:

> *There are ways for resolving physician conflicts, but only when those conflicts are with other physicians. The chief surgeon can step in to resolve conflicts. In extreme cases, there's also a process for terminations that involves legal counsel.*

There were notable exceptions. New England Baptist took advantage of multidisciplinary meetings convened regularly to work out conflicts about patient care, including conflicts involving physicians. An administrator described the process:

> *We have a staff council that's largely responsible for information sharing among the departments. The staff council deals with medical policy and conflict resolution. ... It's an informal body to air differences. It's more for problem*

solving. We have monthly meetings that are attended by all medical staff, including physicians, nursing, and social work.

Like New England Baptist, Baylor University Medical Center also had developed a fairly comprehensive approach to conflict resolution. In addition to the standard grievance procedures for vertical conflicts, Baylor had several avenues for addressing interdisciplinary conflicts, including conflicts between physicians and nonphysicians. The vice president for medical staff services explained:

We have two or three different channels, actually. At one level, the chief of service can handle conflicts and complaints that are brought to his attention. Second, there is the physician relations committee, which deals with conflicts between the hospital personnel and the doctors and sometimes deals with doctor-doctor conflicts. Third, there is a surgical relations committee that deals with specific incidents that occur in the OR (like, for instance, when a doc is abusive to a nurse or another doc in the OR). Each of these committees meets on an as-needed basis and has about seven members: one nurse, one administrator, and the rest are mostly doctors and allied health professionals.

In addition to those channels, Baylor had a unique but complementary approach to conflict resolution:

Because Baylor is a Baptist hospital, its 10 chaplains play a role in conflict resolution. They teach conflict resolution classes to all employees.

Of all the hospitals studied here, Presbyterian Plano had perhaps the most innovative and far-reaching approach to conflict resolution, encompassing employees across all disciplines.

According to an administrator in the office of human resources, the Presbyterian approach had two tracks:

> *We implemented training classes for all employees that teach employees how to deal with conflict resolution, including adopting appropriate behaviors. There is also a "Pledge to My Peers," which is a structured format for resolving conflicts in a peer-to-peer fashion. An example of this is the principle that "the museum door is locked," meaning that employees shouldn't bring up past grievances when airing a new one with a coworker unless it's unavoidable. Aggrieved employees are encouraged to approach the coworker or supervisor or whoever and say, "I would like to speak with you regarding the pledge," which then signifies to the coworker that an appropriate forum—time, place, mindset—for dialogue needs to be sought. It is important to recognize that to be approached is not seen as either punitive or embarrassing.*

She explained the second track for conflict resolution at Presbyterian Plano:

> *The conflict resolution committee serves to debate more serious grievances. The aggrieved employee picks names out of a hat—four line employees and one manager—in which all the names of active potential committee members are placed. These five randomly chosen committee members listen to both sides of the case and then recommend a course of action to the VP of human resources and the executive director of the hospital. In all cases so far, the VP and exec director went along with the committee's recommendation, which was very positive for the already strong morale at Presby Plano. We've doubled our hospital's size in recent years, and we're in danger of changing from a humanistic to a bureaucratic environment, but these ways of dealing with conflict keep workers feeling connected to each other.*

❖ ASSESSING THE IMPACT OF CROSS-FUNCTIONAL CONFLICT RESOLUTION

To assess the impact of cross-functional conflict resolution, we probed each of the nine hospitals to find out whether a formal cross-functional conflict resolution process was in place for nurses, physical therapists, or physicians. This variable was coded from 0 to 1 for nurses, physical therapists, and physicians, where 0 indicated that the work group did not have access to a formal cross-functional conflict resolution process and 1 indicated that the work group did have access.[108] The results suggest that the availability of cross-functional conflict resolution processes significantly strengthens relational coordination among care providers. Exhibit 8-1 suggests that doubling the inclusiveness of cross-functional conflict resolution produced an 18 percent increase in relational coordination among nurses, physicians, residents, therapists, case managers, and social workers. There is a simpler, more graphic way to observe the impact of cross-functional conflict resolution on relational coordination. Cross-functional conflict resolution was plotted for each of the nine hospitals against relational coordination.

Exhibit 8-1   Impact of Cross-Functional Conflict Resolution on Relational Coordination†

	Relational Coordination
Cross-Functional Conflict Resolution	.18 **
Physicians	−.16 ***
Residents	−.02
Physical Therapists	.07
Case Managers	.05
Social Workers	−.07
Surgical Volume	.00
R-squared	.63

† This exhibit is discussed in the "Notes for Exhibits" chapter beginning on page 315.

Exhibit 8-2 illustrates the positive impact of this work practice on relational coordination among care providers.

Using statistical techniques to account for patient differences, we also found that the inclusiveness of cross-functional conflict resolution significantly improved patient care outcomes.[109] Doubling the inclusiveness of clinical conflict resolution produced a 30 percent reduction in the length of hospital stays and an 18 percent increase in patient satisfaction. Combining all four performance metrics into a single measure of surgical performance, we found that cross-functional conflict resolution increased overall surgical performance by 20 percent. Furthermore, our analysis showed that cross-functional conflict resolution affects performance through its effect on relational coordination.[110]

Exhibit 8-3 summarizes these results, which suggest that healthcare organizations can improve performance by expanding the inclusiveness of cross-functional conflict resolution. But as before, cross-functional conflict resolution is only one component of a high performance work system whose overall effects will be explored in Chapter 17.

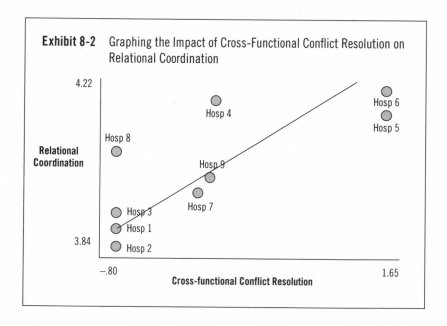

Exhibit 8-2 Graphing the Impact of Cross-Functional Conflict Resolution on Relational Coordination

Exhibit 8-3   Impact of Cross-Functional Conflict Resolution on Surgical Performance†

	Length of Stay	Patient Satisfaction	Postoperative Freedom from Pain	Postoperative Mobility	Surgical Performance Index	Surgical Performance Index
Cross-Functional Conflict Resolution	−.30 ***	.18 ***	.07	.06	.20 ***	−.07
Relational Coordination						.31 ***
Patient Age	−.03	.01	−.01	−.04	.01	.01
Comorbidities	.09	.06	−.01	−.04	−.05	−.05
Preoperative Status	.03	−.01	.20 ***	.28 ***	.17 ***	.16 ***
Surgical Procedure	.01	.11**	.21 ***	.10 **	.16 ***	.16 ***
Psychological Well-being	−.08 +	.14 **	.41 ***	.41 ***	.41 ***	.40 ***
Surgical Volume	.12 **	.08 +	.05	.03	.03	.04
R-squared	.60	.26	.40	.14	.42	.85

† This exhibit is discussed in the "Notes for Exhibits" chapter beginning on page 315.

❖ BOTTOM LINE

High levels of task interdependence create the potential for high levels of conflict, particularly in the context of time and cost pressures. Conflict resolution mechanisms can vary greatly, from training employees to engage in constructive conflict to establishing a panel of peers who will hear conflicts and engage the participants in resolving them. The critical element is that conflict resolution practices are available to resolve conflicts across all functions, including physicians. As with other work practices in this high performance work system, physicians often represent the last frontier. Otherwise well-managed hospitals often neglect to include physicians in cross-functional conflict resolution processes, undermining relational coordination and thus reducing the efficiency of patient care as well as some aspects of quality.

Chapter 9

Invest in Frontline Leadership

We've been downsizing. They wanted to take out management. The motivation for the change was money. Supervision is being done by colleagues now. It's not the same as when it's being done by someone with the time and the knowledge base. There's also consultation to the senior staff that's been lost.

There are competing views on whether frontline supervisors improve or undermine coordination between workers. Organizational theorists such as Richard Hackman and Richard Walton have suggested that active supervision encourages workers to focus more on their vertical ties up and down the organizational hierarchy, distracting attention from lateral ties with their coworkers and thereby undermining teamwork.[111] This view was especially prevalent in the 1980s and 1990s, when empowerment was a popular goal of many organizations and supervisors were widely suspected of standing in the way of achieving this goal.

But theorists in the human relations tradition such as Douglas McGregor and Rensis Likert argued, to the contrary, that supervisors play a critical role in achieving organizational effectiveness through their role in coaching and feedback.[112] McGregor pointed out moreover that providing coaching and feedback can be far more time-intensive than the traditional directive style of supervision: "It is far quicker to hand a man a list of tasks to perform than to discuss with him the reasons for why these tasks need to be done." Consistent with McGregor's argument that it is more time-consuming to engage in coaching and feedback than simply to boss people around, Lyman Porter and Edward Lawler found that supervisors tend to take on a more facilitative style when their span of control is small (fewer employees to manage) and a more directive style when their span of control is large (more employees to manage).[113] This suggests that to enable supervisors to play a less directive role and spend more time engaged in coaching and feedback, it helps to invest in higher levels of supervisory staffing.

What does this have to do with relational coordination? In a highly interdependent work process such as patient care, it is often difficult to disentangle the web of causality to determine how specific members of the care team are contributing in a positive or negative way to patient outcomes. For this reason, coaching and feedback can be powerful in helping care providers improve their coordination by better understanding how their actions can hinder or facilitate the patient care process. However, coaching and feedback are time-intensive and therefore difficult to accomplish in a meaningful way without a deliberate allocation of time to those tasks.

Supervisory staffing trends have moved in the opposite direction. In healthcare, supervisory spans of control have been on the rise. Cuts in supervisory staffing often are motivated by the belief that leaner supervisory structures are more empowering as well as more cost-effective. For those who are convinced that supervisors do not add value, cutting supervisors is equivalent to cutting waste. This has been a persuasive argument in some hospitals. In other hospitals, managers believe that supervisors play a critical frontline leadership role, particularly with respect to coaching and feedback, and that it is worthwhile to invest resources in this critical function. As a result of these differing perspectives, the level of supervisory staffing varied widely across the nine hospitals we studied.

In hospitals with relatively high levels of supervisory staffing, supervisors described their jobs as including substantial amounts of coaching and feedback in addition to formal performance reviews. In a hospital with one supervisor for every six social workers, supervisors played a highly proactive role. In a hospital with one nurse manager or supervisor for every five nurses, the supervisory role also was highly proactive, including staff development that encompassed coaching and feedback in addition to more formal performance reviews. A nurse manager in this hospital explained her role:

> *I spend most of my time helping staff with clinical issues. I help the nurses with problem solving as needed. There are a lot of tricky issues. The senior nurses and I give lots of feedback.*

Her colleague in social work added:

> *People need ongoing praise and correction, constant recognition, and feedback. That should happen on a consistent basis.*

This active supervisory role sometimes was reinforced at higher levels. A director of physical therapy at the Hospital for Special Surgery explained the approach used by her and her assistant director:

> *Teamwork is fostered by the open-door policies that Mary and I have. I've instructed my team that we can be bothered at any time. Often this means that I constantly have people coming in and out during the day. We are very available.*

As was noted above, the coaching and feedback role is more time-consuming than a directive approach or a hands-off approach to supervision. At New England Baptist, with 12 nurses per manager, supervision was fairly hands-on. Some of the softer supervisory responsibilities were taken quite seriously, such as formal performance reviews and conflict resolution. However, coaching and feedback were not considered central to the supervisory function. Instead, those activities were allocated to a senior group of nurses: clinical nurse specialists. Those nurses served as supervisory supplements in the sense of having formal responsibilities for coaching their fellow nurses.

In hospitals in which nurse managers were responsible for 35 to 40 nurses, the supervisory role was more constrained. Many aspects of coaching and feedback could not be performed because of the constraints of the workload. In particular, there was little expectation that nurse managers would allocate time for coaching and feedback. Sometimes it was expected that nonsupervisory senior staff would take over those roles:

> *The supervisory ratio has changed. We have fewer managers per employee. We have five directors of nursing, then each unit has a nursing manager, and that's it. But we have a high utilization of senior staff as team leaders and mentors.*

With no time allocated to these senior staff members to carry out coaching and feedback, however, it was not clear whether that expectation could be met. The head of human resources conceded the difficulty:

> *Managers can only give developmental feedback once a year. But people need ongoing praise and correction, constant recognition, and feedback. That should happen on a consistent basis. You can do that if you manage by walking around. If you read* The One Minute Manager, *that's what it's like.*

From the perspective of central administration, this concept of one-minute management appeared more feasible than it did from the perspective of nursing managers who were working under time pressure. As a nurse manager at Massachusetts General Hospital explained:

> *The bad part is that people are more on their own. It's a more complex environment and more crisis-driven, but we have less time to help people.*

A frontline care provider explained:

> *When we had regular supervision, you would call your supervisor for recommendations in a crisis. Then you would get formal feedback too. It wasn't just a luxury, it was a real value added. When you're running around with tremendous pressure, it's real value added to stop with someone and reflect on what you're doing.*

At a hospital with 60 nurses per manager, supervisors were reported to be responsible for scheduling, formal performance review, and conflict resolution and "technically" were expected to provide coaching and informal performance feedback as well. However, statements that managers were "technically" or "theoretically" responsible for coaching and feedback suggested that they did not do much of it, nor were they seriously expected to, in light of their workload. These supervisory responsibilities existed primarily on paper because of the hospital's lack of investment in the staffing resources needed to perform them. A nurse manager at Massachusetts General Hospital explained:

> *We've been downsizing. They wanted to take out management. The motivation for the change was money. Each department was challenged to work this out. Many of us are looking for new models of supervision. Supervision is being done by colleagues now. It's not the same as when it's being done by someone with the time and the knowledge*

base. There's also consultation to the senior staff that's been lost.

Such cuts seem shortsighted. Cuts in supervisory staffing had been made in some cases not only in response to cost pressures, however, but also because supervisors had become obstacles rather than facilitators. The vice president for nursing at the Hospital for Special Surgery explained:

We shifted from eight units run by head nurses, nurse supervisors, and other intermediate administration to flattening out and just having four units run by nurse managers. So you can say it decentralized our formerly hierarchical structure. It is a flattened model, almost too much. But we needed to get rid of those intermediate supervisors—they were impeding communication between nurses and the unit managers.

A director of physical therapy at Massachusetts General Hospital described a similar rationale for the reduction in supervisory staffing:

There used to be a director, five assistant directors, and six supervisors. You had to do everything through the managers—it was just a big bureaucracy, and I think that the people on the floor felt a bit out of touch because sometimes it seemed like the managers weren't listening to the people on the floor. They've done away with that, and now it's just me.

Instead of retraining supervisors to take on a coaching, facilitative role, supervisory levels were cut instead. Reductions in supervisory staffing then led to the problems described above, in which frontline clinical personnel suffered from a lack of support in carrying out their work. Another option is to train supervisors to play a facilitative role. Such investments have been shown in other complex industries—such as airlines—to be a key element for building shared goals, shared knowledge, and mutual respect among frontline employees.[114]

Like many other leadership skills, coaching and feedback are learned skills. Healthcare organizations therefore need to invest in training supervisors to carry out their coaching and feedback role, an investment that was taken seriously in only a few of the hospitals we studied. As the head of human resources at Beth Israel Deaconess explained:

> *We need groups of employees who can identify a process and streamline it to benefit the patient and organizational efficiency. Probably the most fundamental way we do this is to develop our managers. ... We put a lot of energy into developing managers as creative problem solvers and team builders. This is critical in making the philosophy of empowerment come alive.*

But training supervisors to foster relational coordination through coaching and feedback, though critically important, will not pay off if supervisors are inadequately staffed to carry out those roles.

❖ ASSESSING THE IMPACT OF SUPERVISORY STAFFING

To assess the impact of supervisory staffing, we measured the ratio of supervisors to frontline care providers in each of the nine hospitals for nurses, physical therapists, and physicians.[115] The results suggest that supervisory staffing significantly strengthened relational coordination among care providers. Exhibit 9-1 suggests that doubling supervisory staffing produced a 19 percent increase in relational coordination among nurses, physicians, residents, therapists, case managers, and social workers. There is a simpler, more graphic way to observe the impact of supervisory staffing on relational coordination. Supervisory staffing was plotted for each of the nine hospitals against relational coordination. Exhibit 9-2 illustrates a positive impact of this work practice on relational coordination among care providers.

Exhibit 9-1   Impact of Supervisory Staffing on Relational Coordination†

	Relational Coordination
Supervisory Staffing	.19 *
Physicians	−.16 ***
Residents	−.02
Physical Therapists	.06
Case Managers	.04
Social Workers	−.07 +
Surgical Volume	−.00
R-squared	.58

† This exhibit is discussed in the "Notes for Exhibits" chapter beginning on page 315.

Exhibit 9-2   Graphing the Impact of Supervisory Staffing on Relational Coordination*

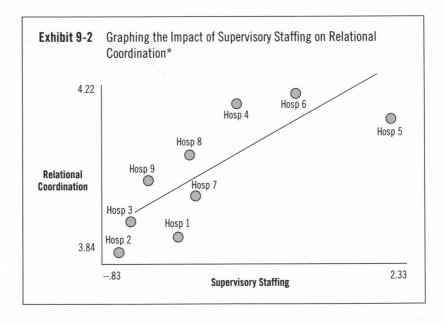

Using statistical techniques to account for patient differences,[116] we also found that supervisory staffing significantly contributed to patient care outcomes. Doubling supervisory staffing enabled a 33 percent reduction in the length of hospital stays and a 20 percent increase in patient satisfaction. Combining all four performance metrics into a single measure of surgical performance, we found that supervisory staffing increased overall surgical performance by 17 percent. Furthermore, our analysis showed that supervisory staffing affects performance *through* its effect on relational coordination.[117]

Exhibit 9-3 summarizes these results, which suggest that healthcare organizations can improve performance by increasing supervisory staffing. Remember however that supervision, like the other work practices we introduce in this book, is only one component of a larger high performance work system whose overall effects will be explored in Chapter 17.

❖ BOTTOM LINE

Supervision should not be seen as antithetical to empowerment; instead, supervisors can facilitate empowerment by supporting care providers to coordinate directly with one another.

Exhibit 9-3   Impact of Supervisory Staffing on Surgical Performance†

	Length of Stay	Patient Satisfaction	Postoperative Freedom from Pain	Postoperative Mobility	Surgical Performance Index	Surgical Performance Index
Supervisory Staffing	−.33 ***	.20 ***	.00	−.02	.17 ***	−.06
Relational Coordination						.30 ***
Patient Age	−.02	.00	−.01	−.05	.00	.01
Comorbidities	.08 +	.07	−.02	−.05	−.04	−.05
Preoperative Status	.03	−.02	.19 ***	.28 ***	.17 ***	.16 ***
Surgical Procedure	.00	.11 **	.22 ***	.11 *	.15 ***	.16 ***
Psychological Well-being	−.10 +	.14 **	.40 ***	.41 ***	.41 ***	.40 ***
Surgical Volume	.11 **	.10 *	.04	.00	.02	.04
R-squared	.65	.39	.37	.12	.33	.84

† This exhibit is discussed in the "Notes for Exhibits" chapter beginning on page 315.

However, supervisors cannot play this role if they are inadequately staffed. Higher supervisory staffing enables supervisors to engage in coaching and feedback, supporting higher levels of relational coordination among care providers and thereby enabling them to achieve improvements in the quality and efficiency of patient care.

Chapter 10

Design Jobs for Focus

Since the publication of Wickham Skinner's classic essay "The Focused Factory" in 1974, management scholars have debated the benefits of organizational focus.[118, 119] The arguments in favor of organizational focus are straightforward: When organizations create areas of focus, their physical and human assets can be tailored specifically to accomplish a narrowly defined set of objectives, whether in a manufacturing or a service setting.[120] The empirical evidence largely has supported this argument, showing that more focused firms perform better on a number of dimensions.[121] Regina Herzlinger's book on market-driven healthcare draws on best practices in other industries to generate lessons for transforming healthcare.[122] One of her central recommendations is that healthcare organizations organize their staffs around areas of patient focus rather than attempting to offer a wide range of diverse services. However, evidence of the performance benefits of focus has been largely anecdotal in healthcare, drawing frequently on James Heskett's case study of Shouldice, the Canadian hospital whose delivery system is organized around repairing hernias, with 100 percent of staff time allocated to patients who need hernia repair.[123]

In our study, administrators at focused hospitals felt that their hospitals had some advantages over more diversified hospitals. The chief operating officer at the Hospital for Special Surgery explained:

> *To get the best outcomes for total joints requires focused care. We have the best radiologists. Also, our operating rooms are orthopedic-focused. Nurses in and out of the OR know the intricacies of orthopedics. We do research on prosthetics. These are the benefits of focus. Because we are a stand-alone orthopedics hospital, we can focus how we want and don't have to fight for resources. Quality improvement is best if it's driven by an innate knowledge of what you are trying to improve. As a focused hospital, we have that.*

A nurse who had left that hospital to work elsewhere gave her perspective on the benefits of focus:

> *Before I came here I worked at the Hospital for Special Surgery, and it was all orthopedics. It was such a different atmosphere because everybody was thinking orthopedics, and here I'll call for a piece of equipment and nobody knows what it is. I'll say: "What do you mean, you don't know what it is? It's very important." Well, it's important to me, but it's not important to people on the other floor. So, you know, that took a lot of adjusting for me.*

Focus may be achieved at the expense of other valued outcomes, however, including integrative capabilities, access to internal labor and capital markets, the ability to respond holistically to customer requirements, and the ability to adapt to changing environments.[124] The net benefits of focus are therefore still open to question, particularly at the organizational level, where the advantages of diversification are most apparent. The same chief operating officer at the Hospital for Special Surgery pointed out some of the disadvantages of focus:

> *A full-service institution can discount orthopedic care and could make it up in OB/GYN, for example, as some of our competitors do. Managed care has powerful effects on us. A full-service hospital can take $1,000 less for a knee replacement. We can't. The marketplace is driving us down. To attract cases, full-service hospitals can use other departments to offset its costs. Given the current trends, we might become one hospital with New York Hospital.*

In addition, he explained, when patients had complications or comorbid conditions, they often required referral to a full-service hospital.

Consistent with these disadvantages, overall organizational focus has decreased slightly among U.S. firms in recent decades. But meanwhile, focus at the suborganizational level has increased over that period.[125] We will see that focus at the level of the job can help to drive higher levels of relational coordination among care providers, with positive effects on the quality and efficiency of patient care.

❖ PATIENT-FOCUSED JOB DESIGN

In designing jobs, the degree and type of specialization are key considerations. Some jobs are designed to be broad, encompassing a wide range of tasks that span a work process from beginning to end. Other jobs are more specialized, focusing on a narrower set of tasks. Two distinct approaches to job design—the technical or mechanistic approach and the psychological or motivational approach—offer competing perspectives on the benefits of broad versus specialized jobs. The technical approach to job design holds that specialization and the simplification of work help organizations achieve maximum efficiency. The psychological approach holds that broad jobs are more intrinsically motivating, satisfying, and conducive to achieving desired outcomes because they provide higher levels of autonomy, significance, and feedback.[126] Neither of these approaches has focused on how job design affects the coordination of work, however. Even seemingly minor changes to job design may affect the work process not just within jobs but also between jobs, by influencing the nature, frequency, and quality of interactions between workers who are assigned to different jobs.

Even in organizations that are highly diversified, delivering a wide array of services, focus can be achieved through focused job design, which pays particular attention to a specific type of patient or condition. This is often called patient-focused job design. With patient-focused job design, workers can achieve greater specialization and skill with regard to the treatment of a particular type of patient or condition. However, greater specialization and skill are not the only benefits. Patient-focused job design also allows employees to become better at coordinating with one another. It strengthens relationships among care providers working with a particular patient population, enhancing the coordination of care by helping providers build shared goals, shared knowledge, and mutual respect. By giving care providers the opportunity to interact repeatedly with the same colleagues and patients over time, focused job design should produce higher levels of relational coordination among care providers, resulting in higher-quality and more efficient patient care.

❖ ASSESSING THE IMPACT OF PATIENT-FOCUSED JOB DESIGN

To assess the impact of patient-focused job design, we measured it in each of the nine hospitals as the percentage of care provider time dedicated to joint replacement patients by the physicians, nurses, physical therapists, and case managers assigned to work with that patient population.[127] Interestingly, patient-focused job design was not related to the degree of organizational focus. Hospitals with high degrees of organizational focus—focusing only on orthopedics, for example, such as New England Baptist, the Hospital for Special Surgery, and the Hospital for Joint Diseases—did not always have high levels of patient-focused job design. Although care providers at those hospitals spent 100 percent of their time with orthopedics patients, the percentage of time they spent with joint replacement patients—as opposed to patients with back injuries, hip fractures, or other conditions—was sometimes higher and sometimes lower than in hospitals that were more diversified. We found that patient-focused job design significantly strengthened relational coordination among care providers whereas organizational focus did not. Exhibit 10-1 suggests that doubling patient-focussed job design produced a 20 percent increase in relational coordination among nurses, physicians, residents, therapists, case managers, and social workers. There is a simpler, more graphic way to observe the impact of patientfocused job design on relational coordination. Patient-focused job design was plotted for each of the

Exhibit 10-1   Impact of Patient-Focused Job Design on Relational Coordination

	Relational Coordination
Patient-Focused Job Design	.20 **
Physicians	−.16 ***
Residents	−.04
Physical Therapists	.05
Case Managers	.08
Social Workers	−.10 +
Surgical Volume	−.10 *
R-squared	.60

nine hospitals against relational coordination. Exhibit 10-2 illustrates its impact patient-focused job design on relational coordination among care providers.

Using statistical techniques to account for patient differences and controlling for differences in overall organizational focus, we found that patient-focused job design also improved patient care outcomes.[128] Specifically, patient-focused job design produced shorter hospital stays and higher levels of patient satisfaction. To illustrate, doubling patient-focused job design produced a 19 percent reduction in the length of hospital stays and a 20 percent increase in patient satisfaction but no significant change in postoperative pain or functioning. Combining these four performance metrics into a single measure of surgical performance, we see that patient-focused job design increased overall surgical performance by 14 percent. Furthermore, our analysis shows that it influences performance through its effect on relational coordination.[129]

Exhibit 10-3 summarizes the results, which suggest that healthcare organizations can improve their performance by adopting a higher level of job focus around specific patient

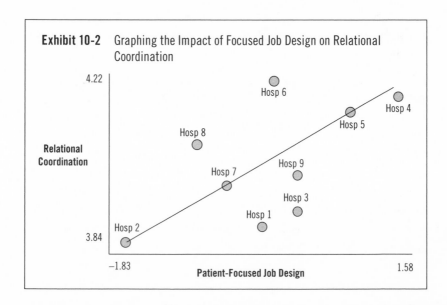

Exhibit 10-2   Graphing the Impact of Focused Job Design on Relational Coordination

Exhibit 10-3   Impact of Patient-Focused Job Design on Surgical Performance

	Length of Stay	Patient Satisfaction	Postoperative Freedom from Pain	Postoperative Mobility	Surgical Performance Index	Surgical Performance Index
Patient-Focused Job Design	−.19 ***	.20 **	.00	−.01	.14 **	−.01
Relational Coordination						.27 ***
Patient Age	−.02	.01	.00	−.05	.00	.01
Comorbidities	.08 *	.07	−.01	−.05	−.04	−.05
Preoperative Status	.03	−.02	.22 ***	.27 ***	.16 ***	.16 ***
Surgical Srocedure	−.02	.13 **	.23 ***	.09 **	.17 ***	.16 ***
Psychological Well-Being	−.08 +	.13 **	.40 ***	.40 ***	.40 ***	.40 ***
Surgical Volume	.31 ***	.01	.04	.01	−.10	.05
R-squared	.38	.19	.31	.08	.24	.83

populations. As with the other work practices, however, patient-focused job design is only one element of a larger system of work practices; these effects are not expected to occur in the absence of other complementary changes.

❖ A SECOND TYPE OF JOB FOCUS: THE HOSPITALIST JOB DESIGN FOR PHYSICIANS

There is a second type of job focus that is particularly relevant for physicians. Relative to other care providers, physicians tend to lack focus around a particular site of work. Whereas other members of the care provider team—including nurses, residents, physical therapists, social workers, and case managers—tend to be hospital-based and therefore work together on an ongoing basis in the same location, physicians traditionally have maintained private practices outside the hospital, coming to the hospital primarily when their patients are hospitalized. They are far less likely than nurses and other care providers to have jobs that are focused on providing care in a single location. This lack of focus makes it hard for physicians to participate in the coordination of patient care. Physicians are expected to be at the center of coordination and decision making, yet they tend to be present in the hospital on an intermittent basis as a result of their external responsibilities. Moreover, as reimbursement levels have been reduced, physicians have been required to see more and more patients in their private practices to maintain their incomes. The care providers we interviewed in the nine-hospital study often described the challenge of tracking down physicians to communicate with them about patient needs. Here is an illustrative example:

> *We have a computer, but if there's a question about a physician order, you need the answer right now; you can't have an answer two hours from now. So you page the resident, or you get the attending physician, or you go find them because they're either here in clinic or they're in the OR, or they're in their office seeing patients, or they're manning a clinic.*

Economists have argued recently that physician job design is indeed a problem and in particular that "organizational independence and clinical interdependence of physicians and hospitals" is one major factor in poor coordination.[130]

One response to these challenges has been the creation of a new job design for physicians called the *hospitalist or hospital specialist*.[131] Rather than following their patients from outpatient care to inpatient care, physicians now have the option of handing them off to a hospitalist—a hospital-based physician—who becomes responsible for a patient's care during the hospital stay. The result of this job design is that some physicians are dedicated to hospital-based care, working repeatedly in the same hospital with the same staff, so that patients can be admitted to the care of a dedicated hospitalist physician rather than remaining under the care of their own private practice physician while they are in the hospital. We expect that this job design will enable hospital-based physicians to develop stronger relational coordination with the rest of the hospital-based care provider team, resulting in higher-quality and more efficient patient care.

❖ ASSESSING THE IMPACT OF THE HOSPITALIST JOB DESIGN

To assess the impact of the hospitalist job design, we went beyond the nine-hospital study of surgical care and took advantage of a natural experiment occurring at Newton-Wellesley Hospital, where hospitalists worked side by side on the same medical units with physicians who were not hospitalists. Our results suggest that the hospitalist job design significantly strengthened relational coordination among care providers. Exhibit 10-4 suggests that the hospitalist job design produced a 66 percent increase in relational coordination between physicians and other care providers, including nurses, therapists, case managers, and social workers.

There is another way to assess the impact of the hospitalist job design on relational coordination. Exhibit 10-5 is a matrix that shows the strength of relational coordination between physicians and each other care provider, showing relational coordination

---

Exhibit 10-4   Impact of Hospitalist Job Design on Relational Coordination†

	Relational Coordination
Hospitalist Job Design	.66 **
Patient Age	−.00
Patient Gender	−.08
Patient Severity of Illness	−.00
Probability of Patient Assignment to Hospitalist	−.86 +
R-squared	.16

† This exhibit is discussed in the "Notes for Exhibits" chapter beginning on page 315.

Exhibit 10-5   Illustrating the Impact of Hospitalist Job Design on Relational Coordination†

	Relational Coordination Reported With				
	Physicians	**Residents**	**Nurses**	**Therapists**	**Case Managers**
Nurses	4.30	3.97	4.40	3.94	4.16
	3.34	3.90	4.31	3.80	3.96
	(.000)	(.194)	(.096)	(.137)	(.015)
Therapists	2.69	2.79	4.07	4.21	3.81
	2.10	2.19	3.89	4.34	3.70
	(.001)	(.001)	(.026)	(.827)	(.183)
Case Managers	4.17	3.20	4.18	3.20	4.62
	3.22	3.29	4.26	3.16	4.38
	(.000)	(.701)	(.830)	(.425)	(.020)

† This exhibit is discussed in the "Notes for Exhibits" chapter beginning on page 315.

first for hospitalist physicians and then, below that number, for nonhospitalist physicians. We can see that the average level of relational coordination between physicians and other key care providers was about 30 percent higher when the physician was a hospitalist than it was when the physician had a traditional job design (see the Physician column of Exhibit 10-5).

Using statistical techniques to account for patient differences, we also found that the hospitalist job design improves patient care outcomes.[132] Specifically, the hospitalist job design reduces the length of stay and the total cost of the stay while also reducing the likelihood of readmission to the hospital. To illustrate, the hospitalist job design produced a 46 percent reduction in the length of hospital stay, a 7 percent reduction in the cost of the stay, a 24 percent reduction in the likelihood of readmission after 7 days, and a 33 percent reduction in the likelihood of readmission after 30 days, with no significant effect on patient mortality. Exhibit 10-6 summarizes these results. These results suggest that healthcare organizations can improve their performance by adopting the hospitalist job design. As with the other work practices, however, the hospitalist job design is not expected to achieve these outcomes on its own. To be successful, it should be

Exhibit 10-6 Impact of Hospitalist Job Design on Medical Performance†

	Length of Stay	Total Costs	Mortality	Readmit within 7 Days	Readmit within 30 Days
Hospitalist Job Design	−.46 ***	−.07 **	−.26	−.24 +	−.33 *
Patient Age	−.01 ***	.002 ***	.03 ***	.00	.00
Patient Gender	.08	−.03 +	−.23	−.07	−.22 **
Patient Severity of Illness	−.36 ***	.11 ***	.20 ***	.09 ***	.10 ***
Patient Days in ICU	.52 ***	.09 ***	−.05	−.08 *	−.08 **
Probability of Patient Assignment to Hospitalist	−1.70 ***	−1.03 ***	−4.85 ***	−1.45 *	−1.89 ***
Patient Ties to Hospital	—	—	—	3.02 **	2.33 ***
R-squared	.11	.37	NA	NA	NA
Chi-squared	NA	NA	.0000	.0000	.0000
Observations	6,699	6,866	6,866	6,866	6,866

† This exhibit is discussed in the "Notes for Exhibits" chapter beginning on page 315.

adopted along with the other high performance work practices described in this book.

❖ BOTTOM LINE

Focused job design enables healthcare organizations to improve coordination among their care providers, improving both the quality and the efficiency of the patient care they offer. Hospitals that are "focused factories" as well as those that are general all-purpose hospitals can design jobs that allow their care providers to focus more time on a particular patient population. Indeed, creating focus at the job level allows organizations to achieve the strategic benefits of diversification while gaining some of the operational benefits of focus.

Another job design innovation specifically for physicians—the hospitalist—can further achieve focus. Other scholars have found that hospitalists generate efficiencies. According to Janet Coffman and Thomas Rundall, "most evaluations found that patients managed by hospitalists had lower costs or charges than patients in comparison groups and that these savings were achieved primarily by reducing length of stay."[133] We have gone further, showing that the hospitalist job design can also produce improvements in quality outcomes. We also have shown how hospitalists produce those results. Our study at Newton-Wellesley Hospital revealed that the hospitalist job design produces higher levels of relational coordination between physicians and other care providers, thereby resulting in more efficient care while also producing improvements in the quality of care. It is clear that focused job design—both the hospitalist job design for physicians and the patient-focused job design for all care providers—can enable healthcare organizations to achieve higher levels of relational coordination, leading to more effective care delivery. But focused job design is only one component of a larger system. Another critical component is flexible boundaries between jobs. As we will see in Chapter 11, jobs should have a core area of focus but with flexible boundaries between them.

Chapter 11

Make Job Boundaries Flexible

There are customs—like the fact that a physical therapist will never deal with bedpans and such—that go above and beyond licensing. These customs have a negative effect, like when a physical therapist in the patient's room will go get a nurse to deal with the bedpan, making things difficult.

Work rules in the form of policies and procedures govern much of workplace behavior. Whether generated by professional associations, by the personnel office, or through union negotiations, they set the boundaries for acceptable behavior. The work rules that most influence relational coordination are those that specify which tasks belong to a particular function or work group and in doing so exclude other work groups from performing those tasks. Exclusive work rules have the positive effect of clarifying roles and ensuring that the person performing the task has the necessary technical competence and training. Traditionally, organizational theorists argued that work rules specifying the exclusive assignment of certain categories of work to certain workers should improve performance by increasing focus and role clarity. Indeed, though often associated with unionization, formal work rules emerged as part of a system of scientific management advocated by Frederick Winslow Taylor that was intended to improve workplace functioning.[134]

Despite their benefits, however, work rules can introduce rigidities into the work flow, thus reducing both job satisfaction and performance.[135] Work rules may be beneficial for tasks with low uncertainty, but they are expected to be detrimental for tasks with high uncertainty.[136] Consistent with this reasoning, Kim Clark and Takahiro Fujimoto showed that overlapping task boundaries were conducive to success in a product development environment characterized by high levels of uncertainty, interdependence, and time constraints.[137] Gil Preuss found that overlapping task boundaries on nursing units were associated with improved information quality and a reduced frequency of medication errors.[138] Whereas specialization is useful for developing expertise and maintaining role clarity, flexibility between specialized jobs allows organizations to achieve optimal performance. Why? Flexibility fosters shared knowledge among people who work in different areas of specialization while helping to build mutual respect and reduce status boundaries.

In healthcare, work rule restrictions take the form of specifying each discipline's scope of work. There are several sources of work rule restrictions. State-level professional licensing organizations for physicians, nurses, social workers, and therapists determine the scope of work of the disciplines they represent. The license that is given out by each state healthcare organization has a practice act that defines the functions a caregiver is able to perform. Individual hospitals also have their own internal organizations, typically distinct for each discipline, to determine the scope of work for the disciplines they represent. Both external and internal regulations evolve over time, and internal regulations are made within the parameters of external regulations.

Licensing requirements that prevent providers from doing work for which they are not trained are intended to protect patients from harm. Some work rules are more a matter of custom or culture, however, and some have little to do with assuring technical competence. The director of rehabilitation at the Hospital for Special Surgery noted that certain customs discourage nurses from helping physical therapists:

> *There are certain cultural tendencies that often inhibit others from doing their work. For instance, therapists train all nurses in mobility, but still nurses are often reluctant to deal with moving the patient, getting the patient out of bed, etc. It's partly because they still feel that they aren't qualified, and partly because that's just considered a PT thing.*

There was also a lack of helping in the other direction. For example, the director of social work at Beth Israel New York explained:

> *There are customs—like the fact that a physical therapist will never deal with bedpans and such—that go above and beyond licensing. These customs have a negative effect, like when a physical therapist in the patient's room will go get a nurse just to deal with the bedpan, making things difficult.*

In cases where specialized skill was not the issue, work rules took on the quality of "it's not my job," fostering a lack of respect for the work of the other discipline and a lack of regard for other people's time.

Similarly, at Massachusetts General Hospital, orthopedics nurses did not get the patients out of bed even though the physical therapists had trained them to do so and even though the Nurse Practice Act, which the nurses followed, did not prevent them from performing the activity. According to the director of physical therapy, "They don't feel they're qualified to do this, whereas we feel that after the first day, it isn't that big a deal." According to him, the physical therapists at Massachusetts General were more flexible about their boundaries in the interests of providing timely patient care:

> *In ortho, physical therapists definitely do the bedpans. You see, length of stay is so compressed and time is so valuable. You'll only delay yourself if you try to hunt down the nurse's aide.*

All hospitals in a particular state face the same externally defined work rules. As a result of the interpretations and initiatives taken by the hospitals' internal committees or union representatives, however, work rule restrictiveness varies from hospital to hospital. Internal committees can be used to make externally defined work rules even more restrictive. The director of social work at Massachusetts General Hospital explained:

> *A scope of practice is developed at MGH for each of the professions. Licensing doesn't tell you exactly what you can or cannot do. Licensing only provides a baseline—can you do hands-on care, can you medicate, and so on. So we've developed a scope of practice that delineates social work's sphere of influence. Could other disciplines do what we do? Theoretically yes, but practically speaking, their lack of a knowledge base limits others from doing consultation, or counseling, or dealing with family conflict. Others could develop that knowledge base, but it would be chaotic. Also, it might create malpractice problems. Social work could walk a joint replacement patient, but if the patient fell, we wouldn't be covered by malpractice [insurance].*

Other parties have worked to *reduce* the restrictiveness of work rules by expanding the scope of work of a particular work group to include work that is also performed by other work groups. The Joint Commission for the Accreditation of Healthcare Organizations, for example, has asked nonprofessional work groups to define their core and noncore functions to determine what kinds of cross-training can be conducted for the purpose of increasing a hospital's ability to respond in emergency situations. An administrator from Massachusetts General Hospital explained that: "a consultant came in to talk about functional silos and about becoming better at working across disciplinary lines." This cross-functional approach focused primarily on so-called nonskilled personnel, however, and had not yet been extended to those in the professional disciplines.

Work rule restrictions vary across hospitals and across work groups within a hospital. In some hospitals, work rules are well established and so taken for granted that they are not questioned. Work rules can be taken for granted to the extent that their restrictiveness is not even perceived. Instead, their limitations have become like customs or even laws of nature. In other hospitals, by contrast, the boundaries between jobs are more dynamic and are treated more flexibly.

One of the most common licensing issues we uncovered was between social workers and the newly emerging care coordinators or case managers. In some ways, case management required both the clinical skills of a nurse and a social worker's knowledge of family dynamics and outpatient resources. However, hospitals most often determined that the core job requirement for being a case manager was the registered nurse license rather than the social worker license. A nurse manager at Beth Israel New York explained:

> *There's a lot of issues with case management. Like how the care coordinator and the social worker define their*

roles. We're still working this out. It's the development of these new unit-based teams that feeds discussion.

Another licensing issue was found between nurses and technicians. A senior vice president at Baylor University Medical Center explained:

The role of nurse versus tech is still flexible, and we're working to keep it that way. There may be areas of limitation, but we are obviously trying to prevent that from happening, when possible. There is a practice counsel that is housewide—they look at policies and procedures, and they are examining the nurse-tech model right now.

A third licensing issue was found between physician assistants (PAs) and registered nurses (RNs) regarding the extent to which physician assistants could relate to nurses as though they were physicians. A care coordinator at Beth Israel New York explained:

The PA is a lower licensing level than the RN. Everything they do is under the auspices of the physician they're working for. I should not say lower. They are different jobs. They are technical people with usually two years of training. If you get a good one, they do very well, but they have no independent function. The doctor has to sign all the orders. The biggest thing is that they don't have the whole feeling for the patient. That piece is a little bit missing, but here they are working very well in their roles. I was very skeptical when I came. I'm used to working with residents, you know, who are physicians, and I was a little bit uncomfortable. At first we had a couple of PAs who felt they were more educated than they were. They thought they were doctors, and they're not. The group we have now is wonderful. They work well within their scope. They know what they don't know. They interact with other people appropriately. They're great.

Specific rules governed the scope of what a physician assistant could do. For example, "since the nurse legally can't take phone orders from the PA, this means that although legally the PA can phone the nurse, he or she basically will restrict him- or herself to written orders."

Some healthcare administrators pointed out the positive aspects of licensing restrictions in terms of role clarity and suggested that there was sufficient flexibility across roles beyond the restrictions set by licensing. A director of case management at the Hospital for Joint Diseases explained:

> *We find the licensing requirements to be an assistance, not a hindrance. If licensing doesn't prohibit it and you do someone else's work, we ask you to document it, and you get paid for it. As far as work rules are concerned, we don't find much conflict.*

More frequently, administrators were supportive of increasing the flexibility of job boundaries to achieve organizational efficiency goals, particularly staffing coverage or preventing delays that would increase the length of stay unnecessarily. According to the director of human resources at Baylor University Medical Center:

> *There is a lot of overlap between the licensing for different disciplines, which is good because that means that different functional groups can cover for each other. But now we are conducting a study of licensing requirements of the allied health professionals and nursing to allow the staff greater flexibility. There is some conflict around IVs and whether nonnursing staff may work with them.*

The common challenge was to limit licensing restrictions to areas of skill requirements, allowing functions to overlap where practical, and encouraging collaboration whenever it would add value. The vice president of human resources at Beth Israel Deaconess described this challenge:

There is probably a good reason why we need a licensed person to do certain things when a certain skill set is needed. Sometimes you want a boiler fixer and not just any mechanic. Where licensing is necessary, it's used as it's supposed to be. Professionals are very proud of their licenses. They are a mark of professional achievement and a recognition of skill. They want those initials on their badges. But take, for instance, a social worker like Michael Hubner. She's made many contributions to her discipline. But she would describe her job now not as a social worker but as someone who brings disciplines together.

In her view, part of the solution was to put the primary focus on the work process and secondarily on the jobs needed to carry it out:

If you create organizational structures that don't have jobs bounded by definitions of professions but instead look at the process that the jobs are part of, then disciplines that need to come together will. That helps to break down territoriality.

This idea was taking off at Beth Israel Deaconess at the time of the study and appeared to have become a reality at New England Baptist and Presbyterian Plano, where there was a clear ethic calling for staff members to use their judgment and put boundaries aside if necessary in the interests of efficiency and patient well-being. An administrator at New England Baptist explained:

We only have work rules insofar as different people are trained to use certain equipment. In general we have collaborative practices that allow people to pick up each other's slack. ... We try to give each person a better understanding of the other's role. We do team care, and we even include the patients as members of the team.

According to the director of patient services at Presbyterian Plano:

> The scope of work is broadening for nurses over time and also for social workers. We had to broaden their scope of work in order to institute case management. Physical therapists are still pretty direct in what they do. It may go to their licensing requirements; I don't know. And physicians are highly delineated... But there is no problem if people need to help each other. People will cross the line if the patient is in jeopardy. You could go to court for going beyond your license. But I would defend you if your intent was to do good for the patient. Law libraries have these cases—I've looked into it. There can also be legal problems if you don't intervene when a patient is in jeopardy. It all comes down to which would you rather defend? That you tried to help, I think. But in some places, it's less acceptable to help.

The chief of orthopedics at Presbyterian Plano concurred:

> This is the best staff I've ever worked with, and I'm not just blowing smoke at you. We have case managers that really take the medical initiative and responsibility. It's a team.

Although we did not measure job flexibility, it appeared anecdotally that some of the hospitals that had achieved the greatest gains in implementing other high performance work practices had also achieved the greatest degree of job flexibility. It also appeared that certain disciplines—in particular physicians and physical therapists—lagged behind their fellow care providers in the achievement of greater job flexibility.

❖ BOTTOM LINE

We saw in Chapter 10 that job focus, particularly keeping jobs focused on a particular patient population or at a particular location of care delivery, contributes to high levels of relational coordination. At the same time, jobs should not become so focused that they become barriers to coordination with others. Healthcare organizations can achieve the right balance by designing jobs to have a core area of focus around a particular patient population or location but also to have flexible boundaries with the other disciplines caring for the same patient population.

Increasing the flexibility of job boundaries is difficult because it threatens people's sense of security and introduces a greater element of the unknown into their jobs. Flexibility also introduces the potential for equalizing the status of one's job with those who are considered to be of lower status or threatening one's status as a professional who has a protected and valued area of expertise. Janice Klein observed that rigid job boundaries are often a source of occupational status and pride and for that reason should not be taken lightly.[139]

Still, rigid boundaries are problematic when they exist between work groups that are involved in a highly interdependent work process. According to a recent Institute of Medicine report, rigid boundaries between the healthcare professions are one of the key inhibitors of care coordination and performance improvement in healthcare organizations.[140] For healthcare organizations that can achieve flexible job boundaries without losing distinct areas of professional expertise, we expect that the benefits will include higher levels of relational coordination across disciplines, leading to higher levels of efficiency and better outcomes for patients.

Chapter 12

Create Boundary Spanners

The case manager does the ... discharge planning, utilization review, and social work all rolled into one. The case manager discusses the patient with physical therapy and nursing and with the physician. He or she keeps everyone on track. The case manager has a key pivotal role—he or she coordinates the whole case.

Boundary spanners are staff members whose primary task is to integrate the work of other people around the needs of a particular project, process, or customer.[141] Boundary spanners are expected to be particularly effective when cross-functional coordination is highly critical and/or existing boundaries are highly divisive, making coordination difficult to achieve.[142] Organization design expert Susan Mohrman argued that boundary spanners are a powerful way to resolve the problems that arise from the division of labor. Whether the work takes the form of a project, a process, a product, or the provision of services to a particular customer, their job is to integrate work across functional boundaries.[143] Project managers play the role of boundary spanner in product development settings, while case managers increasingly play the role of boundary spanner in healthcare settings.[144]

What enables boundary spanners to be effective? Boundary spanners are expected to be more effective when there are fewer products, processes, or customers whose information they are responsible for coordinating at any point in time so they can devote more attention to each one.[145] Attempts to make cross-functional liaisons more productive by increasing their case-loads and increasing their reliance on information technology run the risk of reducing their effectiveness by eliminating some of the inherent benefits of cross-functional liaisons as an inter-active rather than programmed coordination mechanism.[146] In a study of flight departures, larger caseloads for boundary spanners yielded lower levels of relational coordination, lead-ing to longer turnaround times, lower employee productivity, and poorer service quality outcomes for passengers.[147]

In healthcare settings, case managers typically play the boundary spanner role. Whether they are trained as nurses or social workers, case managers are responsible for gather-ing information about a patient from the various providers involved in that patient's care, passing the information along to others who need to be informed, and making decisions on the basis of that information or determining which decisions need to be made and by whom.

Case managers were established in the mid–1990s in hospi-tal settings in response to growing pressure to reduce lengths of stay. Much of their role centered on discharge planning: determining when a patient was ready to leave the hospital and where that patient would go next. At Beth Israel Deaconess, where case management was replacing the traditional social work responsibility for managing discharge, the chief of social work explained:

> *The whole point of case management is to work on medi-cal management and utilization. We had a $52 million problem. The organization was in financial crisis. We are*

using case management to pull waste and cost out of the system. Getting people out in a more timely way. Asking things like do we really need another lab test?

Some case managers were responsible for a broader range of tasks than discharge planning. Those tasks ranged from monitoring the resources used for the care of a patient to active involvement in facilitating the sequence of clinical activities and assuring the timely transfer of information to those responsible for downstream activities.

Case managers varied across the nine hospitals in the number of patients for whom they were responsible. In six of the nine hospitals the caseload was more than 20 patients per case manager, and in one it was as high as 40. The caseload appeared to affect the level of attention a case manager could give and the extent to which he or she could be actively involved in coordinating patient care. At the Hospital for Joint Diseases, with a caseload of 27, the director of case management described the challenge:

> *The case managers work an eight-hour day, actually closer to nine, five days a week. On weekends they take turns carrying a beeper, and there are usually a couple of phone calls during the weekend that they need to take care of. The problem is that case managers are overworked—they have about five to seven too many patients. The time factor interferes with their ability to be proactive.*

At Brigham and Women's Hospital, with a similar caseload, a case manager described her job:

> *I am responsible for about 30 patients. … With this number, I just look at the list for problem patients.*

In other hospitals, case managers had smaller caseloads and were expected to play a broader role that involved coordinating care throughout a patient's stay. That broader role brought case managers into more frequent contact with other members of the patient care team. Rather than simply collecting and processing information, they tended to become more engaged in problem solving and to engage the rest of the team in that process, working to create a shared understanding across the different functions regarding the needs of each individual patient. According to the director of patient services at Presbyterian Plano, where case managers had an average caseload of 17 patients:

> *The case manager does the ... discharge planning, utilization review, and social work all rolled into one. The case manager discusses the patient with physical therapy and nursing and with the physician. He or she keeps everyone on track. The case manager has a key pivotal role—he or she coordinates the whole case.*

A case manager at Baylor University Medical Center with a similarly small caseload explained her job:

> *All of our total joints are case managed. We've done their discharge planning prior to them coming in, we follow through to make sure those discharge plans are still in effect, and we've got things on a care map.*

The Baylor case manager was unusual in that she not only worked within the acute hospital setting but had responsibilities that spanned the continuum:

> *My area of responsibility is for orthopedics patients in the total joint program here, at the rehab, and for our long-term care patients. So I'm completely across the continuum. I work with the doctors' offices on preplanning for elective total joints, so I do a lot of work with the doctors' offices prior to admission. And then I work with the nursing staff in the acute care, coordinating patients' care, whether that's*

in the facility, or whether it's home care, or wherever it's going to be most appropriate for the patient. ... We've got healthcare representatives assigned to the majority of our orthopedics patients. I liaison with them on getting information to our patients. They help me schedule the preoperative class for the patients, so patients are well informed when they are admitted.

According to the Baylor case manager, her role had evolved in response to new pressures in the healthcare environment:

I started out in more of an educational role. But those were the days when the DRGs [diagnostic related groups] were just coming into effect. We didn't have managed care, so it was a completely different focus than what it has developed into now. We didn't have patients across the continuum, and the patients were staying in the hospital three to four weeks for a joint replacement. So as things evolved throughout the years and managed care has changed and all these kinds of things have changed, my job has evolved. We've come to realize that having a consistent person who is involved at every stage is a positive thing.

A lot of what I'm doing is providing a common link in communication. As we all know, every single thing you ever learn about somebody is not written down somewhere. It's about the consistency—this person's told you something that you normally wouldn't write down as a clinical charge, that you can pass down to the next person that's going to be taking care of him or pass on to the next group of nurses.

One major challenge of the job was dealing with physicians:

There's probably more than one or two who aren't good at staying in touch. If they don't get in touch with me, I get in touch with them. I know which physicians are in which offices on what day. I have the direct numbers to the operating rooms. [Laughter.] They can't hide. That is part of my job. When the patient is ready and everything is ready to move, one of my biggest jobs is getting that information from the physician and making sure it happens.

Some really haven't accepted my role, even over all these years. Some still think, "That's a physician's decision making, and somebody else shouldn't be involved." They see it as me telling them how to practice medicine, how to do their job, instead of seeing it as a benefit and a partner-type thing. I am more efficient and effective, really. I know their personalities, I know which ones are there, and I know which ones I have to leave alone and let them come by.

The director of care coordination at Baylor explained the complexity of the role:

The case manager is a very difficult, very complex role. You're balancing a lot of different roles. So it takes just the right person to be able to do it. ... And they have multiple reporting relationships. So it's important that someone is able to deal with that kind of multifaceted negotiation relationship. So right away when someone would say, "I can't report to two bosses," I knew I had the wrong person. Because the nature of this role is having to negotiate things like that all the time.

Indeed, the complexity of the boundary spanner role calls for careful selection and, in particular, careful attention to a candidate's ability to engage in conflict resolution. The director of patient care and quality management at the Hospital for Special Surgery explained:

Teamwork is such an important part of the role. When I'm interviewing, I ask them how they've resolved problems in the past. I give them plenty of time. I've been known to wait through three minutes of silence.

The Baylor director of care coordination explained that hospital's criteria for case manager selection:

[Case managers] have to be very, very, very good communicators and negotiators and very assertive but also have a good sense of timing. They have to be very collaborative. These are sort of the subjective behavioral kind of characteristics we look for. Need to have a great ability to deal with confidential information and sensitive information. Have to have a good analytical ability to deal with financial issues. I especially think they have to be willing to be a patient advocate but also be able to balance the financial parameters and think "out of the box" and have a system perspective.

She also emphasized the need for clinical credibility:

A case manager has to build credibility with the physicians before they can do anything. Absolutely. Absolutely. And that takes a while. It's really clinical credibility. So you almost have to have somebody come in, work clinically, and then go into the advanced case manager role. We almost always promote case managers from within for this reason.

The criteria were similar at Massachusetts General Hospital. According to the chief medical officer:

[Case managers] are selected for good interpersonal skills. They need to be experts in negotiations. They have to negotiate with insurers about what will be paid for. They negotiate with physicians too about when it's time to discharge. They walk a fine line. But they really like the job. It's a well-respected position.

❖ CASE MANAGERS AS A REPLACEMENT FOR PRIMARY NURSES?

Primary nurses were in effect the original cross-functional boundary spanners in the hospital setting. The primary nursing model first was instituted at Beth Israel Deaconess in 1974 under the leadership of Joyce Clifford, and many hospitals around the country followed suit. Under this model each patient was assigned one nurse who would have primary responsibility for that patient throughout his or her stay. As Beth Israel Deaconess' senior vice president of nursing, Joyce Clifford, defined it:

> *Primary nursing is the accountability for a patient over time. The focus of primary nursing is that the patient has one nurse who is accountable 24 hours a day for his or her care, and it's the same nurse who takes over all account-ability. It doesn't mean that he or she does all of the care. There is a handoff to associate nurses, but he or she should feel absolute ownership of the patient's experience.*

Primary nurses at Beth Israel Deaconess were responsible for coordinating inpatient care with the other disciplines, making sure the patient did not fall through the cracks. In addition to facilitating the coordination of inpatient care, primary nursing helped solidify the professional status of nurses by increasing their accountability for patients.

However, as lengths of stay became shorter, people began to question the adequacy of primary nursing for achieving coordination. Hospitals across the country sought to place the responsibility for coordination in the hands of case managers rather than primary nurses. Case managers were different from primary nurses in two critical ways. First, case managers were trained to focus on the efficiency of care as well as the quality of care and therefore focused on the speed with which patients could be moved from intake to discharge without compromis-ing the quality of their care. Second, case management was a more specialized coordination role than was primary nursing. Case managers were focused solely on their coordination role, whereas primary nursing was a hybrid model with responsibility both for coordination and for providing direct care to the patient.

Despite the strong rationale for it, there was intense resistance to the introduction of case management at Beth Israel Deaconess.[148] Many nurses were concerned that case managers would take over a role that had long belonged to primary nurses and that served as a source of pride and professional identity: accountability for patient care and for coordinating that care with the other disciplines. The senior vice president of nursing was particularly concerned about the emergence of case management. "Case managers are taking over the role of primary nurses," she noted. According to the new director of case management, however, that change was for the better:

> *There are some philosophical differences between case management and primary nursing, but from a practical standpoint, nurses are so busy with clinical care, they don't have the time they used to have to manage patient care. And coordination requirements have expanded since primary nursing was first established.*

❖ ASSESSING THE IMPACT OF CROSS-FUNCTIONAL BOUNDARY SPANNERS[149]

To assess the impact of cross-functional boundary spanners more systematically, we measured the staffing and role expectations of case managers and the presence of the primary nursing model.[150] The results suggest that expanding the staffing and broadening role of cross-functional boundary spanners significantly strengthened relational coordination among care providers. Exhibit 12-1 shows that doubling the intensity of the boundary spanner role produced an 11 percent increase in relational coordination among nurses, physicians, residents, therapists, case managers, and social workers. There is a simpler, more graphic way to observe the impact of boundary spanners

Exhibit 12-1   Impact of Cross-Functional Boundary Spanners on Relational Coordination†

	Relational Coordination
Cross-Functional Boundary Spanners	.11 **
Physicians	−.16 ***
Residents	−.04
Physical Therapists	.07
Case Managers	.04
Social Workers	−.06
Surgical Volume	−.02
R-Squared	.44

† This exhibit is discussed in the "Notes for Exhibits" chapter beginning on page 315.

Exhibit 12-2   Graphing the Impact of Cross-Functional Boundary Spanners on Relational Coordination

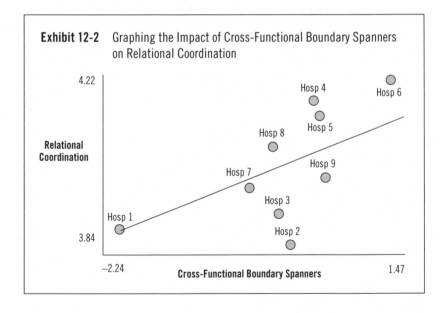

on relational coordination. The boundary spanner role was plotted against relational coordination for each of the nine hospitals. Exhibit 12-2 illustrates a positive impact of this work practice on relational coordination among care providers.

Using statistical techniques to account for patient differences, we also found that cross-functional boundary spanners significantly improved patient care outcomes.[151] Specifically, increasing the intensity of the boundary spanner role resulted in shorter hospital stays and higher levels of patient satisfaction, along with fairly substantial improvements in clinical outcomes. To illustrate, doubling the intensity of the boundary spanner role produced a 19 percent reduction in the length of hospital stay, a 16 percent increase in patient satisfaction, a 13 percent increase in postoperative freedom from joint pain, and a 12 percent increase in postoperative joint mobility. Combining these four performance metrics into a single measure of surgical performance, we found that cross-functional boundary spanners increased overall surgical performance by 21 percent. Furthermore, our analysis showed that boundary spanners achieve their performance effects through their effect on relational coordination.[152] Exhibit 12-3 summarizes these results. These results suggest that healthcare organizations can achieve improved performance results by expanding the staffing levels and scope of responsibilities of their boundary spanners.

Exhibit 12-3   Impact of Cross-Functional Boundary Spanners on Surgical Performance†

	Length of Stay	Patient Satisfaction	Postoperative Freedom from Pain	Postoperative Mobility	Surgical Performance Index	Surgical Performance Index
Cross-Functional Boundary Spanner	−.19 ***	.16 ***	.13 ***	.12 **	.21 ***	.08 +
Relational Coordination						.22 ***
Patient Age	−.03	.01	−.01	−.04	.01	.01
Comorbidities	.10 *	.05	−.02	−.05	−.06	−.05
Preoperative Status	.03	−.01	.20 ***	.28 ***	.17 ***	.17 ***
Surgical Procedure	.02	.10 *	.20 ***	.09 *	.14 ***	.15 ***
Psychological Well-Being	−.08 +	.14 **	.41 ***	.41 ***	.40 ***	.40 ***
Surgical Volume	.20 ***	.07	.04	.02	−.03	.03
R-squared	.42	.22	.82	.58	.59	.85

† This exhibit is discussed in the "Notes for Exhibits" chapter beginning on page 315.

However, boundary spanners are only one component of a high performance work system and are not expected to be effective without the presence of other supportive work parties discussed in this book.

❖ BOTTOM LINE

Healthcare organizations that invest in smaller caseloads and broader coordination roles for their case managers will benefit from higher levels of relational coordination across all the disciplines involved in the care process, with positive implications for both the quality and efficiency of patient care.

Chapter 13

Connect through Pathways

One of the biggest things care paths do is facilitate communication between various people. Pull people out of their silo mentality. Boundaries are sometimes overly restrictive or too vague. It could go either way. Things that everybody wants to do or that nobody wants to do. … It's not just a piece of paper that you end up with. It's getting people to work out the issues. There are a lot of boundary issues.

According to organizational theory, protocols and routines help organizations achieve coordination by prespecifying the tasks to be performed and the sequence in which to perform them.[153] Protocols—in the form of care paths or clinical pathways, for example—can capture the lessons learned from previous experiences, allowing a process to be replicated without reinventing the wheel. When protocols are used to codify best practices, individual capabilities can be transformed into organizational capabilities and therefore into potential sources of competitive advantage.[154] Total quality management, for example, relies heavily on the use of protocols to capture and implement previous learning and thus create a platform for further improvements.[155]

Protocols also serve to standardize work, allowing participants to focus their attention on exceptions to normal procedure. Protocols therefore are expected to be most effective for coordinating work under conditions of low uncertainty.[156] Organization design expert Jay Galbraith stated, "The primary virtue of rules is that they eliminate the need for further communication among the sub-units. ... To the extent that the job-related situations can be anticipated in advance and rules derived from them, integrated activity is guaranteed without communication."[157]

The truth of the matter may be quite different, however. Paul Adler and Brian Borys have argued that protocols can facilitate interaction among parties in a work process rather than serving as a replacement for interaction.[158] Similarly, Martha Feldman and Anat Rafaeli argued that cross-functional protocols can build connections among participants in a work process by building shared meanings and a shared understanding of where one's tasks fit into the overall flow of work.[159] In particular, cross-functional protocols can take the form of process maps that clarify the tasks in a work process and the key interdependencies among those tasks. Rather than using protocols that specify the sequence of tasks to be performed by a particular function, cross-functional protocols elucidate the interdependencies among tasks to be performed by different functions engaged in a common work process.

Cross-functional protocols in the hospitals observed for this study took the form of care paths or clinical pathways. Care paths are in effect process maps that can be used to clarify the interactions and decision points in a cross-functional process. At the time of the study, hospitals were using care paths to prespecify the sequence and timing of tasks to be performed on patients with a particular diagnosis. One key motivation for care paths was to standardize patient care by eliminating variations in physician and hospital staff practices that were determined through external standards or internal consensus to be medically unnecessary.

An additional benefit of care paths is the potential for improving the coordination of patient care. Rather than exchanging information on every aspect of each individual patient's condition and treatment, standardization through care paths allows care providers to make provisional assumptions about the interventions needed by a patient with a particular diagnosis on a particular day of his or her stay. In theory, care paths, like protocols more generally, improve coordination by reducing the need for information about individual cases; they set standard expectations and focus information flow on exceptions to the standard.

In each of the nine orthopedic departments we studied, care paths had already been designed and implemented to improve the care of joint replacement patients. As a result, communication in patient rounds and by case managers could center on exceptions to expected progress rather than on progress that followed the expected path. Communication also was facilitated by increased transparency about which tasks needed to be performed by each function. According to an administrator at Massachusetts General Hospital:

> *We are using the pathways to be more interdisciplinary. ... It was anecdotal before. No standard. With the pathway we've standardized care. ... In orthopedics it's truly cross-functional now.*

In another hospital we heard:

> *Clinical pathways help by informing people about what others are doing. There has been a lot of parallel play around here. We think we know what other people's jobs are, but we don't. With clinical pathways we get learning, solutions, and agreement. This is brilliant all by itself.*

At Massachusetts General Hospital we also heard:

> *Care paths were basically a scheme to bring people together for the interdisciplinary rounds and to help new caregivers get on track faster. It's been a really useful tool for pulling everybody together. Everybody is on the same page.*

The chief of orthopedics at Massachusetts General explained:

> *One of the biggest things care paths do is facilitate communication between various people, pull people out of their silo mentality. Boundaries are sometimes overly restrictive or too vague. It could go either way. Things that everybody wants to do or that nobody wants to do. ... It's not just a piece of paper that you end up with. It's getting people to work out the issues. There are a lot of boundary issues.*

At Beth Israel Deaconess, the chief of orthopedics explained:

> *Interdisciplinary practice guidelines provide a road map for nursing, PT, OT, nutrition. You actually get the patient collaborating on his own recovery. They know these are the goals, and they can assess their own progress. They even hold us accountable for achieving their goals sometimes.*

But despite having similar expectations for clinical pathways, there was substantial variation among hospitals in the number of functions whose tasks were included on the pathways. In one hospital, the clinical pathway included only two functions: nurses and physical therapists. At the other end of the spectrum, the pathway in another hospital incorporated the tasks of seven functions. In some of the hospitals, physician tasks were excluded from the pathway because of physicians' resistance to what they perceived as an attempt to standardize and routinize their work. In hospitals where physician tasks were on the pathway, a large investment of time and effort had been required to get their buy-in. An administrator at Beth Israel Deaconess explained:

> *Our physicians were involved in writing the care paths and coming up with them, but the first one we did took us a year and a half to get it written. And that was because of the fact that we had to involve them. It took us that long to get 42 physicians to reach consensus on what they wanted, what we could put on there. This one didn't want this; this one didn't want that.*

For some physicians it was a status issue. The chief of orthopedics at Beth Israel Deaconess explained:

> *A lot of doctors are fearful of clinical pathways. Power and responsibility are being taken from them. We had big fights. ... Some nurses are smarter than the doctors, but you're dealing with egos. That's the one thing about clinical pathways. Some doctors ask, "How dare you let the nurse follow this line of reasoning?" There are status issues.*

A nurse at the Hospital for Joint Diseases reflected on how much physicians had learned from one another through the process of clinical pathway development:

> *I was amazed when I first started on clinical paths how little doctors have talked to each other about what they do. You'd think that they were small businessmen. They really don't know each other's practices until they sit down and negotiate a care path. At first it's going to be a shock. It's like looking in the mirror if you haven't ever done it.*

The senior vice president of nursing at Baylor University Medical Center described a physician colleague who had a personal experience that transformed him from an opponent to a supporter of clinical pathways:

The head of anesthesia was one of those physicians who bad-mouthed care paths. Said this is cookbook medicine. You shouldn't treat the patient like this. This is bad. We're losing our individuality. Then his dad had to have a total hip replacement. After his dad had his care path, he made an appointment and came in to see me, and he said, "I'm a believer. The whole team knew exactly what the goal was for every day." He said, "It was so consistent, and the messages to the patient were so consistent." He said, "It was wonderful! So thank you!" He changed from the perspective of the physician who needs to have total control to the patient who needs consistency and goals. And he's one of our biggest advocates now.

Indeed, support for clinical pathways from a physician leader was often critical for their acceptance. A case manager at Brigham and Women's Hospital explained:

Pathways are very well accepted at the Brigham now. Better than I would have expected. But Dr. Sledge, I don't know if you gave us any choice! It was vitally important that the chief surgeon supported it; it really was.

Thus, the inclusiveness of clinical pathways in terms of the number of functions whose tasks were included varied across the nine hospitals, depended in part on physician support for a pathway. In addition, the degree of flexibility built into the pathway—and therefore the likelihood that patients would remain on the path—varied greatly. Among the nine hospitals, three of them kept 100 percent of their joint replacement patients on the path, five kept 90 to 97 percent on the path, and one kept only 70 percent of its patients on the path. According to the director of patient services at Presbyterian Plano:

We keep 100 percent of our patients on the care path through discharge. If they fall behind, they don't fall off.

We try to catch that day back. Patients are evaluated at rounds by the case manager and the physician every day, along with the physical therapist. They verify what happened over the previous day and decide when it's time to move on. They'll do what's necessary to achieve the appropriate level of functioning for the number of days postop.

These differences in the scope of application of pathways stemmed from resistance by some physicians to using pathways to guide the care of "their" patients. The differences also stemmed from the belief that some patients were too complex for their care to be governed by a protocol.

When a patient's reaction to previous interventions strayed outside the expected range of variation, that patient typically was treated as a nonstandard case and taken off the care path. A more flexible version of care paths built in customization by advancing the patient from one treatment to the next when certain goals were achieved rather than according to a predetermined schedule. With this flexible version of care paths, patients were less likely to be taken off the care path when a deviation from standard progress occurred and also less likely to be held back when they were progressing faster than the pathway led the caregivers to anticipate. As one administrator explained:

What I've been trying to work with my physicians on is looking at outcomes and not dates. Our physicians are wrapped up, real big, on days. I will sit there, make rounds with a physician, and say, "Why can't Joe Blow go home today? He's walking to the bathroom by himself; he's walked 75 feet." And he'll look at me and say, "I did a whole hip revision three days ago." Well, I'm sorry you did it three days ago, but. ... In an ironic way, care paths have helped to cement that because they are based on number of days postsurgery. Maybe they should be written

> *more on the basis of functional transitions. We have the*
> *functional benchmarks in the care paths and everything.*
> *Right now our care path is a five-day routine. But if the*
> *patient has met the end point at day 3, why are we keep-*
> *ing him an extra two days?"*

The newer clinical pathways have sought to correct this problem by focusing on functional achievement rather than number of days. The chief of social work at Beth Israel Deaconess explained:

> *First-generation care paths were based on day 1, day 2,*
> *where the day of the stay dictated what the tasks were.*
> *Now we've moved to second-generation care paths where*
> *we move from task to task depending on the level of func-*
> *tioning achieved rather than whether it's day 1 or day*
> *2. This takes a more sophisticated team because it's more*
> *customized.*

The director of rehabilitation at the Hospital for Special Surgery, where the concept of functional milestones originated, explained the benefits for physician accountability:

> *Functional milestones are how we benchmark ourselves.*
> *We have a primary PT [physical therapist] in charge*
> *of this patient. The discharge is done physically by the*
> *physicians. But the PT writes on the functional mile-*
> *stones chart over the bed what day that patient is ready*
> *to go home. Even on postop day 1, it can be estimated.*
> *Physicians decide discharge based on social and clinical*
> *considerations. But they are being looked at from that*
> *standpoint. They are being tracked. It could come back*
> *to haunt them if they don't discharge in a timely way.*
> *It should happen very rarely. We are here to treat effec-*
> *tively but also efficiently.*

❖ ASSESSING THE IMPACT OF CROSS-FUNCTIONAL PATHWAYS

To assess the impact of cross-functional pathways more systematically, we measured the number of functions whose tasks were included on the clinical pathways for joint replacement patients and the percentage of patients who stayed on the pathway in each of the nine hospitals.[160] The results suggest that the inclusiveness of cross-functional pathways significantly strengthens relational coordination among care providers. Exhibit 13-1 shows that doubling the inclusiveness of the pathway produced a 12 percent increase in relational coordination among nurses, physicians, residents, therapists, case managers, and social workers. There is a simpler, more graphic way to observe the impact of cross-functional pathways on relational coordination. Cross-functional pathways were plotted against relational coordination for each of the nine hospitals. Exhibit 13-2 illustrates a positive impact of this work practice on relational coordination among care providers.

Using statistical techniques to account for patient differences, we also found that cross-functional pathways significantly improved patient care outcomes.[161] Specifically, this

Exhibit 13-1   Impact of Cross-Functional Pathways on Relational Coordination†

	Relational Coordination
Cross-Functional Pathways	.12 +
Physicians	−.15 ***
Residents	−.02
Physical Therapists	.06
Case Managers	.05
Social Workers	−.07
Surgical Volume	−.01
R-squared	.26

† This exhibit is discussed in the "Notes for Exhibits" chapter beginning on page 315.

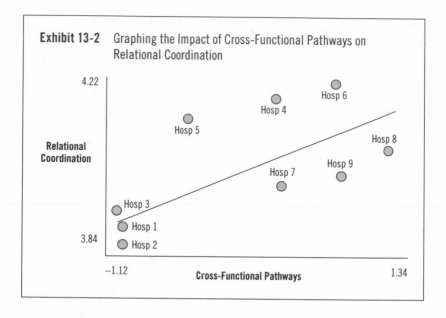

Exhibit 13-2   Graphing the Impact of Cross-Functional Pathways on Relational Coordination

work practice produced shorter hospital stays, higher levels of patient satisfaction, and improved clinical outcomes. To illustrate, doubling the inclusiveness of clinical pathways produced a 23 percent reduction in the length of hospital stays and a 29 percent increase in patient satisfaction. Inclusive clinical pathways also produced a 10 percent increase in postoperative freedom from joint pain and a 9 percent increase in postoperative joint mobility. Combining these four performance metrics into a single measure of surgical performance, we found that cross-functional pathways increased overall performance by 24 percent. Furthermore, our analysis showed that cross-functional pathways achieve their performance effects through their effect on relational coordination.[162]

Exhibit 13-3 summarizes these results. These results suggest that healthcare organizations can improve performance by increasing the number of functions whose tasks are included on the clinical pathway and the percentage of patients who remain on the pathway throughout their episode of care. Physicians often represent the last frontier; otherwise well-managed hospitals often neglect to include physician tasks on the clinical

Exhibit 13-3   Impact of Cross-Functional Pathways on Surgical Performance†

	Length of Stay	Patient Satisfaction	Postoperative Freedom from Pain	Postoperative Mobility	Surgical Performance Index	Surgical Performance Index
Cross-Functional Pathways	−.23 ***	.29 ***	.10 *	.09 *	.24 ***	.05
Relational Coordination						.25 ***
Patient Age	−.03	.01	−.01	−.04	.02	.01
Comorbidities	.10 *	.06	−.02	−.05	−.07 +	−.05
Preoperative Status	.03	−.02	.20 ***	.28 ***	.16 ***	.16 ***
Surgical Procedure	.00	.11 **	.21 ***	.10 **	.16 ***	.16 ***
Psychological Well-being	−.07	.13 **	.40 ***	.40 ***	.39 ***	.40 ***
Surgical Volume	.16 ***	.03	.05 +	.03	.01	.05
R-squared	.36	.28	.54	.34	.48	.83

† This table is discussed in the "Notes for Exhibits" chapter beginning on page 315.

pathway, undermining relational coordination and therefore reducing both the efficiency and the quality of patient care. However, like the other practices we have explored, clinical pathways are part of a high performance work system and are expected to work best when adopted as part of that system.

❖ BOTTOM LINE

We have seen that the more inclusive cross-functional pathways are of the care providers who are engaged in the care of the same patients, the more they strengthen relational coordination. Cross-functional pathways that are designed in accordance with these principles help care providers to conceptualize how their tasks are distinct yet interdependent, helping to build shared goals and shared knowledge and thus high levels of relational coordination. Through their impact on relational coordination, clinical pathways increase the efficiency of care, for which they are best known, but also increase patient satisfaction and key clinical outcomes.

Chapter 14

Broaden Participation in Patient Rounds

Ultimately the residents thought these meetings were an efficient use of their time. They thought: We have all the people that we probably need to talk to today about discharge planning at one table. What a gold mine. We can get all of this done, and then we won't get paged five times by them for the rest of the morning.

Cross-functional meetings are a coordinating mechanism that is intended to foster real-time coordination, incorporating information as it becomes available.[163] Meetings provide a forum for interaction among people who are engaged in the same work process. Whether scheduled or unscheduled, meetings give the participants in the process an opportunity to coordinate their tasks interactively, on the spot.[164] Face-to-face interactions are expected to have particular relevance in ensuring effective communication because of their high bandwidth, immediacy, and ability to build connections among participants through the use of nonverbal cues.[165] Although informal or unscheduled meetings sometimes are said to be more productive than formal meetings,[166] informal meetings tend to take place among those who are similar. Formal, or scheduled meetings may be needed to ensure interactions among staff members from different functions who would otherwise tend not to meet.

Patient rounds are a type of cross-functional meeting in which physicians, residents, nurses, and others responsible for the care of a patient get together to discuss the patient's case either at the bedside or in a separate conferencing area. The goal of rounding is for people who are involved in the care of a particular patient to get information from the patient and from one another so that better decisions can be made about subsequent care or the patient's discharge. We found that the combination of care providers who rounded separately or in combination varied greatly across hospitals, based on historical practice and scheduling issues.

In most of the hospitals studied here, two types of patient rounds were conducted. Physician rounds, in which an individual physician visits each of his or her patients, typically were conducted on a daily basis. These rounds usually were conducted by the physician alone or with a resident. In one hospital, however, physicians were accompanied on their daily rounds by a nurse, a case manager, a social worker, and a therapist. Face-to-face communication was therefore achieved on a daily basis among the core members of the healthcare team.

Interdisciplinary rounds traditionally were held weekly, typically in a conference room. These meetings usually included a nurse manager, a case manager, and nurses from the unit. In some hospitals the rounds included other disciplines—for example, a resident to represent the physician perspective, a physical therapist, a nutritionist, a pharmacist, and even a chaplain. As the length of patient stays dropped, however, weekly meetings became less useful. Often by the time the group could sit down and discuss a patient's needs, the patient had been discharged or had gone beyond his or her target length of stay. Some hospitals responded by eliminating interdisciplinary rounds, while others increased their frequency to two or more times per week.

A social work administrator described how rounds changed in her department:

> *Social workers have always done some kind of rounding. So did nurses, and so did doctors. But all at different times. We also had once-a-week meetings to get together to discuss patients. But it was time-consuming and not an effective use of time. It wasn't "in the moment" problem solving. So it was a waste, because it was mostly retrospective review. Now we do it every day. The meetings now are not this long, total review—it's what's going to happen today, what we can do to make to make it happen. It is forward-looking, not retrospective. It helps me plan my day. Before a lot of that information got scattered. Your whole day was spent telling the same story to different people.*

The more frequent rounds tended to be less inclusive, however. A third observed approach was to hold more inclusive meetings less frequently but supplement the meeting schedule with a highly active case manager who facilitated daily communication among those involved in the care of a patient. According to a case manager at Baylor who played a highly active role in care coordination:

> *We do patient rounds twice a week for all the patients that we have in the hospital. And when we have new patients coming in, we see them within 24 hours to start their discharge planning and their discharge process. Rounding means a record review as well as talking to the patient, and it's done by myself and a social worker.*

In addition, physicians at Baylor conducted their own rounds and connected with the case manager before and afterward:

> *We have 42 orthopedic physicians that are all private physicians with private practices. They round themselves*

personally, and they have PAs that round with them. If I'm on the floor and the timing is right, I may round with them. But a lot of times, they will come by my office before they start making rounds and say, "Update me on what your plans are, where we are with these patients and everything." Or they'll call me on the phone. Then afterward they'll call me with new orders or leave them here so I'll know if the patient is medically ready for discharge.

At Beth Israel Deaconess, interdisciplinary rounds had been held for several years to discuss patients weekly among the relevant care providers. The frequency of the meetings was increased to daily to improve their effectiveness as a mechanism for coordinating patient care. At the same time, several disciplines that had not been included in the past began to be included. The meetings were held on the units in the patient care stations and were led by the nurse manager, who came to the meeting with computer printouts listing each patient on the unit as well as the patient's diagnosis, age, insurance, and length of stay to date. After each patient's name there was a space for writing notes. The nurse manager presented the patient's functional status, the utilization review nurse followed with insurance information, the social worker added any important psychosocial background, and then other healthcare providers (including the resident, the primary nurse, and the physical and occupational therapist) elaborated with additional details as necessary.

According to the chief social worker for patient care coordination at Beth Israel Deaconess, the merits of these meetings were not immediately obvious to some of the clinical staff:

Some of the staff were kind of dragging their feet to get over to the table, because they weren't quite sure what they were supposed to do when they got there. The idea of meeting every single day, I think, seemed preposterous to people. "Every day? We can't meet every day on these patients." But pretty quickly they saw, in fact, that it was a really good use of their time usually, because it's not long. It should take only a half hour, and they should review all 30 patients on the floor. Most patients are really a quick once-over. Some patients may need a more in-depth assessment. It should take just a couple of minutes to do each patient. The idea is, This is what's going on, what's the plan? Where are we going? Who is going to make the call? Next.

One other benefit of these meetings was the increased sense of cohesion among providers:

Staff feel much more of a team on the floor. They feel as though they have teammates now and they are not just sort of lone people doing their job, like this is my job. Now every single day we have an opportunity to talk to those people in the morning and kind of catch everybody up.

There seemed to be a benefit for the patients as well:

I think they should notice that there is less confusion about who is doing what and when. I think in a busy teaching hospital it's hard because there are so many people that come in and out of patients' rooms and they are not always talking to each other very well, and the patients notice that. They notice that and say, "Well, wait a minute, somebody was just here an hour ago, and they said this is what I have been doing, and now you're saying something different." I think the patient should notice that there's less of that now.

It became apparent that despite the increased use of boundary spanners, clinical pathways and information systems for coordination, cross-functional meetings continued to be valuable for coordinating patient care. Rather than replacing the need for meetings, these other work practices helped to make the meetings more efficient. Meetings could be held more frequently to facilitate timely communication and avoid unnecessary delays in patient discharge. However, they could also be conducted more quickly thanks to the standardized routines captured in the clinical pathways that allowed decisions to be made by exception. Attention in these meetings therefore could be focused on patients who were experiencing deviations from expected progress. According to a director of care coordination:

> *That's the purpose of the care coordination round. There's the interdisciplinary round with the entire care team— nurses, therapists, etc.—and then there are the care coordination rounds, and the coordinators hold these daily, at least once a day. That's why they are so quick. They just maintain sort of an oversight to make sure things are progressing as expected. For instance, many of the patients are on critical pathways. So we evaluate that case to make sure it's proceeding as expected against the pathway.*

Similarly, upgraded information systems made these meetings more efficient, enabling all care providers to arrive with a higher level of shared information than they had previously.

❖ ASSESSING THE IMPACT OF CROSS-FUNCTIONAL ROUNDS

To assess the impact of cross-functional rounds more systematically, we measured the inclusion of nurses, physical therapists, and case managers in physician rounds and the inclusion of physicians, physical therapists, and case managers in nursing rounds in each of the nine hospitals. Each of these variables was coded on a scale from 0 to 2, with 0 indicating that the work group did not participate in the rounds, 1 indicating that they participated sometimes, and 2 indicating that they participated usually or always.[167] The results suggest that cross-functional rounds significantly strengthen relational coordination among care providers. Exhibit 14-1 shows that

Exhibit 14-1   Impact of Cross-Functional Rounds on Relational Coordination†

	Relational Coordination
Cross-Functional Rounds	.20 ***
Physicians	−.17 ***
Residents	−.03
Physical Therapists	.07
Case Managers	.04
Social Workers	−.07 +
Surgical Volume	−.12 **
R-squared	.76

† This exhibit is discussed in the "Notes for Exhibits" chapter beginning on page 315.

doubling the inclusiveness of the rounds produced a 20 percent increase in relational coordination among nurses, physicians, residents, therapists, case managers, and social workers. There is a simpler, more graphic way to observe the impact of cross-functional rounds on relational coordination. Cross-functional rounds were plotted for each of the nine hospitals against relational coordination. Exhibit 14-2 suggests a positive impact of this work practice on relational coordination among care providers.

Using statistical techniques to account for patient differences,[168] we also found that the inclusiveness of cross-functional rounds significantly improved patient care outcomes. Specifically, this work practice produced shorter hospital stays and higher levels of patient satisfaction and some improvement in clinical outcomes. To illustrate, doubling the inclusiveness of patient rounds produced a 26 percent reduction in the length of hospital stay, a 28 percent increase in patient satisfaction, and a 6 percent increase in postoperative freedom from joint pain. Combining these performance metrics into a single measure of surgical performance, we found that inclusive cross-functional rounds increased overall surgical performance by 23 percent. Furthermore, our analysis shows that cross-functional rounds

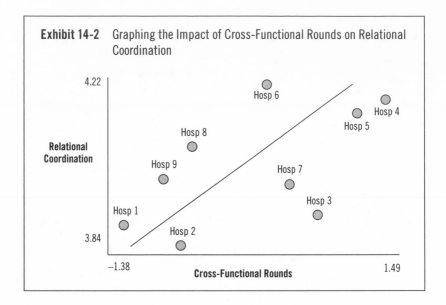

Exhibit 14-2   Graphing the Impact of Cross-Functional Rounds on Relational Coordination

Exhibit 14-3   Impact of Cross-Functional Rounds on Surgical Performance†

	Length of Stay	Patient Satisfaction	Postoperative Freedom from Pain	Postoperative Mobility	Surgical Performance Index	Surgical Performance Index
Cross-Functional Rounds	−.26 ***	.28 ***	.06 +	.02	.23 ***	.00
Relational Coordination						.26 ***
Patient Age	−.02	.00	−.01	−.05	.00	.01
Comorbidities	.08 *	.07	−.01	−.04	−.04	−.05
Preoperative Status	.03	−.01	.20 ***	.28 ***	.17 ***	.16 ***
Surgical Procedure	.01	.11 **	.21 ***	.11 **	.15 ***	.16 ***
Psychological Well-being	−.08 *	.14 **	.41 ***	.41 ***	.41 ***	.40 ***
Surgical Volume	.31 ***	.03	.01	−.00	−.12 **	.04
R-squared	.56	.69	.34	.07	.51	.83

† This exhibit is discussed in the "Notes for Exhibits" chapter be\ginning on page 315.

achieve their performance effects through their effect on relational coordination.[169]

Exhibit 14-3 summarizes these results. These results suggest that healthcare organizations can achieve improved performance by increasing the inclusiveness of patient rounds. However inclusive patient rounds are just one component of the larger high performance work system and are expected to be more effective when used in conjunction with the other practices.

❖ BOTTOM LINE

There are costs to convening many people on a frequent basis, but those costs are less than the value gained if the meetings provide a convenient forum for high quality communication among the participants whose tasks are most highly interdependent, helping to strengthen shared goals, shared knowledge, and mutual respect. We also have seen that these meetings do not have to be time-consuming to be effective. In fact, by supplementing patient rounds with case managers (as described in Chapter 12), clinical pathways (as described in Chapter 13), and shared information systems (as described in Chapter 15), these meetings can be short, focused and efficient, making it feasible for a broader array of functions to participate.

Chapter 15

Develop Shared Information Systems

I can spend half of my day tracking down patients. I will hear somebody mention somewhere in the hallway about a patient with this condition, and they're not on my printout, so I've got to walk to every floor and say, "Do you have this patient?" And they go: "Oh, that patient's on the vascular service, but yeah, I think Dr. [Smith] already operated on him." It's ridiculous. When I take two days off or, God help us, if I take off one week's vacation, it takes me two days when I come back to find out what happened to the patient on the OR schedule. Did they in fact come in, when did they go home, why they canceled, where they are, what happened to them. It's a horror. I can't read a progress note; I can't read half of the orders. I mean, if it's a routine orthopedic patient, I know what they're going to order, I know what they're going to write, so I can read those. But if the patient develops a medical complication and I can't read that doctor's note, I don't know what he's saying in there.

Organization design theorists have discovered that information systems are beneficial not only for accomplishing individual tasks but also for achieving coordination between tasks.[170]

Information technology expert N. Venkatramen has argued that information systems facilitate coordination by providing a "uniform infrastructure of information" to all people who participate in a particular work process.[171] An underlying argument is that the growth of information technology is widening the range of feasible organization designs through dramatic reductions in the cost of transferring information and the constraints of time and place for connecting people. Organizations can be flatter, with less need for vertical differentiation, when there are direct horizontal linkages across tasks and functions that are facilitated by IT. Rather than functional hierarchies to collect and transmit information between functions, information can flow directly, on an as-needed basis, among those who are directly affected by it.

The patient medical record is a longstanding means for exchanging information about a patient's condition among care providers. It traditionally has taken a paper form and has been affected by the limitations that accompany paper files. Medical records are bulky and are moved around from provider to provider with some inconvenience. Paper medical records cannot be used simultaneously by various providers, and so their use encourages discrete care providers to work in sequence rather than simultaneously on a patient, introducing delays into the process. Paper records are prone to being lost, and even when they are in the right place at the right time, critical information may be missing, illegible, or buried in the pile of paper.

Much organizational innovation in healthcare at the time of this study centered on automating medical records to improve access to critical patient information by care providers involved in patient care. Success had not met expectations, though a great deal of expertise was developed in this area and despite the fact that some hospitals had made heavy investments in hardware, software, and systems development. Automated systems did not alleviate the problems of paper medical records as much as expected. Automated medical records were far more transportable from provider to provider than were paper records, and that was particularly important as more patient care occurred beyond the walls of the hospital. However, confidentiality restrictions limited the ability to share records among all relevant parties. In addition, automated records had more limited transportability than paper records in one sense: Computers could not be transported easily to the patient's bedside to access information and enter new information during a patient encounter. The need to print out the electronic record to take to the bedside and then make handwritten notes and enter them into the system later introduced several additional steps that reduced the benefits of electronic records. Like paper records, electronic records could be lost, and critical information could be missing or illegible, particularly when users were poorly motivated to use the technology. There was also the major problem of acceptance by care providers who were accustomed to working with paper records.

In theory, each of these problems could be overcome. Most of the problems were present whether patient records were paper or electronic, because they involved underlying issues of workplace relationships and information exchange. The error was to believe that those underlying workplace issues had technological solutions when in fact their roots were deeper. Automation can help solve some of the underlying problems by helping people think creatively about workplace relationships and envision new solutions, but not if the underlying problems are ignored or seen as solvable simply through automation. As Adam Seth Litwin argued based on his study of a major implementation effort at Kaiser Permanente, the automation of medical records invites a reexamination of the underlying work flows, paving the way for fundamental innovations that are otherwise more difficult to implement.[172]

Not surprisingly, we observed variation among the nine hospitals in the degree of automation that had been achieved. All nine hospitals already had automated administrative information such as financial charges and insurance coverage of the patient. All nine hospitals also had automated records of lab work that had been requested for each patient, and seven had automated records of current medications. However, only two hospitals had automated information regarding a patient's medical history, and only one was tracking the patient's current condition, inpatient procedures, or inpatient consults. Several categories of clinical information that were critical for the coordination of care remained on paper records in nearly all of the nine hospitals studied. One administrator described the obstacles to getting clinical information online:

> *Information systems are important for coordination, I think, but right now they are more a hope than a reality. Our chief information officer is building a clinical and administrative information system allowing patients to receive care anywhere across the continuum. ... Right now you would have to dictate your diagnosis, have someone edit it, and so on. If it were entered directly, this wouldn't be an obstacle. For automation to work, it's important to get a format that's understood across specialists.*

A case manager described the mix of paper and electronic information in her hospital:

> *I make appointments with down-line facilities, then put in a request to the physician for a discharge summary to be written. Transcription services will do a summary of the patient's paper record; the doctor just gets on the phone and describes the patient's stay, looking at the paper record. It comes back online as part of the patient's electronic record. Either the case manager or the nurse puts the request for the patient discharge summary into the computer. Transcription Services notifies my office that the patient is being discharged. Then the summary will be faxed to the downstream facility.*

Some hospitals had highly disorganized information systems, which created a stressful, ineffective work environment for care providers and potential disasters for patients. At Beth Israel New York an orthopedics care coordinator explained:

It makes it very difficult. I can spend half of my day tracking down patients. I will hear somebody mention somewhere in the hallway about a patient with this condition, and they're not on my printout, so I've got to walk to every floor and say, "Do you have this patient?" And they go: "Oh, that patient's on the vascular service, but yeah, I think Dr. [Smith] already operated on him." It's ridiculous.

Other hospitals had automated systems that were divided between administrative information and clinical information with little interface between them. An administrator at the Hospital for Special Surgery explained:

We have two separate systems right now. The front end is clinical, and the back end is financial. We have an interface system, a one-way interface from clinical to financial. We are changing it to meet HMO needs. There are still two systems, but with a two-way interface. Another problem is that the clinical system is more administrative than clinical. Eventually we will replace that too. Standardization of care through clinical paths makes it easier to develop a good clinical information system. We can isolate things better. But a lot of clinical systems aren't there yet. Our CEO won't touch a system unless we are guaranteed success.

Brigham and Women's Hospital had one of the most comprehensive approaches to information systems of any hospital in the study. According to the vice president of information systems, the systems went far beyond the administrative and billing information that previously had been automated to include extensive clinical information:

We define clinical systems as any system that is used by a clinician in providing care. It's definitely an integral part of how people work here, both on the clinical side and on the administrative side. Order entry, a clinical information system which is where you get patient information, whether it is lab results or something else—I would say it's easier to tell you what is not automated in the patient information. What is not automated is that we haven't done history and physicals and put those online. The nursing flow sheets are not online. These are the two major areas. Again, all of the lab results, operating reports, and discharge summaries are online. Actually, we are now having their notes uploaded so you can get a full view of a patient's care through the ambulatory record.

Even with such a sophisticated information system, however, this hospital was "drowning in paper." The vice president explained:

We actually have a pretty nice system, which we call Demand Print, so that when we put information into an inventory record, it then queues out to print when that record is being requested. So that part of the issue with medical records is that you are constantly drowning in paper because the law really says that we have to have it in paper and available and stored that way. So we print now when a record is requested, but there are some practices that don't even request paper records any longer.

The benefits of automation were not always apparent in terms of immediate time savings. However, proponents at Brigham and Women's argued that the other benefits for better-coordinated care were tremendous:

In some cases, it has added time for order entry, but the additional time has been outweighed by far less aggravation in trying to locate a record. ... People are really recognizing the power of having a system like provider order entry because you can do incredible medical management just by providing information at the point of care. And we have a pretty extensive program so that we can tell you that you just ordered this, but do you know that three hours ago it was already ordered and why are you doing it again? The computer automatically covers that. And if there is an alert that we need to get to physicians, they can actually get an e-mail page to let them know that they need to look at the order entry system lab result that came back.

The problem with success was keeping up with the demand from care providers for further automation and improvements in the automation:

Now we've been so successful with data entry that we can't keep up with the demand from our providers. There are probably about 55 things that people currently want to change to our current application. We put together an order entry advisory committee, a group of physicians and nurses that come together on a monthly basis, and they prioritize what's the most important thing on the list now that we need to do.

Even well-designed systems worked only to the extent that all the key parties participated in the same system. In some hospitals, physician participation was incomplete, and there was no clear way to enforce participation from those who did not voluntarily participate:

You can't track down all of the physicians here because some of the physicians have their own system. That's another problem—they don't talk. Independent physicians have their own independent systems, and they only talk to themselves. I mean, so there's a big problem. Some of them are on the e-mail system, and some of them aren't.

Automation of information exchange also has the potential to introduce new problems. Although some authors, such as Henry Lucas and Jack Baroudi, have argued that automated information systems replace the need for boundary spanners and meetings, others such as Nitin Nohria and Robert Eccles have argued that excessive reliance on automated communication runs the risk of weakening relationships among parties over time if face-to-face or voice contact is replaced by electronic communication.[173] Communication primarily through formatted, automated interfaces runs the risk of failing to transmit contextual information that is critical to understanding the case at hand or to developing an understanding over time of the overall work process. Morten Hansen discovered similarly that electronic networks were more conducive to building extensive weak ties than to building intensive strong ties. Because strong ties are needed to transfer complex or tacit information, as Deborah Ancona and David Caldwell have argued, electronic networks by themselves do not replace the need for more personalized forms of coordination.[174] Some have argued that information technology actually increases the need for personal, face-to-face interactions and furthermore that it can help to structure and facilitate face-to-face interactions after an initial learning curve.[175]

Automated communication therefore is expected to be successful only if used in conjunction with interactive coordinating mechanisms such as cross-functional boundary spanners and meetings. As the director of social work for the Hospital for Joint Diseases explained:

> *I think you need a central meeting where people can get together and share those ideas. Because people can make recommendations in a computerized system so that others on the team can start to get a feeling for what assessments are being made by the different disciplines. But you need to get together to finalize those plans. There's information that essentially you might not want to document. You know,*

you're just making an assessment, and you want to share
that assessment with several people before you start to docu-
ment on a formal record. And by putting something into
the system, it might become part of a formal record when
really it was just an idea.

Even with future system upgrades, it was not clear to what
extent the increased reliance on electronic communication
could replace the need for face-to-face communication to
resolve differences. A case manager explained the challenges
in her department:

Doctors aren't available in orthopedics. They are in the
OR starting at seven-thirty. We communicate through
the computer or by paging. The physicians write their
orders in the computer, so they are in their computers
all the time and they get messages there. They put their
orders into computers, and then the nurses check in to read
them. It doesn't seem to be a problem. But it's very dif-
ficult to talk with the doctors. My job is to get on their case
[about patients who are ready for discharge, for example],
but there's not really a way to do it.

In addition, e-mail was not always sufficiently timely for the
decisions that had to be made in this time-constrained environment. One administrator explained:

Waiting for an e-mail—I mean, the therapists don't have
e-mail. They're walking around; they're not computer-
based. At each of the satellites we have a computer, but
if there's a question about a physician order, you need the
answer right now; you can't have an answer two hours
from now. So you page the resident, you get the attending,
or you go find them because they're either here in clinic or
they're in the OR, they're in their office, you know, seeing
patients, or they're manning a clinic.

Other hospitals used simple but powerful information systems to manage patient care that were based on the concept of visual control and used a clinical pathway as its foundation. The director of rehabilitation at the Hospital for Special Surgery explained:

> *Our functional milestones chart gives us a quick visual control on where the patient is at. There's a board over each bed that corresponds to the functional milestones to let us know how many resources the patient needs. It shows with color-coded stickers what level of mobility the patient has achieved. You can just eyeball where the patient is at. You might just be there to help someone. It makes the patients feel that there's some connection. It is there to encourage the patient also. Patients are very clear that they have achieved a goal. It reinforces what their level is and reinforces what their ultimate goal is, and that when they've achieved it, they can be discharged.*

He continued:

> *Believe it or not, the therapists carry six or seven different types of stickers in their pockets, and as they hit goals, they put the sticker on. Now, this sounds ridiculous, I know. This stupid piece of paper has been the most value-added thing we've probably ever come up with. The physicians love it. Why do they love it? Because above the bed, at a glance, they can see where somebody is, and they don't have to read the chart. They get an overall sense, the date he's supposed to be discharged is highlighted, and the patients get involved because they're actually participating with this activity log. They start to become competitive with each other. "Did you get a green sticker today? I have a green sticker." The families are starting to ask the patient, "How come you don't have so many stickers?"*

The effectiveness of this nonautomated information system is a reminder of the power of visual control, a fundamental innovation from the Toyota Production System. The effectiveness of this simple system is also a reminder that for the purposes of developing relational coordination, the key to an effective information system is to provide a common infrastructure of information whether it is automated or not.

❖ ASSESSING THE IMPACT OF CROSS-FUNCTIONAL INFORMATION SYSTEMS

It is apparent from our research that no one measure will capture perfectly all aspects of information systems that are critical for achieving well-coordinated patient care. To assess the impact of cross-functional information systems more systematically, however, we measured the range of administrative and clinical capabilities included in the information systems at each of the nine hospitals.[176] We saw earlier in Exhibit 4-2 that most hospital information systems in the study included lab results and insurance information but that fewer than half included medical history, inpatient procedures, provider order entry, or inpatient consult history. Only a third included inpatient consult history or discharge summary, and only one included the patient's current condition and functioning. Our statistical results suggest that more inclusive information systems significantly strengthen relational coordination among care providers. Exhibit 15-1 suggests that doubling the inclusiveness of information systems produced a 15 percent increase in relational coordination among nurses, physicians, residents, therapists, case managers, and social workers. There is a simpler, more graphic way to observe the impact of information systems on relational coordination. Information systems were plotted for each of the nine hospitals against relational coordination. Exhibit 15-2 illustrates a positive impact of this work practice on relational coordination among care providers.

Exhibit 15-1   Impact of Cross-Functional Information Systems on Relational Coordination†

	Relational Coordination
Cross-Functional Information Systems	.15 **
Physicians	−.15 **
Residents	−.00
Physical Therapists	.06
Case Managers	.05
Social Workers	−.06
Surgical Volume	.02
R-squared	.46

† This exhibit is discussed in the "Notes for Exhibits chapter beginning on page 315.

Exhibit 15-2   Graphing the Impact of Cross-Functional Information Systems on Relational Coordination

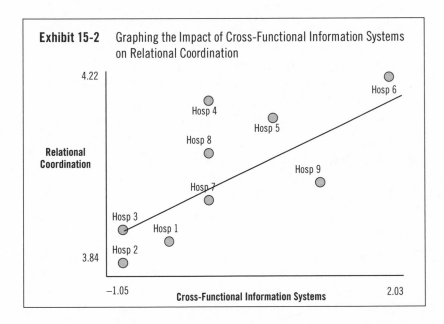

Using statistical techniques to account for patient differences, we also found that the inclusiveness of information systems significantly improved patient care outcomes.[177] Specifically, inclusive information systems produce shorter hospital stays and higher levels of patient satisfaction, along with some of the most substantial improvements in clinical outcomes of any of the work practices we have examined. To illustrate, doubling the inclusiveness of information systems produced a 30 percent reduction in the length of hospital stay, an 18 percent increase in patient satisfaction, a 10 percent increase in postoperative freedom from joint pain, and a 12 percent increase in postoperative joint mobility. Combining these four performance metrics into a single measure of surgical performance, we found that cross-functional information systems increased overall surgical performance by 23 percent. Furthermore, our analysis shows that cross-functional information systems achieve their performance effects through their effect on relational coordination.[178]

Exhibit 15-3 summarizes these results. These results suggest that healthcare organizations can improve performance by increasing the inclusiveness of their information systems. Like the other practices explored in this book, however, information

Exhibit 15-3   Impact of Cross-Functional Information Systems on Surgical Performance†

	Length of Stay	Patient Satisfaction	Postoperative Freedom from Pain	Postoperative Mobility	Surgical Performance Index	Surgical Performance Index
Cross-Functional Information Systems	−.30 ***	.18 **	.10 *	.12 **	.23 ***	−.05
Relational Coordination						.30 ***
Patient Age	−.04	.01	−.00	−.04	.02	.01
Comorbidities	.11b *	.06	−.02	−.05	−.06	−.05
Preoperative Status	.03	−.01	.20 ***	.28	.16	.16
Surgical Procedure	.00	.11 **	.21 ***	.10 **	.16 ***	.16 ***
Psychological Well-Being	−.07 +	.14 **	.41 ***	.41	.40	.40
Surgical Volume	.09 *	.08	.08 *	.06	.06	.03
R-squared	.50	.12	.58	.45	.46	.84

† This exhibit is discussed in the "Notes for Exhibits" chapter beginning on page 315.

systems are only one component of the larger high performance work system and are not expected to be effective on their own.

❖ BOTTOM LINE

By providing a common infrastructure of information, information systems can increase shared knowledge across functions, enabling participants to engage in more timely and accurate communication with each other. The key is to develop information systems that are accessible to a broad array of care providers and that include both administrative and clinical information. So far, this goal has not been widely achieved by healthcare organizations. As James Rebitzer and colleagues have pointed out: "The IT revolution has been slow coming to hospitals and only in recent years have large expenditures in electronic medical systems begun."[179] In addition, these information systems do not work by themselves; they are part of a larger high performance work system. It is therefore critical that these information systems be used to supplement rather than replace more interactive work practices such as boundary spanners and patient rounds. Information systems that are designed in accordance with these principles will enable healthcare organizations to develop high levels of relational coordination and to improve both the quality and efficiency of patient care.

Chapter 16

Partner with Your Suppliers

Now we are much more dependent upon other facilities to be an extension of our care. People leave sicker and quicker. We need to have some level of competency on the other side. Historically we've been possessive with our patients. That's been an impediment. We think we do it best. It's our pride. But you can't do it that way. You have to give your trust over to the next setting.

Thus far in this book, we have learned a great deal about how healthcare organizations can improve coordination across care provider functions. We have described a high performance work system that helps to build strong networks of relational coordination between doctors, nurses, therapists, social workers, and case managers. To the extent that this high performance work system focuses only on building coordination within a single organization, however, its impact will not be sufficient to address current industry challenges.

As organizations vertically disintegrate and outsource services that once were produced internally, coordination across organizational boundaries has become increasingly important for achieving desired performance outcomes. Because market mechanisms are often insufficient for coordinating interdependencies, organizations must design and invest in mechanisms for managing cross-organizational relationships.[180] Management scholar Rosabeth Kanter has argued that pressures for cross-organizational coordination are reshaping the world of business and requiring new capabilities for business success.[181] Supply partnerships can add value by providing a more coherent, seamless experience for the customer while minimizing wasted time and resources, creating a competitive advantage for both partners in the supply partnership, as we have seen in both the auto industry and the apparel industry.[182] Russell Johnston and Paul Lawrence have called these partnerships *value-adding partnerships*, arguing that companies engaged in these partnerships have advantages over companies that try to negotiate with one another in the absence of a partnership, and that they also have advantages over vertically integrated companies that bring all activities in house.[183] Value-adding partnerships are "a set of independent companies that work closely together to manage the flow of goods and services along the entire value-added chain." These partnerships allow each party to focus on what it does best while generating better outcomes than either party could achieve in a more traditional supplier relationship.

Healthcare organizations and their customers can benefit enormously from supply partnerships. As a result of shorter lengths of stay enforced by payers, patients have been leaving hospitals in a more vulnerable condition. Patients therefore are increasingly likely to receive follow-up care in other settings, such as rehabilitation hospitals and skilled nursing facilities, or at home with the help of home care providers. As more care is provided outside the hospital, other healthcare organizations have begun to play an increasingly important role in the healthcare value chain. It is therefore critical for healthcare organizations to take the relational coordination that they have achieved internally and extend it beyond their own walls to coordinate the whole episode of care for their patients.[184]

Pressures for shorter lengths of stay have increased the need for coordination between the hospital and other care providers to ensure a timely and accurate handoff of both the patient and the medical, administrative, and social information relevant to his or her care. Discharging patients properly requires a relationship with the downstream providers who will care for the patients after discharge both to ensure that slots will be available on short notice and to ensure that once gone, patients will be in good hands. The careful handoff of information is critical to ensuring that patient recoveries continue on course and without error. Handoffs also must be well orchestrated to reassure the patient that he or she is not being tossed callously "over the wall."

But well-orchestrated handoffs are not easily achieved. The director of case management at Beth Israel Deaconess explained:

> *Discharge is an interesting nexus. That's where all the failures are. That's where you blow it. That's also where all the drama is. There is a letting go of safety into the unknown.*

Furthermore, financially and legally, hospitals often have little responsibility for what happens to their patients after discharge. As the director of patient care and quality management at the Hospital for Special Surgery explained: "For now, our responsibility ends with discharge, provided we're sending patients to acceptable places." However, financial contracts that make hospitals responsible for the entire episode of care—sometimes called *bundling*—are on the rise, focusing greater attention on efforts to coordinate postdischarge care. Some payers have begun to negotiate contracts in which the hospital and its physicians take on the responsibility and risk for a pool of patient lives. Under these arrangements, the hospital and its physicians, usually through a physician-hospital organization, are paid a fixed monthly fee to provide care for a patient. Hospitals therefore accept responsibility for the cost and quality of not just the hospital stay but the entire continuum of care. Under such contracts, hospitals benefit from managing the continuum of care, creating greater pressure to form relationships with providers of downstream services. An administrator at the Hospital for Special Surgery explained the shift:

> *If we're going to globalize our coverage and we're going to assume the responsibility for an episode of care, that puts us in a different situation. Right now, we want to get people out in as timely a manner as possible with the safest and most adequate plan. But whatever that plan is, we haven't been concerned about that. We've gotten them home care. How many visits they've made in home care, and how much it cost, or whether they've gone to subacute, or how long they spent there hasn't been of concern to us. The issue for us has been finding a good place that will accept people very quickly. The financial connection kind of muddies the waters a bit. ... Now we'll have to take into account the cost and the efficacy of the discharge plan.*

Accepting the financial risk for an entire episode of care also increases the incentive to coordinate with other parties in the continuum. One administrator explained:

> *If you're going to take the risk of global pricing, you're going to have to be able to control the things that you can, which includes home care, outpatient therapy, subacute, rehab, and so on. You've got to coordinate the handoff now, okay? You never had to worry about that before. We just asked you where you lived, you said Boston, we called up somebody in Boston, and they did it and billed Medicare. Now [with global fees] I have to have a relationship*

with you where now I have to feel sure that you're going to do quality care and meet my needs.

Despite increasing pressures to coordinate care across organizational boundaries, the obstacles were powerful, including subtle power issues such as the desire to *control* one's supply chain rather than *coordinate* with one's supply chain partners as evidenced in the previous quote. Large hospitals traditionally maintained a strong internal focus—a hospital-centered view of healthcare—that placed postdischarge providers in a peripheral position. Just as care providers in different functions have been divided by differences in power and status, so have the healthcare organizations that work at different stages of the care continuum. Acute care hospitals traditionally have enjoyed a higher status than rehabilitation hospitals, which in turn have enjoyed a higher status than skilled nursing facilities or home care organizations. Just as differences in care provider status have posed obstacles to the coordination of care, so have differences in organizational status.

Furthermore, just as finger-pointing can occur instead of problem solving when problems arise with the patient within the hospital setting, the same dynamic can occur when problems arise after the patient's discharge. Michael Hubner, former chief of social work at Beth Israel Deaconess, described her experience:

> *When something goes wrong with the patient, someone falls through the cracks, no one wants to take responsibility. You get "You didn't tell me that the patient needed ... " and "You should have found out. ..." It's not pretty.*

In other words, much of what we have learned about relational coordination within healthcare organizations is just as relevant when we consider relational coordination between healthcare organizations. At its best, relational coordination across the supply chain is characterized by frequent, timely, accurate, problem-solving communication reinforced by shared goals, shared knowledge, and mutual respect. More often, however, coordination across the supply chain is characterized by infrequent, delayed, inaccurate communication focused on blaming rather than problem solving when things go wrong, reinforced by fragmented goals, fragmented knowledge, and lack of mutual respect. In the following sections, we see how Beth Israel Deaconess, Brigham and Women's, the Hospital for Joint Diseases, and New England Baptist worked to build supply partnerships with their patients' upstream (primary care) and downstream (postacute) providers.

❖ SUPPLY PARTNERSHIPS AT BETH ISRAEL DEACONESS

Beth Israel Deaconess[185] historically prided itself on its strong organizational culture, creating an internal focus that was perhaps even stronger than that of other hospitals. A number of events challenged that internal focus, however, changing the way Beth Israel Deaconess saw itself in relation to the rest of the healthcare system. Shorter lengths of stay enforced by health maintenance organizations (HMOs) and Medicare in the late 1990s meant that patients were leaving more quickly and sicker than previously. Discharging patients properly required some kind of relationship with the downstream providers who would care for the patients after discharge to assure both that slots would be available on short notice and that once gone, patients would be in good hands. Second, some payers were beginning to negotiate capitated contracts with local hospitals in the Boston market, in which the hospital and its physicians took on the responsibility and risk for a pool of patient lives. Under those arrangements, Beth Israel Deaconess and its physicians, usually through a physician-hospital organization (PHO), were paid a fixed monthly fee to provide care for a patient. Beth Israel Deaconess thus became responsible for the cost and quality not only of the hospital stay but also of the broader continuum of care. Under capitation, Beth Israel

Deaconess therefore benefited from managing the continuum of care by forming relationships with providers of downstream services. Third, two major hospitals in the Boston market joined in 1995 to form an integrated delivery system called Partners that included both upstream and downstream providers. Potential competition from Partners put additional pressure on Beth Israel Deaconess to form an integrated delivery system of its own.

To develop relationships with its downstream providers, Beth Israel Deaconess's leadership formed a subacute strategy task force. Through that task force, innovations that had been developed to coordinate patient care internally were leveraged to facilitate the coordination of patient care with external providers. According to Michael Hubner, the leader of that task force:

> *It's time-intensive to build a relationship with an external provider. So we started to think about it differently. We started looking for the organizations that met our criteria, such as shared values, who we could develop relationships with. The task force came up with a memorandum of understanding for the organization and gave it to the vice presidents. We said, "Please empower us as a group to take the lead on developing relationships with outside providers." They agreed that all subacute activities would go through our group.*
>
> *We have done a lot of work on thinking through what are the opportunities for really getting together with other providers and thinking about the whole care trajectory so that when a patient leaves our doors and goes somewhere else, they don't repeat the last day of what happened here. Now we have more faith in the information we get from the other providers, and they can take what they get from us as solid data and not need to rethink or redo things. So that if we say a patient is able to ambulate, they accept that, and vice versa. It's really thinking about*

the patient's view of the system as opposed to our separate views of it. It's really the same process we've gone through internally to build trust and improve information sharing among everybody involved in the patient's care while they are here.

The task force identified Youville Hospital and Rehabilitation Center as an effective provider of rehabilitation care for Beth Israel Deaconess's postsurgical patients and worked to develop a memorandum of understanding with Youville. As the task force for subacute strategy worked to improve coordination with Youville, they often found that the coordinating mechanisms that had been developed to improve coordination internally could be extended to facilitate coordination with Youville.

Cross-Organizational Pathways and Protocols

One innovation was to extend clinical pathways beyond inpatient care to encompass the coordination of care with external providers. According to Claire Paras, the director of clinical pathway development:

Clinical pathways have brought costs and variation down. ... Some thought they were cookbook medicine. Physicians resented being told what to do. Now the resistance is gone somewhat. Still, clinical pathways are too limited to inpatient care. The opportunities are to move them outside the walls. It's trickier, though. Inpatient care we have control over. ... These are second-generation clinical pathways. ... We are developing one now with Youville.

Similar to Beth Israel Deaconess' earlier experience with establishing cross-functional clinical pathways, cross-organizational clinical pathways were also difficult to get off the ground, according to Paras:

Youville and our cardiac team met to talk about seamless care. But it's easier to talk about it than to do it. We release a patient to rehab. Then they are back to square one. They get reassessed, just like in the past. It's debilitating to the patient and costly. Clinical pathways are not that easy to develop. You need to reach consensus on types of treatment. There is a replacement of individual judgment with a standardized protocol. It's not only the handoffs but also agreeing on treatment. Our ortho group went out of alignment a little with Youville on preadmission requirements. So those efforts came to a halt, at least temporarily.

One physician leader argued that extended clinical pathways were not feasible:

Some of my colleagues have this ideal of extending the clinical pathways from here to the downstream facility. But it's an ideal. Ultimately it's their place, and we can't tell them what to do.

That physician leader did note, however, that the same objections had been expressed initially in regard to internal clinical pathways and then were largely overcome.

Cross-Organizational Information Systems

Another innovation was the development of a cross-organizational information system. Beth Israel Deaconess's electronic medical record was in principle far more transportable from provider to provider than were paper records and could have been used to facilitate the coordination of patient care beyond the walls of the hospital. Shared access to Beth Israel Deaconess's electronic medical records would have allowed a patient's medical record to be pulled up on a computer screen in either hospital so that it could be viewed by both parties at any point during the patient's care. However, confidentiality restrictions initially limited the ability to share patient records across organizational boundaries. Although there were great hopes throughout the industry of using the electronic medical record to coordinate patient care across organizations, for a time the results were very limited.

But Beth Israel Deaconess was able to extend the use of electronic mail to its external partnership with Youville. A social worker explained:

> *The efficiency of our work processes determines whether we make timely referrals. We got Youville onto e-mail because the transfer of information was terribly inefficient. We had to go through so many steps. Social work communicated with Youville through Placement, and they responded to us through Placement. We got ourselves on the same e-mail system with Youville and have been able to bypass Placement.*

The care providers involved in the partnership found that the e-mail link between Beth Israel Deaconess and Youville did not replace the need for meetings:

> *At first we were sending e-mail messages back and forth about patients, scheduling them for admission. But then something went wrong and it came to a halt. What we realized was that we were neglecting our relationship with Youville. It takes more than an information system.*

Still, some argued that integrated information systems were the critical factor that facilitated the development of an integrated delivery system. The chief of social work explained:

> *One question we are addressing is, Are we going to be an integrated delivery system or not? Where will we refer our patients? This involves systemwide capacity and make-or-buy decisions. Theoretically you can have a virtually integrated system that isn't coowned. The glue that holds it together is information systems [ISs] rather than*

*coownership. IS in the form of a unified patient record
and a unified system for assessment the cost and quality of
care delivery. We don't have this yet.*

Cross-Organizational Meetings

Interdisciplinary patient rounds already had been expanded
inside Beth Israel Deaconess to include daily rather than weekly
meetings and to include the participation of additional functional groups. With their external partner Youville, the Beth
Israel Deaconess staff anticipated initially that the coordination of care would occur largely through the extended clinical
pathway and the use of e-mail. Once the initial planning meetings were complete, representatives from the two organizations
stopped meeting. When a misunderstanding occurred, the
parties realized that the e-mail interface could not completely
replace the need for meetings. A social worker explained:

> *So we are back to holding regular meetings and work
> groups with them to get to know each other and feel com-
> fortable about the relationship.*

As a result of this learning, regular cross-organizational
rounds were established, including personnel from Beth Israel
Deaconess and Youville, in which patients' progress was discussed and decisions were made regarding their treatment.
This discovery that information systems could increase the
efficiency of meetings but not completely replace them is supported by much of the literature on knowledge sharing, as we
learned in Chapter 15.

Cross-Organizational Boundary Spanners

As we saw in Chapter 8, the case manager role was developed at Beth Israel Deaconess in the late 1990s to supplement
an earlier boundary spanner role: the primary nurse. The
case manager role was extended to include responsibility for
coordinating patient discharge and handoffs to downstream

providers; indeed, this was one of the key advantages of case management over primary nursing.

To facilitate coordination with postdischarge care providers, most hospital units at Beth Israel Deaconess were assigned both a social work case manager and a nurse case manager. Nurse case managers were responsible for determining the level of care needed by the patient, whether it was continued acute care, rehabilitative care, or home care. The nurse case manager was also responsible for identifying and following up with patients who needed services at home. Social work case managers were responsible for arranging postdischarge services a patient might need when he or she returned home, such as Meals on Wheels and transportation services. The social work case manager was also responsible for handling the patient's insurance issues and dealing with any concerns the family might have. Together the case managers coordinated care among providers internally and with external providers while ensuring that the patient's care would be reimbursed by the payer.

Weakening of the Supply Partnership

Even successful partnerships can lapse over time if insufficient attention is paid to maintaining them. Several years after the memorandum of agreement between Beth Israel Deaconess and Youville, the director of social work lamented the demise of the effort:

> *Now there is very little outpatient follow-up. It's a bit of a fault of our system. It's really due to insufficient staffing of case management. They just hand off the patient to the downstream provider and do not follow up. With the competitive pressures we were facing, relationships became less important and it was more about the bottom line. We let our memorandum of agreement with Youville expire. We went from "How do we build relationships to take care of the patient?" to "How do we cut costs?"*

The exception, she noted, was with patients whose physicians were contractually at risk for the cost of their care as a result of capitated contracts with managed care organizations. Those patients were managed throughout the care continuum by Beth Israel Deaconess's department of community case management:

> *Those patients get a lot of oversight. The case managers have very advanced computer systems, following patients wherever they are generating costs. When they are admitted to Youville, for example, our case managers check in—they don't go visit, but they are constantly in touch to monitor what is happening.*

When cost was of the utmost importance because of at-risk contracts, the cross-organizational coordinating mechanisms were kept in place and even strengthened. However, this occurred only for those patients, whereas the broader systems for cross-organizational coordination were allowed to languish. According to the director of social work:

> *People will learn that it's shortsighted to ignore the relationships with our downstream providers, but it is taking a while.*

❖ SUPPLY PARTNERSHIPS AT BRIGHAM AND WOMEN'S

The coordination of care was limited in many of the same ways at Brigham and Women's Hospital. Hospital case managers were very successful at coordinating the discharge from acute care, as we learned in Chapter 8. However, when it came to coordinating across the continuum, their effectiveness was limited. A physician leader at Brigham and Women's explained:

> *The care coordinator doesn't follow the patients after they leave here. The care coordinator relinquishes control at*

*this point. There is always the possibility for failure of
communication. We need better handoffs. We are working on this now.*

Clinical pathways were limited in the same way: "Our clinical pathways have become well accepted, and they are working
well. But they must start earlier and end later if we want to
achieve coordination across the continuum."

To achieve better coordination across the continuum,
Brigham and Women's began to build a postacute care pro-
vider network and track the quality of care after discharge.
According to the director of care coordination:

*Our first step was choosing facilities and agencies and then
deciding that we would invest in them and partner with
them in the care of patients and we would share patient
information and cost information and clinical information
between us. We set clinical standards and service standards
for those agencies, and we meet with them on a regular
basis. The meetings include Brigham physicians and care
coordination staff and then similar staff and administrators from the downstream agencies. It's sort of a mix of
program development, because this is a new endeavor for
us, as well as quality review.*

Brigham and Women's Hospital's early efforts differed from
those of Beth Israel Deaconess in at least one fundamental way:
its decision to make the primary care physician the common
thread for coordinating patient care across the continuum.
According to the vice president of network development:

*We've made a very conscious decision that we're not going
to succeed as a healthcare system unless we include the
primary care doc in the management of our patients,
whether we get further capitated or not. We've put all
our energy into that. It's not just to get them to make*

the referrals; it's to get them involved in really thinking about the patients. We've developed a few strategies on the front end to support patients and kind of bond and link the idea of primary care docs. We've put a huge emphasis on feedback into the system, back to the PCP.

Coordination across the continuum by the primary care provider (PCP) was even intended to include coordination within the hospital itself. The vice president of network development explained:

As part of our PCP agenda we've been trying to bring the image of the primary care doc in the organization as the coordinator of inpatient care to the forefront. That's been a big issue on our part. They're taking responsibility for admitting and writing orders and taking care of their patients while they're in the hospital. They don't hand off the patient when they are admitted to the hospital: All our primary care docs are around here all day long, and they're very involved in care. And in fact, people get smacked around pretty hard if the primary care doc's patient gets admitted and they're not called. We're working very hard on making these connections. We've got reward systems in the ED [emergency department] for the docs calling the PCP and saying, "Guess what, your patient showed up unannounced." There's a whole system. That's the primary care focus.

It is not clear whether those efforts worked, however, as we will see below.

❖ SUPPLY PARTNERSHIPS AT THE HOSPITAL FOR JOINT DISEASES

In other hospitals, partnerships were developed with home care agencies through which patients and their home environments were evaluated by home care even before a patient was admitted for surgery. The director of social work at the Hospital for Joint Diseases explained:

> *A week prior to surgery, the home care agency goes in and completes an evaluation not only of the patient's home care needs but of the home environment. I mean, we might find out the patient is coming for elective bilateral hip replacement, living in a fifth-floor walk-up, they're 80 years old, and live alone. Obviously, some things need to be resolved before that patient comes in for elective surgery, or that's one that won't stay on the pathway.*

At the Hospital for Joint Diseases, several home care agencies were given on-site status to facilitate the supplier relationship:

> *There is no business arrangement other than that they're on-site. The reason why we have them on-site, it's a benefit to us. It is early home care evaluation and lower length of stay, as well as quick assessment and patient satisfaction. And we find that sometimes you get better services from on-site companies when there is competition about who can offer what. Visiting Nurse Service has been on-site since we located on 125th Street. Catholic Center was brought in based on the needs of our Orthodox Jewish population, then Revival Home Health Care was brought in as well and has been here for about two years now, and the other companies an average of eight years.*

Just as we found at Beth Israel Deaconess, these supply partnerships enabled the parties to develop clinical pathways that extended beyond acute care to include subacute, rehab, and home care:

> *We have actually asked each of the three companies that are on-site to have a representative come to our critical pathway meetings so that they can be part of the planning, be consistent in the educational piece also, so that they're*

teaching the patients the same thing that we've teaching them. Because different hospitals do different things from day 1 to day 3, and we want to make sure that everyone is consistent, including the home care. It's a continuum of care, and it's not broken down any longer into the inpatient piece, the home care piece, or the outpatient piece. It's all one continuum.

Although these agreements did not bind anyone to anything, they could become quite strong over time. The associate director of quality management explained:

Our transfer agreement doesn't really seem to bind anyone to anything. It's, you know, a legal mechanism for acknowledging this relationship, but it really is not what's important. The way that we get specialized and preferential treatment from the downstream providers is based more on our networking and our developing relationships. We have a special relationship with some facilities. And it's based on volume of referrals, you know. If people are very accommodating to us, we give them more referrals.

❖ SUPPLY PARTNERSHIPS AT THE NEW ENGLAND BAPTIST

Even at New England Baptist, where 1,200 joint replacements were conducted per year and most patients were sent to an on-campus skilled nursing facility after discharge, handoffs had not been perfected. The director of the Bone and Joint Institute in New England Baptist explained:

The skilled nursing facility has a clinical pathway that includes our social worker. But the pathway is not working well. The pathway is not linked to our pathway here in acute. It needs to be, yes, but it's not. It should be one pathway from day 1 through discharge. But the legal requirements of a skilled nursing facility lead to different databases. There's a whole issue of whether the staff should document to the pathway. Here in acute, we use it to document. Our nurses see the advantage. But the nurses in the skilled nursing facility don't use it; don't take it seriously. As a result, we get clogged up between here and there. The skilled nursing facility is backed up. We have to increase their beds or increase our length of stay. We have to make it more seamless.

The New England Baptist approach to home care was proactive, looking for partnership arrangements with home care agencies that were willing and able to meet its high standards:

The patients who don't go to our skilled nursing facility typically go home. So then we have to coordinate with the home care agency. Some agencies do it well, others don't. Our physicians are concerned about quality. So we have an RFP (request for proposal) to partner with home care agencies within our quality parameters. Forty-three agencies have been invited. We will track outcomes.

She was not entirely optimistic about the results: "We did a test run before with the parameters laid out. It was with a national company, but they bombed. Problems weren't addressed. Primarily they were poor handoffs." In her view:

Unless you want to own the whole feeding chain, you can't control it. We know more patients need to go home, but given the lousy way that things happen ... no one knows what the other one does in this business. Home healthcare is a different world from acute care.

❖ IS COMMON OWNERSHIP THE SOLUTION?

Many in the healthcare industry have expressed the same sentiment: If we could own the whole supply chain, perhaps we could control it better. Jamie Robinson and Larry Casalino argued that "the potential advantages of integrated delivery systems in which medical groups and hospitals remained autonomic and antagonistic are obvious." In particular, "an integrated delivery system can function as a seamless system within which patients can move freely from outpatient to inpatient to sub-acute to home health services."[186]

Could it really be that simple? We conducted a study of patients who received care at Brigham and Women's Hospital—part of the Partners integrated delivery system—to find out whether patients who received all their care within the Partners system had better coordinated care than those who received only part of their care within the system.[187] The results were inconsistent. Patients who received rehab care within the same integrated delivery system as their surgery reported better coordination of care than did those who received rehab care out of network. However, patients who received home care within the same integrated delivery system as their surgery reported worse coordination of care than did those who received home care outside the system.

These findings suggest that integrated delivery systems—common ownership of all providers in the supply chain—are not a magic solution for coordination problems. There continues to be variability in cross-organizational coordination that can be better addressed by extending elements of an organization's internal work practices to include its key supply partners whether or not they are under common ownership. Ownership cannot take the place of this important design task. Even economists are coming to realize that coordination across the continuum of care requires more than contractual relationships.[188]

❖ ARE PRIMARY CARE PHYSICIANS (OR FAMILY MEMBERS) THE SOLUTION?

Others have argued that the primary care physician can play a critical role in achieving coordination across the continuum of care. To gain more insight into this potential role, we conducted a follow-up study at Brigham and Women's Hospital, a hospital that had adopted an explicit strategy in which the primary care physician would play the role of coordinator, as we saw above.[189] We assessed coordination across the supply chain from acute care to rehab to home care and found a fragmented system with the primary care physician playing only a weak role in the coordination of care.

Exhibit 16-1 shows, in the shaded areas, the strength of relational coordination among providers who worked with the same patient at the same stage of care.[190] Relational coordination among care providers in acute care, rehab care, and home care tended to be relatively strong, typically higher than 3 on a five-point scale. In contrast, the nonshaded areas show the much weaker relational coordination that we found between providers who worked with the same patient at different stages of care (between acute and rehab, rehab and home, and acute and home), typically much lower than 3 on a five-point scale. The crosshatched areas along the bottom rows and far right columns show relational coordination carried out by other participants in the care system: participants who potentially could play the role of boundary spanner or systems integrator, including the primary care physician, the patient's family member, and the managed care case manager. When we examined relational coordination between these system integrators and the care providers in acute, rehab, and home care, we saw that some of these ties were strong (higher than 3 on a five-point scale) but that most were quite weak.

In particular, the patient's family member or informal caregiver exhibited high levels of relational coordination with at least one care provider in every stage of care. The managed care case manager had strong ties only with the acute care case manager, most likely as a result of managed care's focus on getting the patient out of the hospital as quickly as feasible. But the primary care physician was the least well-connected, exhibiting low levels of relational coordination with everyone, including the family member or informal caregiver.

Exhibit 16-1 Relational Coordination for Surgical Patients across the Continuum*

		Acute Hospital			Rehabilitation Hospital				Home Care		System Integrator		
		Surgeon	Case Manager	Physical Therapist	Physiatrist	Nurse	Case Manager	Physical Therapist	Nurse	Physical Therapist	Primary Care Physician	Informal Caregiver	Managed Care Case manager
Acute Hospital	Case Manager	3.5	1.3	4.3	1.1	2.2	2.6	2.3	2.5	2.2	2.5	3.6	3.9
	Physical Therapist	3.4	3.8	4.1	1.1	1.2	1.1	1.4	1.1	1.3	1.1	1.9	1.2
Rehabilitation Hospital	Case Manager	2.1	2.2	1.9	3.6	4.3	4.5	4.4	2.2	1.9	1.8	3.3	2.7
	Physical Therapist	2.3	1.7	2.1	3.8	4.2	4.2	4.6	1.5	1.8	1.4	3.0	1.5
Home Care	Nurse	2.7	1.5	1.3	1.2	1.2	1.2	1.3	4.5	4.0	2.1	3.4	1.5
	Physical Therapist	3.5	1.8	1.9	1.6	1.6	1.5	1.9	3.8	4.3	2.0	3.3	2.1
System Integrator	Primary Care Physician	2.2	1.5	1.3	1.4	1.7	1.8	1.7	1.5	1.4	1.2	1.9	1.3
	Informal Caregiver	3.3	1.8	2.4	2.1	3.0	2.1	2.8	3.3	3.6	1.9	–	1.2
Observations		519	456	467	296	298	298	283	418	400	445	337	267

* This exhibit is discussed in the "Note for Exhibits" chapter beginning on page 315.

Despite the fact that Brigham and Women's Hospital explicitly intended the PCP to play a central role in coordinating care, the PCP played the weakest role. The only participant who played a consistent system integrator role across the continuum of care was the informal caregiver: the family member of the patient.

Not all patients experienced such a fragmented care continuum. Our results showed that PCPs and managed care case managers *increased* their coordination role weak relational coordination across the continuum resulted in negative clinical outcomes primarily for patients who were older or had poorer overall health. We also found that integrating family caregivers into the care team made a positive difference: High levels of relational coordination between family caregivers and other care providers resulted in greater caregiver preparation, predicting better clinical outcomes for patients.[191]

❖ BOTTOM LINE

The challenge of coordinating care across organizations is even more daunting than the challenge of coordinating care within organizations, but in many ways the two challenges are similar. Like relational coordination within healthcare organizations, relational coordination between them is often characterized by infrequent, delayed, inaccurate communication focused more on finger-pointing than on problem solving, reinforced by fragmented goals, fragmented knowledge, and status hierarchies.

The good news is that many of the solutions are also quite similar. Many of the practices that we have explored for fostering high levels of relational coordination within organizations can be extended to foster high levels of relational coordination between them. In particular, clinical pathways, boundary spanners, patient rounds, and information systems can be extended from their origins as internal practices to connect with the external providers who are engaged in caring for the same patients, including the patient's family. It is a story of dynamic capabilities, of organizations taking the best practices that they have established internally and extending them "beyond their own walls," building supply partnerships that enable them to deliver more efficient and higher quality patient care than they could deliver on their own.

Chapter 17

Combine Work Practices to Build a High Performance Work System

Throughout Part 2, we have explored high performance work practices that strengthen relational coordination among care providers, enabling them to deliver high quality patient care while using resources efficiently. Chapter 16 showed how those practices can be extended beyond an organization's boundaries to include its key supply partners, including even the patient and his or her family. We have seen however that healthcare organizations vary greatly in their implementation of those work practices. One common pattern we observed was the repeated failure to apply these work systems fully to physicians. Whether it was selection for teamwork, cross-functional performance measurement, cross-functional rewards, conflict resolution, patient rounds, or clinical pathways, physicians were often the least likely of any care provider discipline to be included. This failure to include physicians helps to explain why relational coordination between physicians and the rest of the care provider team was systematically weaker than for any other care provider discipline (see Chapter 3) despite the fact that physicians play a central role in delivering patient care.

In the preceding chapters, we estimated the impact of each individual work practice on relational coordination and on the quality and efficiency of patient care. We found that the size of these estimated effects varied from work practice to work practice. On the low end, we found that doubling the intensity of the boundary spanner role was estimated to increase relational coordination by 11 percent; on the high end, doubling the inclusiveness of team meetings was estimated to increase relational coordination by 20 percent. Because the hospitals in our study have adopted these work practices in combinations or *clusters*, however, our statistical estimates cannot assess the impact of each individual practice as accurately as we would like. It is more accurate to measure their impact together, as a high performance work system.

When we combine all the individual practices into a high performance work system, how does that system affect relational coordination? Exhibit 17-1 suggests that doubling the strength of this high performance work system produces a 44 percent increase in relational coordination among nurses, physicians, residents, therapists, case managers, and social workers. When relational coordination is plotted for each of the nine hospitals against the strength of their high performance work systems, as shown in Exhibit 17-2, the plot suggests a strong positive impact of the high performance work system on relational coordination among care providers.

We also can assess the impact of this high performance work system on patient care outcomes.[192] We find that doubling the strength of this work system enables a 68 percent reduction in the length of hospital stays and a 53 percent increase in patient satisfaction. The same change in this system also contributes to an 18 percent increase in postoperative freedom from joint pain and a 14 percent increase in postoperative mobility, two of the most desirable clinical outcomes of joint replacement surgery. Combining these four performance metrics into a single measure of surgical performance, we found that the high

Exhibit 17-1   Impact of a High Performance Work System on Relational Coordination†

	Relational Coordination
High Performance Work System	.44 ***
Physicians	−.15 ***
Residents	−.01
Physical Therapists	.07 +
Case Managers	.04
Social Workers	−.07
Surgical Volume	−.01
R-squared	.92

† This exhibit is discussed in the "Notes for Exhibits" chapter beginning on page 315.

Exhibit 17-2   Graphing the Impact of a High Performance Work System on Relational Coordination

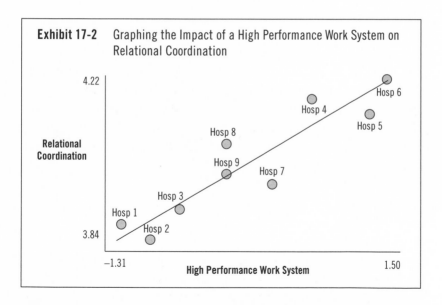

performance work system increased overall performance by 54 percent. Furthermore, our analysis showed, consistent with our qualitative evidence and our theoretical expectations, that this high performance work system achieves its performance outcomes *through* its effect on relational coordination.[193]

Exhibit 17-3   Impact of a High Performance Work System on Surgical Performance†

	Length of Stay	Patient Satisfaction	Postoperative Freedom from Pain	Postoperative Mobility	Surgical Performance Index	Surgical Performance Index
High Performance Work System	−.68 ***	.53 ***	.18 *	.14 +	.54 ***	−.05
Relational Coordination						.29 **
Patient Age	−.02	.01	−.01	−.04	.01	.01
Comorbidities	.09 *	.07	−.01	−.04	−.04	−.05
Preoperative Status	.02	−.01	.20 ***	.28 ***	.17 ***	.16 ***
Surgical Procedure	.01	.11 **	.21 ***	.10 **	.15 ***	.16 ***
Psychological Well-being	−.09 *	.15 **	.41 ***	.41 ***	.41 ***	.40 ***
Surgical Volume	.15 ***	.09 +	.05	.02	.03	.05
R-squared	.76	.58	.44	.16	.71	.83

† This exhibit is discussed in the "Notes for Exhibits" chapter beginning on page 315.

Exhibit 17-3 summarizes these results. Some of the performance effects are quite large, and all of them are statistically significant. This means that healthcare organizations can be quite confident of achieving improved performance results if they strengthen their high performance work system. These results are summarized visually in Exhibit 17-4, including our earlier findings on job satisfaction.

❖ BOTTOM LINE

It is clear that many healthcare organizations, along with their patients and their care providers, would benefit greatly from building the high performance work system described in Part 2. The question we face in Part 3 is how to get from here to there.

In Chapter 18, we will see that external pressures can motivate higher levels of coordination among care providers. However, we will also see that external pressures can only go so far to change behaviors. To sustain care provider efforts over

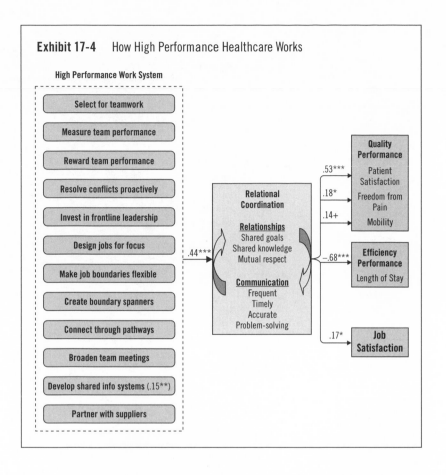

Exhibit 17-4   How High Performance Healthcare Works

time, organizations need to invest in strengthening their high performance work systems. Chapter 19 describes the synergies among the individual work practices that render a fragmented piecemeal approach likely to fail, and proposes instead a systems approach to building a high performance work system. Chapter 20 describes the role that labor-management partnerships can play in supporting the change process. Chapter 21 concludes by describing three powerful barriers to high performance healthcare at the industry level—fragmented payment systems, fragmented physician-hospital relationships and fragmented information systems—and suggesting key elements to include in the current overhaul of U.S. health policy.

Part III

Getting from Here to There

Chapter 18

Respond to Pressure with Resilience[194]

> *We're all being put with a gun to our head, that if you continue doing things the way we did things, we are going to be a nonentity. ... You can't lose a million dollars a week and survive. ... And we're frustrated. ... We don't get the time with the patients that we once got. ... It's not a happy place for us. ... But if you don't make the changes, you're going to be doing catering.[195]*

Healthcare organizations are facing intense pressures to change. Although these pressures for cost reduction and quality improvement are impersonal, they often are experienced in a very personal way. Pressures from an organization's environment are experienced as work stressors: conditions that increase challenges or demands while limiting one's ability to respond to them.[196] These pressures present threats in the form of impending events with potential negative consequences intensified by time pressure.[197] Although threats take many shapes and forms, a key consequence of threats in the workplace is the creation of stressful conditions for those who work there.[198]

The chief operating officer of Hospital for Special Surgery gave his perspective on how these threats emerged, first in the form of the diagnostic related group (DRG) system for cost accounting and then more intensively in the form of managed care:[199]

> *The DRG system … was the beginning of trying to provide quality care in a cost-effective way. We began to realize that if we could do things more efficiently, or if I did not spend the money, I got to keep it. Then managed care came into existence in New York and throughout the rest of the country, and that's what started to change things. The public got tired of paying these exorbitant healthcare costs. They saw waste. The perception was that there was waste in the healthcare industry. So there was a public outcry for change under Clinton. And people were starting to get upset that they were paying money and not getting the value. Now we are at 25 percent managed care penetration and about a 25 percent discount. To get those managed care contracts you have to accept those discount rates, even if it hurts.*

Managed care pressures translated into work stress in the form of heavier workloads, according to the associate director of quality improvement at the same hospital:

> *With managed care, there's a need to get more patients. We are giving managed care a discount, and in order to continue to make money with that discount, you have to admit more patients. So the volume is going up. So we have more patients to see with the same amount of staff, and we want to shorten the length of stay for those patients. So there's much more pressure to see more patients. More of our patients need help, because as you lower the length of stay, it's almost a direct correlation to the number of patients who need transitional care. So there's more to*

do with more patients in less time. And that's created a tremendous pressure on the staff.

These simultaneous pressures for cost reduction and quality improvement also create role conflict. Role conflict occurs when care providers, many of whom were attracted to health-care work by their desire to give the best care possible to patients, find themselves having to watch the bottom line. A director of quality management at the Hospital for Joint Diseases explained:

Our role with patients has been based on one where we are trusted and perceived as people who are doing everything to maximize the care that people get. We have always considered ourselves to be patient advocates, but now it's more complicated than that.

Some argue that managed care has destroyed relationships with patients, which for many care providers served as an attraction to the job and a source of job satisfaction. A social worker at Beth Israel Deaconess explained: "Caregivers can't have that totally personal relationship with the patient anymore. There isn't the time. Sometimes we are still angry about the transition."

In addition, competition often is experienced as a source of stress. The chief of social work at Beth Israel Deaconess explained:

One of the most difficult pieces of all this is that as health-care institutions, we did not see each other as competitors except in the sense of friendly competitors. We were intellectual competitors, not economic competitors. We would just call someone in our neighboring institution to talk. But this is not the case anymore. Work processes are proprietary information now because they are the key to efficiency—some say the key to quality—and the key to survival.

A director of regulatory affairs in the Hospital for Joint Diseases expressed a similar concern:

> *Don't forget, we're in competition now. Everyone's try-ing to stay alive. The leadership here is fairly aggressive and fairly knowledgeable of what the expectations for the practitioner are. You have to think about competition; you have to think about marketing now. And this is all new to us. You know, how do we attract the HMOs? How do we convince people that they need to come here for the very best care? How do we do that, and how do we do it eco-nomically? We're hoping that if we're thoughtful enough and quick enough—which can be a problem, you know— we can address the needs that we're currently facing.*

The uncertainty that comes from such a turbulent environ-ment is also stressful. An administrator at the Hospital for Joint Diseases confessed:

> *It's all an unknown, really, you know. At this point every-body, I think, is kind of going by the seat of their pants saying, "You know, what's it really going to turn out to be?" It's a pretty interesting time. I'm not sure if I like it, though.*

This uncertainty includes the very real threat that the organi-zation will not survive the increased pressures.

❖ IS PRESSURE ALWAYS A BAD THING?

Organizational psychologist Robert Karasek argued that the blocking of goal attainment by work stress results in reduced job satisfaction, reduced well-being, and increased absence and turnover.[200] Work stress also can reduce task performance. In sum, the research "has indicated that persons tend to perform better and express more positive affective responses in work settings in which constraints are absent compared to when they are present."[201] This sounds like bad news for the health-care industry.

However, work stress also can have a positive impact on performance. We know from Gary Latham and Edwin Locke that challenging goals can have a positive impact on performance when those goals are specific yet reachable.[202] Situational constraints more broadly, such as pressures for performance and resource constraints, are work stressors that can have either positive or negative effects on performance. The effects of work stressors can be positive if they allow people's abilities to be utilized to the fullest or negative if they constrain the utilization of abilities.[203]

Clearly, the critical question is: What determines whether work stressors have a positive or negative impact on performance? Often, a U-shaped relationship has been found between pressure and performance. Up to a certain point, pressure leads to higher performance; after that point, additional pressure leads to rapid declines in performance. The location of that turning point varies for different people. Interestingly, coping mechanisms play a critical role in determining how much pressure people can take before the impact becomes negative.

❖ HOW PEOPLE COPE WITH PRESSURE

Coping mechanisms are ways in which people cope with pressure. People with effective coping mechanisms can withstand quite a bit of pressure before falling apart. In the absence of coping mechanisms, however, it takes relatively little pressure to push someone over the edge. Coping mechanisms stretch the boundary of how much pressure a person can take before falling apart.

Some coping mechanisms help people deal with pressures in their individual jobs. Robert Karasek found that when jobs are demanding, workers with control over their jobs thrive but workers without control experience dissatisfaction and stress.

Job control is therefore a coping mechanism that enables people to achieve good outcomes even in demanding jobs.[204] With sufficient job control, people with high job demands do not experience the blocking of goal attainment but are stimulated by those demands to achieve higher performance and gain more satisfaction from their work.[205] Another coping mechanism that reduces the negative effects of work pressures is self-efficacy or the belief that one has the skills needed to complete the task at hand successfully.[206] Both job control and self-efficacy enable workers to respond effectively to work stress by increasing the possibility of goal attainment.

❖ HOW ORGANIZATIONS COPE WITH PRESSURE

Although these individual coping mechanisms may be suitable for addressing individual stressors such as a difficult job or a difficult boss, they may not be adequate for addressing larger collective threats such as pressures from managed care. When stressors emanate from an organization's external environment—such as the pressures that are facing the healthcare industry today—it is questionable whether individual coping mechanisms such as self-efficacy and job control are an adequate response. Fortunately, some scholars have moved beyond individual coping mechanisms to explore collective coping mechanisms. Steve Jex and Paul Bliese found that collective efficacy reduces the negative effects of work stressors on job satisfaction, just as individual efficiency does.[207] Because collective efficacy increases the possibility of collective goal attainment, not just individual goal attainment, it may enable workers to cope with stressors that require more than an individual response.

Other collective coping mechanisms like cohesion and social support are effective because collectives provide a kind of psychic support that allows their members to share stress and therefore reduce the intensity of that stress for any individual member. In a laboratory study in which participants were subjected to equivalent levels of stressors, John Aiello and Kathryn Kolb found that members of cohesive groups reported the least stress.[208] Others have found that social support reduces the negative effects of work stressors.[209] In our study, a case manager explained how she and her colleagues deal with stress collectively:

> *We all get frustrated with each other at times, but then we can sit down and talk about it, you know. We all know the constraints that we work under. We all know the stresses that we have and the workloads that we have. Sometimes you gotta—when you get together, you got to let everybody vent for a few minutes, and then say, "OK, now everybody's got it out, let's get down to the nitty-gritty."*

Wanda Orlikowski and Joanne Yates found that participants tend to engage in more timely communication with each other in response to increased external performance pressures, and Stelia Anderson and Larry Williams found that participants tend to increase both helping and help seeking under stressful conditions.[210] Similarly, Dierdre Wicks found that external pressures tend to diminish the importance of status differences between healthcare providers from different disciplines, and Ingrid Nembhard and Amy Edmondson found that reduced status differences tend to improve working relationships.[211]

A nurse administrator whose hospital was experiencing significant pressures for reduced resource utilization explained:

> *[Pressures from managed care] have been a leveler for a lot of nurse-physician relationships. It seems to me like they're in the soup together.*

As a result of the new pressures, the clinical staff had united around the common threat. In the view of this nurse administrator:

> *Their hierarchy seems to have broken down a little bit. It's lumped the nurses and physicians together more.*[212]

Reductions in status differences thus may result in more positive relationships among key participants, enabling them to respond collectively to external threats.

❖ BEYOND COPING TO RESILIENCE

Individuals and organizations can do more than simply cope with adverse conditions. Resilience is a trait that enables individuals or organizations to persevere or even thrive in the face of threat. Organizational scholars Kathleen Sutcliffe and Timothy Vogus defined resilience as the ability to flourish or thrive amid adverse conditions when rigidity might be expected.[213] Resilience results when organizations retain resources in a form that is sufficiently flexible to cope positively with the unexpected. Relationships are one resource that enables resilience. Organizations with positive work relationships are more resilient, recovering more quickly from external threats.[214] This is true in part because relationships are a source of information-processing capacity, another resource that contributes to organizational resilience. As Sutcliffe and Vogus explain, organizational resilience can be fostered through problem-solving networks, social capital, and relationships because the "greater usage of respectful interaction can accelerate and enrich the exchange of information and the capacity to process it."

❖ IS RELATIONAL COORDINATION A RESILIENT RESPONSE TO MANAGED CARE PENETRATION?

In Part I we learned that relational coordination gives healthcare organizations the capacity to meet the extreme information-processing demands that they face. Relational coordination also serves a source of social cohesion due to the shared goals, shared knowledge, and mutual respect that underlie it. Perhaps the information-processing and relational dimensions of relational coordination together can enable care providers to cope resiliently with the threat of managed care.

Using data from the nine hospitals that have been featured throughout this book, we have added two new variables to our model of high performance healthcare. We can now ask whether pressures from managed care and the resulting work stress tend to foster higher levels of relational coordination among care providers, or whether instead these pressures tend to undermine relational coordination. The nine hospitals in this study were located in three different states: Massachusetts, New York, and Texas. Managed care penetration levels (percentage of the population insured by managed care, whether private, Medicaid, or Medicare) were measured for each state. At the time these patient and provider data were collected, Massachusetts had the highest managed care penetration of all 50 states, ranking first at 55 percent; New York ranked twelfth at 38 percent; and Texas ranked thirty-first at 22 percent.[215] External pressure was measured as the percentage of managed care penetration in each hospital's operating environment.

Work stress was measured as constraints posed by patient insurance on a provider's ability to accomplish his or her job, as perceived by care providers. In our survey of care providers we asked: "Does patient insurance coverage interfere with your ability to meet the needs of patients?" Responses were recorded on a 3-point scale: "does not interfere," "interferes somewhat," and "interferes to a great extent." Relational coordination was measured in our survey of care providers using seven items, as explained in Chapter 3, including frequent, timely, accurate problem-solving communication as well as shared goals, shared knowledge, and mutual respect.

❖ WHAT WE FOUND

The work stress reported by care providers was significantly higher in some hospitals than in others.[216] In particular, care providers in hospitals that faced higher levels of managed care penetration reported higher levels of work stress than did those in other disciplines. Physicians, physical therapists, and case managers reported significantly higher levels of work stress than did nurses and residents, perhaps because they were more likely to be held accountable for decisions regarding patient discharge. Interestingly, across all disciplines, care providers tended to respond to higher levels of work stress by engaging in higher rather than lower levels of relational coordination. However, while physicians reported the highest level of stress from managed care, they also reported the lowest levels of relational coordination with their colleagues.

Exhibit 18-1 shows the results of testing our expanded model of high performance healthcare. The first column (Work Stress) shows that doubling managed care penetration increased work stress by 18 percent. The second column shows that doubling managed care penetration increased relational coordination by 9 percent. The third column indicates that work stress increased relational coordination among care providers and that managed care penetration increased relational coordination *through* its effect on perceived work stress.[217]

Exhibit 18-1   Impact of Managed Care Penetration on Relational Coordination[†]

	Work Stress	Relational Coordination	Relational Coordination	Relational Coordination
Managed Care Penetration	.18 **	.09 *	.05	−.00
Work Stress			.13 **	.11 **
High Performance Work System				.42 ***
Physicians	.24 ***	−.16 ***	−.19 ***	−.17 ***
Residents	−.05	−.05	−.04	−.01
Physical Therapists	.20 ***	.05	.03	.05
Case Managers	.10 +	.04	.03	.03
Social Workers	.07	−.06	−.02	−.03
Surgical Volume	.08	.00	−.00	−.01
R-squared	.68	.18	.30	.97

† This exhibit is discussed in the "Notes for Exhibits" chapter beginning on page 315.

Nevertheless, the fourth column shows that the high performance work system introduced earlier in this book still has by far the largest impact on relational coordination of any factor in this model. Even after we take into account the helpful effects of external pressures and work stress, doubling the strength of this high performance work system is predicted to increase relational coordination by an additional 42 percent. As we already know from Part II, this unique high performance work system enhances both the quality and the efficiency of patient care through its impact on relational coordination. The results are summarized visually in Exhibit 18-2.

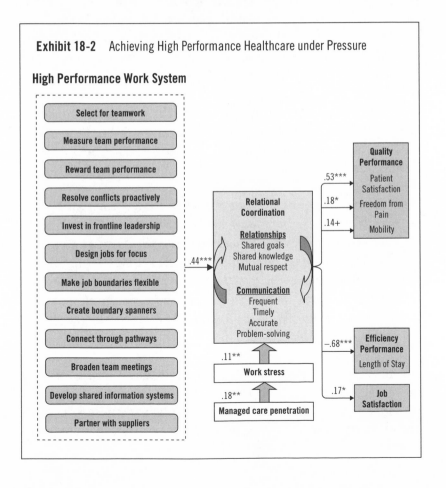

Exhibit 18-2   Achieving High Performance Healthcare under Pressure

High Performance Work System

❖ EXTERNAL THREATS ARE NOT ENOUGH

Given that this unique high performance work system plays such an important role in changing behavior, compared to the role of external threats, we cannot help wondering what motivates its adoption. Do managed care pressures and the resulting work stress help healthcare organizations in their efforts to implement high performance work systems? We tested the relationship between managed care penetration and high performance work systems, and between work stress and high performance work systems. Both correlations were positive but statistically insignificant, suggesting that these factors may not significantly influence a healthcare organization's ability to implement high performance work systems.[218] Perhaps these external pressures make healthcare leaders *more interested* in adopting new work systems, as we learned in our interviews, but they may not make implementation any easier to achieve.

Indeed, some hospital leaders feared that the external pressures they faced would destroy collaboration rather than foster it. The chief operating officer at the Hospital for Special Surgery stated his concerns:

> *External pressures for cost reduction make it more difficult to achieve improvements in teamwork and coordination. We got improvement cross-functionally, but now external demands are threatening it. ... Maybe these outside pressures can test the mettle of the team. With higher demands, maybe we will really focus on goals and outcomes. But if the values and vision become muted, then you lose it.*

Our evidence suggests that these external pressures are more likely to strengthen relational coordination among care providers rather than tear it apart. However, these pressures are not sufficient by themselves to achieve lasting changes in care provider behavior. Our results suggest that a supportive set of high performance work practices is needed as well.

❖ BOTTOM LINE

Although care providers tend to respond resiliently to external threats, their resilience can be strengthened and sustained if they receive support from their organizations in the form of a high performance work system. As Aaron Wildavsky argued in *Searching for Safety*, an effective response to an external threat includes both reactive coping and proactive structuring.[219] Healthcare organizations should act to support resilience, not sit back and expect care providers to do it on their own. My study of the airline industry showed that organizations make choices that either undermine or foster resilience in the face of crisis. The actions that Southwest Airlines took to build relational and financial reserves before and in response to the September 11, 2001, terrorist attacks provided a clear lesson in resilience.[220] Now we know more about resilience. We see that a high performance work system, much like the one found at Southwest Airlines, can also help healthcare organizations respond resiliently to external threats.

The bottom line is that external threats can help to strengthen relational coordination among care providers, but these threats are not sufficient to achieve dramatic and sustained improvements. The high performance work system described in this book is a far more powerful driver of relational coordination and desired performance outcomes. In Chapter 19 we will address perhaps the most important question in this book: How can healthcare organizations implement this high performance work system in order to respond to the challenges they are facing?

Chapter 19

Transform Your Organization in a Systemic and Sustainable Way

There are a lot of moving parts here. It's like an intersection in Paris, like the Champs d'Elysee. We have been rooted in traditional medicine, with complex systems and specialization. To shift gears is a huge deal! It's like trying to turn the Queen Anne around: You have to go way out to sea just to turn it around."

Although external pressures help to jump-start the development of relational coordination among care providers, it is clear that external pressures are not sufficient by themselves. The unique high performance work system described in this book is a far more powerful driver of relational coordination and desired performance outcomes. To respond effectively to external pressures for change, healthcare organizations cannot rely on care provider stress alone but instead should engage in deliberate efforts to implement a high performance work system that supports relational coordination among care providers.

Implementing this work system is not rocket science, but neither is it an easy task. In Part 2, we identified 12 distinct work practices. When implemented in mutually reinforcing systems or bundles, those practices can shape care provider behavior in a consistent and positive direction, building high levels of relational coordination. We call this system of work practices a high performance work system to indicate that it is a system of mutually reinforcing practices that work together in a cumulative way to support care provider behaviors that lead to high levels of organizational performance.[221] It is a unique type of high performance work system because it fosters the critical missing ingredient that high performance other work systems tend to neglect: social capital or relationships among employees that enable them to coordinate their work.

Because this high performance work system encompasses 12 distinct practices, many of which may run counter to those that are currently in place, implementing it can be a daunting task indeed. Strengthening relational coordination requires changing not just one or two work practices but the whole system of practices. As we know from the organization design experts Michael Tushman and David Nadler, it is necessary to change the whole system of practices in order to maintain alignment among them.[222] Each work practice reinforces the others, and so changing one without changing the others increases the risk that the change will not have the desired effect.

❖ OBSTACLES TO SYSTEMS THINKING

Clearly, a systemic approach to change is called for, but systems thinking is not common. More frequently, people tend to focus on one piece of the problem in isolation rather than looking for comprehensive solutions that will address the underlying systemic issues. According to one hospital administrator:

> *Unfortunately, and I hate to say this, I think that our [staff] sort of look at minutiae and don't look at the whole picture and often don't realize that it's the system that is the problem, and then this happens, and they're complaining about this and this and this, and I'll say, "Let's stop and look at this." And it's the system, not these three little minor things, that's the problem. It's the system that created these unnecessary tasks or inefficient tasks for the person to do, and that's what we really needed to address. A lot of our [staff] don't seem to be able to identify that. Their suggestion is that they need more help. They have too much to do. Never thinking that what we're doing is useless or asking why are we doing this.*

This tendency to focus on pieces of the problem rather than the system can increase when external pressures result in increasing workloads for staff and even in burnout and exhaustion. Anita Tucker and Amy Edmondson found that when care providers struggle to meet their goals, armed with inadequate resources, they tend to rely on quick fixes or workarounds rather than seeking systemic solutions to their problems. However, as Tucker and Edmondson found, these quick fixes or workarounds often exacerbate rather than alleviate the problems they were intended to solve.[223]

Clearly, healthcare organizations need to step back and invest in a holistic process of change. They can proceed in this direction by launching an improvement process that is much like the Plan Do Check Act (PDCA) process found in Total Quality Management, or the Plan Do Study Act (PDSA) process that is more common in healthcare.[224] Let us explore the seven steps that are summarized in Exhibit 19-1.

Exhibit 19-1	Process for Achieving High Performance Healthcare
Step 1	Identify leadership for change
Step 2	Choose a focal work process and map it out
Step 3	Measure key quality and efficiency outcomes
Step 4	Measure relational coordination and identify weak links
Step 5	Measure the high performance work system and identify gaps
Step 6	Transform work practices systemically
Step 7	Repeat the process (Steps 3–6)

❖ IDENTIFY LEADERSHIP FOR CHANGE

Leaders play a critical role in organizational change; indeed, some definitions suggest that the essence of leadership is the leadership of change. According to experts James Kouzes and Barry Posner, leadership is "the art of inspiring people to want to struggle for the achievement of new aspirations."[225] The key here is "want to": Leadership does not mean forcing change or manipulating people to change but inspiring them to want to change. We also know from theories of distributed leadership that leaders are not just CEOs, vice presidents, and other top managers. Effective organizational change can and should be led by people at every level and in every functional area of the organization, including leaders who represent employee occupational and professional interests.[226]

If leadership resides throughout an organization, who are the most critical leaders for building the unique high performance work system described in this book? We have found significant gaps in the high performance work systems in the hospitals we have studied. What we observed over and over again were not just random gaps in those hospitals' work systems but repeated failures to extend those systems fully to physicians. Whether it was selection for teamwork, measuring performance broadly, rewards for teamwork, conflict resolution, patient rounds, or clinical pathways, physicians were the least likely of any care provider discipline to be included in cross-functional, high performance work practices. As a result, physician relational coordination with the rest of the care provider team tended to be weaker than for any other function despite the fact that physicians play a central role in delivering patient care.

What does this finding imply for the leadership of change? One might argue that under these circumstances, physicians are the least likely leaders of change. As the participants who tend to be the missing link, physicians are arguably the least well positioned to lead the change process. However, because physicians have tended to be the missing link, one might argue that in fact the reverse is true: Physician leadership is essential to the change process and indeed is the key to effective change. Consistent with this argument, Charles Heckscher and his colleagues concluded that "a more effective change process is one led by physicians who embrace the values of collaborative systems."[227]

This argument is persuasive, to be sure, but physician leadership is clearly not sufficient. Two of the three hospitals in the middle tier of our nine hospitals in terms of their high performance work systems, relational coordination, and patient care outcomes had extraordinarily strong physician leadership over a sustained period, yet they remained in the middle tier. Two of the hospitals in the highest tier had moderate to high levels of physician leadership but also had high levels of leadership from nursing and from central administrative functions such as human resource management. Top leaders—including the chief executive, director of nursing, chief medical officer, director of finance, and director of human resource management—can build a philosophy that places attention and value on relationships of shared goals, shared knowledge, and mutual respect, particularly between physicians and other care provider disciplines, where they tend to be the weakest. The vice president of human resources at Beth Israel Deaconess explained:

> *What's in the background that makes interdisciplinary teams work here? It starts with our strong organizational philosophy. Our practices then become ways of assuring that the philosophy will tick—that all the pieces of the puzzle will come together. We have a longstanding philosophical thrust, starting with the CEO, that we should be a really good place for both patients and employees. ... When a patient is admitted to the emergency room, she shouldn't have to worry about how she'll get to surgery, how she'll get to the recovery room, then the unit, then to home care or a nursing home. Someone should ensure that it's coordinated for her.*

This kind of philosophical foundation provides fertile ground for leaders throughout the organization to develop a high performance work system that fosters high levels of relational coordination, producing consistently high quality, efficient patient care.

Not all organizations have this philosophical foundation as a starting point. Regardless, Step 1 is to identify leaders from multiple disciplines and at multiple levels of the organization who understand the importance of relational coordination for achieving high performance healthcare and who are willing to join together to lead the process of change.

❖ CHOOSE A FOCAL WORK PROCESS AND MAP IT OUT

Once an organization has identified leadership for change, Step 2 is to choose a focal work process around the care of a particular patient population and map it out. We learned in Chapter 2 that coordination is a challenge embedded in the complex nature of the work itself and the specialization that has emerged to address that complexity. As a result of specialization, multiple parties are involved in the care of any individual patient for any specific episode of care. The tasks performed by the different providers are often highly interdependent, meaning that physical or informational outputs from one task are needed for the successful completion of other tasks. These task interdependencies result from the division of labor, interdependencies among subsystems of the body, and interdependencies between clinical interventions and the resources used to carry out those interventions.

The process map therefore should identify all care provider functions groups that participate in the focal work process and illustrate the interdependencies among them, paying attention to flows of patients, materials, and information. Often clinical pathways can help with this task, though there are other tools that managers and consultants use to map out work processes. In particular, James Womack of the Lean Enterprise Institute and others have worked together with the Institute for Healthcare Improvement to develop tools for this purpose.[228] The key outcomes of process mapping should be to identify the care provider functions that are involved in the focal work process and to gain greater clarity about the interdependencies between their tasks.

❖ MEASURE KEY PERFORMANCE OUTCOMES

Once a focal work process has been identified and mapped, Step 3 is to identify the key outcomes of that process. The key outcomes are likely to include the efficiency of resource utilization (length of stay, costs per day of stay, total costs per stay, staffing per patient), the quality of care (patient satisfaction and clinical outcomes), and the job satisfaction of participants in the work process. In many cases, these are outcomes that already are being measured, but they may or may not be measured in a way that is specific to the focal work process and the patient population it serves. Organizations may need to work with their information systems departments to develop a convenient way to obtain these measures on a regular basis. Job satisfaction can be measured by including a question or set of questions on the employee survey described in the next step.

❖ MEASURE RELATIONAL COORDINATION AND IDENTIFY GAPS

Step 4 is to measure relational coordination among the care provider functions that are involved in the focal work process. A sample of the survey instrument is shown in Exhibit 19-2. This survey can be adapted by referring in each question to the focal work process or target patient population and including the name of each participating care provider function in the left-hand column. The survey can be sent to individual care providers at their home addresses or placed in their mailboxes at work. A cover letter signed by one or all of the leaders of the change process should be included, making it clear why it is essential for each care provider to respond to the survey and what will be done with the data. An outside party can be engaged to receive and enter the data to provide anonymity to respondents; there is no need to know the individual identity of the respondents, but it is essential to capture their functional identity (see question 8 on the sample survey instrument) to code the data properly.[229]

These data can be used to build a matrix diagram to visualize patterns of relational coordination among the care provider functions in the focal work process. This type of diagram is known as a dependency structure matrix and originally was developed by Donald Steward and then developed further by Steven Eppinger and colleagues to understand complex engineering and design processes.[230] See Exhibit 19-3 for a matrix diagram from our nine-hospital study. This diagram shows relational coordination with physicians, nurses, therapists, case managers, and social workers as reported by the care providers in the left-hand column. It shows that physicians in the nine-hospital study tended to have the weakest relational coordination with other care providers and that their strongest link was with the physical therapists. This matrix can be built for any focal work process to discover both the strong and the weak links, enabling participants to focus the improvement process on strengthening the weak links.

Exhibit 19-2   Sample Relational Coordination Survey*

1. How *frequently* do you communicate with these care providers about [   ] patients?

	Never	Rarely	Occasionally	Often	Constantly
Physicians	1	2	3	4	5
Residents	1	2	3	4	5
Nurses	1	2	3	4	5
Case Managers	1	2	3	4	5
Therapists	1	2	3	4	5
Social Workers	1	2	3	4	5

2. Do people in these groups communicate with you in a *timely* way about [   ] patients?

	Never	Rarely	Occasionally	Often	Always
Physicians	1	2	3	4	5
Residents	1	2	3	4	5
Nurses	1	2	3	4	5
Case Managers	1	2	3	4	5
Therapists	1	2	3	4	5
Social Workers	1	2	3	4	5

3. Do people in these groups communicate with you *accurately* about [   ] patients?

	Never	Rarely	Occasionally	Often	Always
Physicians	1	2	3	4	5
Residents	1	2	3	4	5
Nurses	1	2	3	4	5
Case Managers	1	2	3	4	5
Therapists	1	2	3	4	5
Social Workers	1	2	3	4	5

4. When problems occur in the care of [   ] patients, do people in these groups blame others or work with you to *solve the problem?*

	Blame Others			Solve the Problem	
Physicians	1	2	3	4	5
Residents	1	2	3	4	5
Nurses	1	2	3	4	5
Case Managers	1	2	3	4	5
Therapists	1	2	3	4	5
Social Workers	1	2	3	4	5

(cont'd)

Exhibit 19-2   Sample Relational Coordination Survey *(Continued)*

5.   How much do people in these groups *know* about the work you do with [   ] patients?

	Nothing	Little	Some	A Lot	Everything
Physicians	1	2	3	4	5
Residents	1	2	3	4	5
Nurses	1	2	3	4	5
Case Managers	1	2	3	4	5
Therapists	1	2	3	4	5
Social Workers	1	2	3	4	5

6.   How much do people in these groups *respect* the work you do with [   ] patients?

	Not at All	A Little	Somewhat	A Lot	Completely
Physicians	1	2	3	4	5
Residents	1	2	3	4	5
Nurses	1	2	3	4	5
Case Managers	1	2	3	4	5
Therapists	1	2	3	4	5
Social Workers	1	2	3	4	5

7.   To what extent do people in these groups *share your goals* for the care of [   ] patients?

	Not at All	A Little	Somewhat	A Lot	Completely
Physicians	1	2	3	4	5
Residents	1	2	3	4	5
Nurses	1	2	3	4	5
Case Managers	1	2	3	4	5
Therapists	1	2	3	4	5
Social Workers	1	2	3	4	5

8.   Please identify the work group you belong to:
   a.   Physician _____   d.   Case Manager _____
   b.   Resident _____   e.   Social Worker _____
   c.   Nurse _____

* This exhibit is discussed in the "Notes for Exhibits" chapter beginning on page 315.

Exhibit 19-3   Differences in Relational Coordination between Functions*

| | Relational Coordination Reported With | | | | |
	Physicians	Nurses	Physical Therapists	Case Managers	Social Workers
Physicians	3.82	3.94	4.03	3.75	3.70
Nurses	3.81	4.48	4.27	4.03	3.92
Physical Therapists	3.85	4.25	4.71	4.06	3.94
Case Managers	3.83	4.36	4.43	4.45	4.37
Social Workers	3.93	4.01	4.03	4.17	4.36
All	3.85	4.21	4.29	4.09	4.06

* This exhibit is discussed in the "Notes for Exhibits" chapter beginning on page 315.

❖ MEASURE THE HIGH PERFORMANCE WORK SYSTEM AND IDENTIFY GAPS

Step 5 consists of conducting an inventory of the work practices in your high performance work system. Exhibit 19-4 provides an interview protocol for measuring these practices. Your organization may be out front in the implementation of some work practices, while seriously lagging on others. Alternatively, you may find that your organization is relatively strong on all work practices, but that physicians or nurses or members of another key function have been neglected. The care provider functions with the weakest relational coordination links, as revealed in the previous step, are likely to be the functions that are inadequately covered by your high performance work practices. Pay particular attention to selection for teamwork, rewards for teamwork, involvement in cross-functional performance measurement systems, supervisory staffing levels, and so on, for these functions. Extending your high performance work practices to include these functions is likely to produce the biggest payoffs.

Exhibit 19-4   High Performance Work System Interview Protocol*

Selection for Cross-Functional Teamwork (0 = not important, 1 = somewhat important, 2 = very important)

Is teamwork ability with other functions an important selection criterion for physicians?

Is teamwork ability with other functions an important selection criterion for nurses?

Is teamwork ability with other functions an important selection criterion for physical therapists?

Cross-Functional Performance Measurement (1 = by discipline, 5 = cross-disciplinary) (1= retroactively, 5 = proactively)

Is quality assurance carried out separately by discipline or in a cross-disciplinary process?

Is quality assurance carried out retroactively or proactively?

Is utilization management carried out separately by discipline or in a cross-disciplinary process?

Is utilization management carried out retroactively or proactively?

Cross-Functional Rewards (for physicians: 0 = individual only, 1 = surplus sharing, 2 = risk sharing) (for others: 0 = none, 1 = individual only, 2 = some team)

Are rewards for physicians based purely on individual performance or on surplus sharing or risk sharing with the hospital as well?

Are rewards for nurses based purely on individual performance or on some cross-functional performance criteria as well?

Are rewards for physical therapists based purely on individual performance or on some cross-functional performance criteria as well?

Cross-Functional Conflict Resolution (0 = no, 1 = yes)

Do physicians have access to a cross-functional conflict resolution process?

Do nurses have access to a cross-functional conflict resolution process?

Do physical therapists have access to a cross-functional conflict resolution process?

Supervisory Staffing (supervisors/frontline care providers)

What is the ratio of physician leaders to staff and nonstaff physicians?

What is the ratio of nursing supervisors to nurses?

What is the ratio of physical therapy supervisors to physical therapists?

Patient-Focused Job Design (time spent with this patient population/total work time)

Of the physicians who work with this patient population, what percentage of their time do they spend, on average?

Of the nurses who work with this patient population, what percentage of their time do they spend, on average?

Of the physical therapists who work with this patient population, what percentage of their time do they spend, on average?

(cont'd)

Of the case managers who work with this patient population, what percentage of their time do they spend, on average?

Cross-Functional Boundary Spanner (patients/case managers) (0 = no, 1 = yes)

How many patients are assigned to each case manager?

Are case managers responsible for discharge planning?

Are case managers responsible for clinical coordination of care?

Do you have primary nursing?

Cross-Functional Pathways (0 = no, 1 = yes)

Do physicians have tasks on the pathway?

Do nurses have tasks on the pathway?

Do physical therapists have tasks on the pathway?

Do case managers have tasks on the pathway?

What percentage of patients is kept on the pathway throughout their stay?

Cross-Functional Team Meetings (0 = never, 1 = sometimes, 2 = usually or always)

Do nurses attend physician rounds?

Do physical therapists attend physician rounds?

Do case managers attend physician rounds?

Do physicians attend nursing rounds?

Do physical therapists attend nursing rounds?

Do case managers attend nursing rounds?

Cross-Functional Information Systems (0 = no, 1 = yes)

Does your cross-functional information system include lab results?

Does your cross-functional information system include insurance information?

Does your cross-functional information system include financial data?

Does your cross-functional information system include a medical history?

Does your cross-functional information system include inpatient procedures?

Does your cross-functional information system include provider order entry?

Does your cross-functional information system include inpatient consult history?

Does your cross-functional information system include the discharge summary?

Does your cross-functional information system include current condition/functioning?

* This exhibit is discussed in the "Notes for Exhibits" chapter beginning on page 315.

❖ TRANSFORM WORK PRACTICES SYSTEMICALLY

Once the gaps in the high performance work system have been identified, the final challenge (step 6) is to transform those work practices systemically. Keep in mind that the work practices in a high performance work system tend to be mutually reinforcing. As a result, investments in one work practice are not likely to pay off fully and indeed may be wasted unless investments are also made in changing the others. For these reasons, it is wise to conduct an assessment of all work practices in one's high performance work system before engaging in any major investments. Once it is understood in a holistic way where the gaps are and how those gaps are interrelated, an investment plan can be mapped out to address the gaps in a holistic way. With this systemic approach, each investment can be enhanced by the synergies it achieves with other related investments.

The high performance work practices introduced in this book reinforce each other in many ways. Consider just a few examples. First, there are potential synergies between selecting for teamwork and measuring team performance. It is difficult to successfully transform a traditional performance measurement system to one that is cross-functional and focused on problem solving if care providers continue to be selected for their individual clinical skills without consideration for their teamwork skills. Likewise, it will be difficult to implement cross-functional performance measurement fully if physicians continue to have a compensation structure that rewards them for excess patient days in the hospital. Selecting care providers for teamwork skills may be a wasted investment if other existing work practices undermine and discourage teamwork, such as rigid job boundaries and rewards for function-specific outcomes rather than overall patient outcomes.

Other synergies among high performance work practices may be less apparent but just as real, such as investments in information systems that can support cross-functional performance measurement. An administrator in one hospital described the lack of good information systems as an obstacle to efforts by himself and his colleagues to adopt a more proactive cross-functional approach to quality measurement:

> *We are hoping to move from anecdotal, you know, you-won't-believe-this-is-happening, to more fact-based studies. So that means we have some real significant problems with data. We have lots of it. It's all over the place. Sometimes we don't know what it means. Sometimes we don't know how to interpret it, and more often than not, the information we have is not the information we need. So that's a big challenge for us.*

Clinical pathways also have synergies with measuring team performance. Cross-functional clinical pathways can be used to measure variances from quality and utilization goals at the process level, thus providing a source of cross-functional data for improving the underlying processes rather than merely pointing the finger at individual care providers. Also, cross-functional performance measurement can produce insights into how the pathway can be updated over time to reflect improvements in best practices.

Likewise, there are powerful synergies among patient rounds, clinical pathways, and cross-functional boundary spanners. We found that patient rounds are most effective when they are inclusive, but inclusive meetings can require a tremendous investment of staff time. Cross-functional clinical pathways can streamline meetings by allowing participants to focus on variances from the pathways, making meetings far more efficient. Case managers, if adequately staffed, can serve as boundary spanners to convene and lead these meetings, and can also supplement meetings with ongoing communication in between. Case managers can also serve as the driver behind the use of clinical pathways, helping to negotiate the decision points that inevitably arise. Investing in one of these three work practices without investing in the others could clearly reduce the potential gains.

There are also potential synergies between cross-functional conflict resolution and frontline leadership. Cross-functional conflict resolution is a critical ingredient of a high performance work system whose purpose is to build relational coordination. However, conflict resolution requires a significant investment of time and often suffers from a lack of attention from frontline supervisors. Supervisors who are staffed sufficiently to engage in coaching and feedback can identify conflicts early on and take a proactive problem-solving approach in conjunction with their colleagues in other functions, using conflicts to build higher levels of understanding and teamwork between functions as well as improvements in the underlying work process.

Most of all, it is critical to invest in high performance work practices for all functions that are core to the patient care process. Investments in high performance work practices for nurses, therapists, case managers, and so on, will not achieve their full benefits if the organization is not simultaneously investing in high performance work practices for the physicians with whom they work. For example, the benefits of investing in cross-functional conflict resolution between nurses, therapists and case managers are expected to be lower if the conflict resolution process is not extended to include physicians, and if other work practices in the organization continue to reinforce physician autonomy, allowing some physicians to remain unaware of and unaccountable for their treatment of others.

More specific guidance for leading systemic change is beyond the scope of this book; however, guidance can be found in books such as Michael Tushman and Charles O'Reilly's *Winning Through Innovation: A Practical Guide to Leading Organizational Change and Renewal*.[231]

❖ REPEAT THE PROCESS

The process we have laid out here is not a one-time fix: Like any good improvement process, and like the PDCA process after which it is modeled, it is a cycle of improvement. The final step (step 7) is to repeat steps 3 through 6: Measure quality and efficiency outcomes to see how they have changed, reassess relational coordination to find out whether the weak links have become stronger, and then refine the high performance work system to strengthen the weak links that remain.

❖ BOTTOM LINE

Achieving high performance healthcare is not rocket science but it is not easy either. The work practices that support high performance healthcare are hard to implement not because they are technically complex, but rather because they go against patterns of behaviors and relationships that have become deeply ingrained in healthcare organizations. Throughout the healthcare system, however, many people are now ready for change. There is now widespread recognition that doing the same thing is not an acceptable alternative. The changes recommended in this book can provide healthcare organizations with the capacity to meet the current challenge of improving the quality of patient care, while simultaneously improving its efficiency.

Employees, along with their professional associations and their unions, are key partners in this change process. Researchers have already documented the positive impact unions can have on the implementation and effectiveness of high performance work practices.[232] In particular, economists Sandra Black and Lisa Lynch have shown that a combination of formal and informal mechanisms for expressing employee voice help increase the productivity effects associated with implementing high performance work practices compared with implementing the same practices with just informal voice mechanisms or none at all.[233]

Neither highly adversarial battles over union organizing nor ongoing adversarial labor-management relations are conducive to implementing and sustaining high performance work practices. However, labor-management partnerships that are based on mutual respect for worker, union, and employer rights and responsibilities have been shown to help by facilitating employee participation and by helping to build relationships within and across organizations.[234] In Chapter 20 we explore the potential for these partnerships to assist in the process of change.

Chapter 20

Make Unions Your Partners, Not Your Adversaries[235]

Labor-management partnerships have demonstrated their potential to support superior performance in healthcare, as in other settings, through the adoption of high performance work practices. Yet labor-management partnerships remain the exception in American labor relations and are hard to sustain.

There is universal agreement that along with expanding access, healthcare reform will have to address quality and cost problems. There is also a growing consensus that addressing these problems requires a coordinated, engaged workforce and labor-management relations that support coordination as well as engagement. To date, however, no proposal for healthcare reform has included a coherent workforce and labor-management relations strategy. Healthcare labor relations currently mirror the pattern found in the rest of the U.S. economy, with adversarial labor-management relations being the norm and efforts to build partnerships the exception. Data from a representative national sample of labor-management relationships show that less than 10 percent are engaged in comprehensive efforts to transform relationships at the workplace. However, those who follow this path report higher levels of innovation in bargaining and greater implementation of high performance work practices.[236] In this chapter we will consider several prominent partnership efforts in healthcare and contrast them with the more adversarial norm.

❖ SEIU AND THE NEW YORK LEAGUE OF VOLUNTARY HOSPITALS AND NURSING HOMES

One longstanding example of a labor-management partnership was initiated by Service Employees International Union (SEIU) Local 1199 and a multiemployer association, the New York League of Voluntary Hospitals and Nursing Homes. Those organizations created a formal partnership in 1997 called the Labor Management Project. The project formally covers over 125,000 SEIU members working in dozens of nonprofit hospitals and nursing homes that are members of the league. The Labor Management Project is a cooperative relationship aimed at improving patient care, helping workers retain their employment if hospitals close, protecting and increasing public funding for the healthcare system, and achieving union-building goals.

Labor-management partnership activities take a variety of forms within the project, depending on the interests and readiness of management and union leaders in each participating organization. In some organizations, the focus has been on improving labor relations through the use of tools such as interest-based problem-solving skills. Other organizations have gone much further by expanding opportunities for workers to improve the quality and safety of patient care, patient satisfaction scores, and the quality of jobs. In some cases, unions such as the Committee of Interns and Residents and the New York State Nurses Association have joined in partnership activities. The results so far have been largely positive. At five medical centers in New York City, partnerships have resulted in increased patient satisfaction, increased employee satisfaction, reduced grievance rates, and cost savings.[237]

❖ SEIU AND ALLINA HEALTH SYSTEM

Allina Health System in Minnesota and SEIU Local 115 recently signed a partnership agreement after a larger multiemployer and multiunion effort proved too difficult to sustain. Allina was originally part of a multiemployer and multiunion partnership involving 15 hospitals, SEIU, and the Minnesota Nurses Association. The original partnership lasted for about five years, supporting hospital-specific teamwork and employee engagement efforts that reduced medical errors and improved the quality of care. Eventually, the multihospital-multiunion partnership dissolved, in part because of conflicts within the employer group and between the two unions. Allina management and SEIU then embarked on their own attempt at partnership.[238] This partnership is still at an early stage and has focused on improving service quality and other aspects of performance, workforce development, income security, and management neutrality to minimize labor-management conflict around union organizing.

❖ KAISER PERMANENTE LABOR-MANAGEMENT PARTNERSHIP

The largest, most complex, and most ambitious labor-management partnership in the United States today is between Kaiser Permanente and the Coalition of Kaiser Permanente Unions (CKPU).[239] The partnership began in 1996 when top executives at Kaiser and national union leaders representing nine different national unions and 27 locals agreed to work together to reverse a deteriorating labor-management relationship and improve the quality of patient care, along with other performance goals.

This partnership has endured for over a decade during which the parties negotiated two highly innovative national-level collective bargaining agreements. The negotiations made extensive use of interest-based problem-solving tools and processes to address a wide range of healthcare and workforce issues, including the appropriate scope of professional practice, service quality, performance improvement, work-family balance, workforce development, attendance and absenteeism, and fringe benefits. The parties also negotiated a comprehensive agreement governing the introduction of new electronic medical records technologies, a very high priority for Kaiser Permanente and an issue that raised considerable concerns about employment security and adjustment within the workforce.

Since the establishment of the partnership, grievance rates have declined and employee satisfaction with Kaiser as a place to work and as a healthcare provider has increased. At the same time, employee satisfaction with their unions has also increased. The parties also jointly designed the work system for a new hospital and opened it in record time, negotiated a restructuring of an optical laboratory to keep it open and to improve its productivity and profitability, and jointly addressed a number of budgetary crises. These efforts helped Kaiser turn around its financial performance: Kaiser registered eight years of profits from 2000 to 2007 after several years of losses.

One of the key goals of the partnership was to use partnership principles and processes to engage frontline workers more fully in ongoing efforts to improve the patient care process. At the end of the partnership's first decade, approximately 40 percent of the unionized workforce reported being involved in some form of partnership activity. The only analysis of the effects of employee involvement on patient outcomes completed to date showed that higher levels of involvement were positively associated with improvements in child and adult immunization rates, breast cancer screening rates, and lipid testing rates.[240] In addition, employee engagement led to greater performance improvements resulting from new medical information technologies.[241]

An important feature of the partnership agreement is the provision governing labor and management behavior when new groups of workers seek to organize. This issue has been one of the Achilles' heels for partnerships. The partnership agreement at Kaiser Permanente addresses this issue by specifying:

> *The parties to this agreement believe that Kaiser Perma-*
> *nente employees should exercise free choice and decide for*
> *themselves whether or not they wish to be represented by*
> *a labor organization.*

In 1999 the parties further specified the procedures governing this process in a memorandum of agreement that prohibits managers and union representatives involved in organizing from portraying each other negatively or engaging in misrepresentation or personal attacks and requires all parties to keep organizing campaigns free from fear and intimidation and discrimination against individual workers. The agreement also covers arrangements for determining bargaining units, rules governing union access to employer property, procedures for using card check to verify majority status, and a dispute resolution process that resolves issues arising during an organizing campaign through arbitration, including, if necessary, the outcome.

This process has worked well. Over the first eight years, approximately 29 new bargaining units covering 7,400 workers gained recognition. Unions were successful in gaining recognition through the card check process in about 80 percent of cases (in 20 percent a majority declined to sign authorization cards).[242] This 80 percent rate is consistent with the success rates with card check agreements in other settings.[243]

The research team from MIT, Rutgers and University of Southern California that studied the first decade of the Kaiser Permanente labor-management partnership judged it a success but still a work in progress. The partnership turned around dangerously deteriorating labor-management relations; deepened the organizational capacity of Kaiser to meet challenges and crises as they arose; demonstrated that workers, unions, managers, and physicians could work together in delivering high quality healthcare; and produced significant benefits for management, employees, and unions. This partnership thus represents an important model of successful collaboration to improve healthcare by engaging the workforce and its union representatives.

❖ TRADITIONAL ADVERSARIAL RELATIONSHIPS IN HEALTHCARE

Partnerships like those at Kaiser Permanente, the League of Voluntary Hospitals in New York, and Allina in Minnesota are still the exception in healthcare labor relations. Many more examples exist of highly contentious labor-management relationships.

Consider the situation at Yale–New Haven Hospital. In March 2006, SEIU Local 1199 New England, Yale–New Haven Hospital, and community leaders signed an agreement that governed the organizing of low-paid service workers and included a requirement of neutrality by the employer and a code of conduct for both parties at the hospital. The agreement also provided for training for local residents. This agreement was the product of a bitter fight the union had waged for several years. The union had allied itself with New Haven residents and local politicians and clergy to examine the hospital's financial practices and block the building of a new cancer center and had argued that poor pay and poor patient care were linked. While those events were taking place, Yale University, although formally separate from the hospital, was pulled into the battle. After the neutrality agreement was signed, the union began an organizing campaign, but in December 2006 an arbitrator postponed the election on the basis of her finding that the hospital had violated both federal labor law and the organizing agreement by allowing managers to conduct mandatory workplace meetings about the organizing drive. The prolonged conflicts at the hospital eventually doomed efforts to build a partnership at both the hospital and the university.

Cedars-Sinai, one of the largest hospitals in Los Angeles and one that is recognized as a leader in healthcare research and teaching, provides another example of the lengthy conflict that can occur when an employer resists its employees' attempts to unionize. Cedars-Sinai traditionally has been a high-wage employer, stating its intent to pay in the upper 20 percent of the area's wage distribution. At the same time it consistently has fought unionization of its staff, starting in 1976 with interns and residents who sought to organize. The hospital successfully argued before the National Labor Relations Board that interns and residents were not employees covered under the act because they were also students being trained by the hospital. In 2002, the hospital again successfully fought a unionization effort, this time by challenging the results of an election in which the majority of nurses voted to join the California Nurses Association. The hospital and the Nurses Association have continued their standoff ever since. The Nurses Association has argued that the hospital intimidates union supporters and relies on union avoidance consultants to the detriment of patient care. In return, the hospital's chief executive has argued that it is the union that "engages in very aggressive tactics" and stated that "we believe that our ability to deal directly with our staff, nurses and others is the best way for us to achieve the institution's mission and achieve high quality health care."[244]

Another example of a drawn-out organizing battle involves a 650-person service and maintenance unit at Enloe Medical Center in California. After a long and intense organizing battle involving a corporate campaign by the union, workers voted to be represented by SEIU in 2004. Management then spent an estimated $3 million in legal fees contesting the election results. Only after three years of consistent rulings by the National Labor Relations Board and the United States Court of Appeals upholding the election results, layoffs of over 170 employees, and the replacement of the CEO did the parties sit down to begin bargaining for a first contract. Four years after the election, bargaining for that contract continued under threat of a strike by the union.[245]

❖ BOTTOM LINE

The bottom line is that labor-management partnerships have demonstrated their potential to support high performance outcomes in healthcare organizations through the adoption of high performance work practices. Still, labor-management partnerships remain the exception in American labor relations and are hard to sustain. Although SEIU has negotiated neutrality agreements in a limited number of hospital chains, most hospitals have remained resistant to union organizing. Where partnerships have been formed, they face opposition from unions that are committed to traditional adversarial relations and from antilabor groups, who argue that these partnerships violate existing labor law. These sources of opposition need to be addressed directly if labor-management partnerships are to become part of our healthcare system.

The current industry environment presents numerous obstacles to achieving high performance healthcare—fragmented payment systems, fragmented hospital-physician relationships, fragmented information systems, as well as adversarial labor law. The next chapter concludes this book by exploring these powerful barriers to high performance healthcare and suggesting key elements to include in the current overhaul of U.S. health policy.

Chapter 21

Support Change at the Industry Level

The market mechanisms, contractual arrangements, governance structures, and information technologies that enable coordination elsewhere in the economy often function poorly in the healthcare setting. As a result, organizational fragmentation is a serious and persistent impediment to improving healthcare quality.[246]

It is often argued that our national health policy—or lack thereof—is driving the quality and efficiency problems that are plaguing the U.S. healthcare system. In this book I have shown that coordination is a major driver of quality and efficiency and that the underlying causes of the coordination challenge go to the very nature of the work. I have also shown the potential for healthcare organizations to respond to those challenges by developing a set of work practices that build strong networks of coordination among care providers internally and with care providers externally. These unique high performance work systems can go a long way toward increasing both the quality and the efficiency of patient care, while increasing job satisfaction for care providers themselves.

Still, the industry environment presents several powerful obstacles to achieving high performance healthcare, including fragmented payment systems, fragmented hospital-physician relationships, fragmented information systems, and adversarial labor law. Let us consider each of these obstacles to high performance healthcare as well as potential policy solutions.

❖ FRAGMENTED PAYMENT SYSTEMS

Often we move too quickly to the argument that payment systems are to blame for the lack of well-coordinated care. There are clearly more fundamental drivers of the coordination challenge, and not all of them can be addressed through a well-designed payment system. Arguably, our payment systems did not create fragmentation; rather, they tend to reinforce that fragmentation because they were designed to accommodate the fragmentation that traditionally characterized the healthcare industry. As health policy analysts Gail Wilensky, Nicholas Wolter, and Michelle Fischer have argued, the challenge of care management and cost control is "magnified by reimbursement systems that *reinforce* silos of care rather than system approaches."[247]

Payment systems have also served as a force for improving the coordination of care. We have seen evidence in this book that managed care contracts have been pushing providers to coordinate care more intensively both internally within their own organizations and externally with their supply partners. Because payers are vigilant about ensuring that each patient is eligible for acute care and does not remain in an acute care facility any longer than is medically necessary, acute care providers have had to coordinate more closely with one another to ensure the timely discharge of patients. This payer vigilance also intensifies the pressure on acute care providers to coordinate with downstream facilities to move patients as quickly as possible to the next level of care. To achieve timely discharge, care providers have had to work with downstream facilities to ensure that they have availability to accept a patient at the time of discharge. Thus, pressure from managed care has contributed to increased coordination between acute care and subacute care providers.

However, this pressure only goes so far. As long as the pressure is simply to get the patient out the door and into the next level of care, little attention may be paid to the quality of the handoff. Indeed, as the director of patient care and quality management at the Hospital for Special Surgery explained in Chapter 16: "For now, our responsibility ends with discharge, provided we're sending patients to acceptable places." Financial contracts that make hospitals responsible for the entire episode of care—sometimes called bundling—have been on the rise, focusing greater attention on efforts to coordinate postdischarge care. Some payers have begun to negotiate contracts in which the hospital and its physicians take on the risk and responsibility for a pool of patient lives.

Under these arrangements, the hospital and its physicians, perhaps through a physician-hospital organization, are paid a fixed fee to provide care for a patient. Hospitals therefore accept responsibility for the cost and quality not only of the hospital stay but the entire episode of care. Under such contracts, hospitals benefit from managing the entire episode of care, therefore increasing their incentives to form relationships with providers of downstream services. An administrator at the Hospital for Special Surgery explained the shift:

> *If we're going to globalize our coverage and we're going to assume the responsibility for an episode of care, that puts us in a different situation. Right now, we want to get people out in as timely a manner as possible with the safest and most adequate plan. But whatever that plan is, we haven't been concerned about that. We've gotten them home care. How many visits they've made in home care, and how much it cost, or whether they've gone to subacute, or how long they spent there hasn't been of*

concern to us. The issue for us has been finding a good place that will accept people very quickly. The financial connection kind of muddies the waters a bit. ... Now we'll have to take into account the cost and the efficacy of the discharge plan.

Payment systems that reward the coordination of care across the continuum—not just getting the patient out on time but ensuring that the patient receives cost-effective high quality care after discharge—will help to break down rather than reinforce the fragmentation of patient care. Under these global contracts, healthcare organizations that know how to coordinate care with their supply partners will have the advantage.

There is some disagreement about the importance of ownership for effectively coordinating care. Some economists imply that common ownership across the supply chain may be needed to achieve coordination. However, as shown in Chapter 16, common ownership of all providers in the supply chain may help establish control, but it does not solve coordination problems. We know from other industries that supply partnerships can work extremely well with or without common ownership. The key is for healthcare organizations to extend their high performance work practices—their boundary spanners, information systems, meetings, protocols, shared performance measurements, and shared rewards—to include their supply partners, thereby building networks of relational coordination with them.

How can health policy support these organizational initiatives to deliver less-fragmented care? A payment system that rewards organizations for contributing to the overall quality and efficiency of an episode of patient care—not just their own piece of it—would clearly be a step in the right direction. In the case of chronic illness, in which the relevant episode of patient care may extend over the lifetime of the patient, this shift in the payment system is even more critical for rewarding coordination across the continuum. Such a payment system would reward healthcare organizations for implementing high performance work

practices and extending them to include key supply chain partners, thus achieving high performance healthcare for chronic
as well as acute conditions. Another promising innovation in
the payment system is the *medical home model* that would reimburse primary care provider organizations for playing an active
role in coordinating patient care both internally and with their
supply partners.[248] These payments could help to fund needed
investments in work practices that support relational coordination among care providers. The medical home model has the
potential to address the gaps identified in Chapter 16, where we
saw that primary care providers tend to play the weakest role of
all potential system integrators, forcing family members to pick
up the slack.

❖ FRAGMENTED HOSPITAL-PHYSICIAN RELATIONSHIPS

We learned throughout this book that the biggest weakness
in hospitals' high performance work systems is their failure
to include physicians. As a result, physician relational coordination with the rest of the care provider team was systematically weaker than for any other care provider discipline,
despite the fact that physicians play a central role in delivering patient care. Consistent with this finding, Randal Cebul,
James Rebitzer, Lowell Taylor, and Mark Votruba argue that
"organizational independence and clinical interdependence of
physicians and hospitals" is a major factor causing poor coordination of patient care.[249] More specifically:

> *The doctor-patient relationship and the doctor's medical
> practice are usually separate and legally distinct from the
> rest of the hospital. Reimbursements made for inpatient
> care are made separately to physicians and hospitals.*

This organizational independence may constitute an obstacle
to building high performance work systems that include physicians. We saw in Chapter 7 that hospitals with strong systems of shared rewards with their physicians, whether through

gain-sharing or risk-sharing arrangements, experienced higher levels of relational coordination along with better patient outcomes. We also saw in Chapter 10 that physicians employed as hospitalists were able to focus their time and attention on the needs of hospitalized patients because they were not torn between the hospital and their private practices. Hospitalist physicians experienced far higher levels of relational coordination with their colleagues from other disciplines, and their patients experienced fewer readmissions and lower total costs of care. Although some hospitals have discovered these and other ways to integrate physicians more completely into the delivery of patient care, it is worthwhile to explore the industry-level factors that may pose obstacles to their efforts.

One factor that promotes physician independence has been the deliberate effort over time by physicians' professional associations to protect professional power and autonomy for their members. Paul Adler, Seok-Woo Kwon, and Charles Heckscher outlined the history of physician independence and the obstacles that it poses for the coordination of care delivery.[250] The Institute of Medicine has argued that the problems we observed in the coordination of care stem from a focus on "role definition, certification and licensure, or doing one's own work as the top priority" by physician professional associations and the health professions more generally.[251] As Randall Cebul and colleagues pointed out:

> *These attitudes ... are inculcated in education programs that emphasize individual decision making in their respective disciplines and do not offer much training for work in complex collaborative setting.*

These are deficits that healthcare organizations can and do address when they adopt work practices to build relational coordination among physicians and hospital-based staff, as we have seen throughout this book. Support from healthcare professional associations would facilitate efforts to build high performance healthcare, making it less of an uphill battle.

Physicians, nurses, therapists, and other healthcare professionals who have made gains toward improved coordination in their workplaces can take lessons learned from their experience back to their professional associations to advocate for a new approach.

Another force that promotes physician independence, Randall Cebul and colleagues argue, is the absence of an employment relationship between physicians and hospitals.[252] An employment relationship would help to align interests between physicians and hospital-based staff, they argue, by facilitating the development of high performance work practices that include physicians as well as other hospital-based staff. This employment relationship is not common in the United States, they argue, due in part to two longstanding legal doctrines that are unique to the U.S. healthcare system: the corporate practice of medicine doctrine and the doctrine of vicarious liability. The corporate practice of medicine doctrine was intended to prevent corporate entities from controlling the practice of medicine and hence discouraged physician employment relationships. As of 1991, only five states clearly prohibited the hiring of physicians by hospitals, but those states accounted for nearly 25 percent of U.S. hospitals.[253]

The doctrine of vicarious liability increases the liability of an organization for work done by its employees compared with work done by independent contractors. Furthermore, an organization's liability for the work of independent contractors increases if those contractors are supervised actively by the organization. As a result, hospitals have less legal liability for malpractice when they maintain a hands-off relationship with the physicians who treat their patients. This legal doctrine is clearly an obstacle to developing a tighter relationship between hospitals and physicians. To overcome this obstacle, a hospital must be assured that the benefits of a tighter relationship with its physicians will be greater than the potential costs of increased liability. In a sense, it is a chicken and egg dilemma. As we have seen, involving physicians in a hospital's high performance work system has the potential to increase both the quality and efficiency of care. Although a hospital's potential risk may increase under a tighter relationship as a result of increased liability for physician actions, its actual risk should decline because of the increases in quality as well as efficiency that are expected to result from integrating physicians into its high performance work system. Relaxing the legal doctrines of corporate medicine and vicarious liability, as well as getting professional associations on board as advocates of interdisciplinary collaboration, would reduce the obstacles to achieving high performance healthcare.

❖ FRAGMENTED INFORMATION SYSTEMS

Some have argued that one of the key reasons for our fragmented system of care is the fragmentation of current health information systems. As we have seen in Chapter 15, healthcare organizations can build inclusive information systems that give care providers shared access to clinical and administrative data, thus facilitating relational coordination and improving both the quality and efficiency of patient care. But industry-level obstacles have made these efforts an uphill battle.

One important obstacle is the absence of accepted standards of performance measurement and common codes for sharing information. Healthcare management experts Amy Burroughs and Regina Herzlinger made this point by comparing measurement standards in the healthcare market with measurement standards in the equity market:

> *The healthcare market is virtually devoid of the kind of information that characterizes the U.S. equity market. There is little information about individual problems and little analysis of their performance in comparison to others. There are few, if any, measurement standards and no mechanisms for independent professional auditing of the data. Finally, no government agency has enforcement powers comparable to those of the SEC [Securities and Exchange Commission] for the production of healthcare information.*[254]

This comparison could just as well be made between the healthcare industry and the airline industry. When I began conducting research on healthcare, I found that there was no industry-level database comparable to the Form 41 that is produced quarterly by the U.S. Department of Transportation to provide detailed cost, revenue, employment, and operational measures or the Air Travel Consumer Report that is produced quarterly by the Federal Aviation Administration to provide detailed quality metrics such as on-time performance, cancellations, lost bags, and customer complaints. Despite the clear national interest in ensuring the delivery of high quality cost-effective healthcare—arguably at least as important as ensuring the delivery of air travel or well-functioning financial markets—there is no comparable government-sponsored data collection effort in place for the healthcare industry. In this sense, healthcare remains a cottage industry, often flying below the radar of national regulatory oversight, unlike any other industry of its size and importance.

A second industry-level obstacle, perhaps related to the first, is the absence of common codes for sharing information, which prevents electronic medical records from easily interfacing between physician practices and hospitals and between acute, subacute, and home care provider organizations.[255] According to the Institute of Medicine, the lack of common standards for coding data has been one of the key obstacles to the implementation of shared information systems. As the institute pointed out:

> *Past efforts to develop automated medical record systems have not been very successful because of the lack of common standards for coding data, the absence of a data network connecting the many healthcare organizations and clinicians involved in patient care, and a number of other factors.*[256]

The lack of shared information systems between provider organizations makes it difficult to manage the continuum of care even when other high performance work practices are in place to support it. We have seen efforts to develop information system linkages across the continuum of care, as described in Chapter 16, but these efforts tend to be limited to integrated delivery systems such as Partners HealthCare, a system that includes two of the hospitals featured in this book: Massachusetts General Hospital and Brigham and Women's. Even when integrated information systems are in place, other obstacles often come into play, limiting their use. In our study of the Partners integrated delivery system, we learned that physicians often failed to use the information system to which they had access, continuing to see themselves as independent parties with interests separate from those of other parties in the integrated delivery system.

❖ ADVERSARIAL LABOR LAW[257]

Labor law in the United States was designed for an industrial workforce with clear lines of demarcation between workers and managers and among occupational groups. It assumes and *reinforces* an adversarial relationship between workers and managers. The legal doctrines that stem from this assumption discourage and limit the workforce coordination and engagement that are needed to address quality and cost issues in healthcare. If meaningful healthcare reform is to be achieved, these limitations on the ability of workers to organize effectively and add their voices to a collaborative approach to healthcare must be addressed.

When employers and unions have tried to find a way to avoid the acrimonious and economically damaging labor disputes that often mark organizing and bargaining, several legal theories have been asserted to undermine those attempts. Those arguments threaten the ability of workers and employers to use collaborative techniques in three primary areas: (1) organizing and recognition procedures, (2) contract negotiations, and (3) day-to-day interactions among employees, supervisors, managers, and physicians.

First, U.S. labor law assumes adversarial labor-management relations in organization and recognition procedures. Employers and unions historically have entered into neutrality agreements when it has become clear that a collaborative rather than an adversarial relationship makes economic sense for both parties. A neutrality agreement generally refers to a commitment by an employer to remain neutral during an organizing drive rather than actively opposing the union. Thus, a neutrality agreement may include a provision that the employer will remain silent regarding its views on unionization or will give union organizers free access to the premises. Neutrality agreements often are accompanied by an agreement providing that the employer will recognize the union as the collective bargaining representative of the employees after a majority showing of support through a card check.[258] However, neutrality agreements have been challenged under U.S. labor law on the grounds that they constitute a form of employer assistance to the union.

Second, U.S. labor law assumes adversarial labor-management relations in contract negotiations. While negotiating a neutrality agreement, employers and unions may wish to discuss the terms of a potential contract, but that discussion is prohibited under current law. An employer and a union generally are forbidden to negotiate an agreement that would establish wages, benefits, and other terms and conditions of employment before the union receives the support of a majority of employees. This restriction means that while negotiating a neutrality agreement, an employer and union may not agree about the conditions of a contract that would apply if and when the union demonstrated majority support even though those terms and conditions are something all parties, including employees deciding whether to support the union, might benefit from knowing in advance.

Third, U.S. labor law assumes adversarial labor-management relations with respect to day-to-day interactions among employees, supervisors, managers, and physicians. Employee coordination and engagement are important in healthcare regardless of the union or nonunion status of the employees. However, labor law puts into question the legality of employee engagement in nonunion or partially unionized settings. Healthcare reform legislation should make clear that the use of collaborative working groups, which would include both employees and supervisors or managers, should not be considered a violation of labor law as long as those working groups are not employer-dominated. Without such a provision, efforts to encourage employee coordination and engagement will be subject to legal attacks, particularly in nonunion workplaces.

In sum, U.S. labor law doctrines inhibit employer-employee collaboration in healthcare in three critical areas: procedures for organizing and recognizing labor organizations, rules governing the negotiation of labor-management agreements, and rules governing day-to-day interactions. In all three of these areas, the existing legal doctrines are out of sync with modern concepts of high performance work systems. These doctrines often constrain employee coordination and engagement while providing no encouragement for building enduring collaborative relationships. Because collaboration between employers and employees is critical for achieving high performance healthcare, a new approach to labor law is needed.

❖ INDUSTRY LEADERSHIP FOR CHANGE

Clearly, the industry-level obstacles we have explored here—fragmented payment systems, fragmented hospital-physician relationships, fragmented information systems, and adversarial labor law—are interrelated and in many cases mutually reinforcing, much as the work practices in an organization's high performance work system tend to reinforce each other for better or worse. It therefore makes sense to address these obstacles in a holistic, systemic way.

Just as a multistakeholder, distributed leadership team is critical for leading the change process within an organization, such a leadership team is also critical for leading the change process at the industry level. To be effective, this leadership team should represent all key stakeholders in the industry. As I have argued with my colleagues Greg Bamber, Thomas Kochan, and Andrew von Nordenflycht in *Up in the Air: How the Airlines Can Improve Performance by Engaging Their Employees*, industry-level leadership is critical for ensuring that a highly competitive industry can produce outcomes that meet the needs of its key stakeholders, including workers, managers, investors, and customers.[259] Without that leadership, competition can lead the industry in a direction that is not sustainable because of its inability to meet the legitimate demands of stakeholders.

Indeed, there are several underlying similarities between the airline and healthcare industries that make for a constructive comparison: the complexity of the underlying work, the functional specialization and expertise required to deliver high quality outcomes, the coordination challenges created by that functional specialization, and the increasing cost pressures that intensify the challenges faced by participants at all levels. In both the airline and healthcare industries, worker interests are represented—whether through professional associations or unions—in a way that can pose obstacles to the change process or, conversely, in a way that can support the change process, as we have seen in partnership efforts at Kaiser Permanente.[260] Engaging these occupational and professional associations to support the policy changes recommended in this chapter would be a promising path for moving forward.

But these policy changes, as important as they are, are not a precondition for changes by individual healthcare organizations. Rather, policy changes and organization-level changes can proceed in parallel. As healthcare organizations work together with their workers and their supply partners toward building more robust, inclusive work systems to deliver high performance healthcare to their patients, they will be better positioned to support changes in the policy arena.

Notes for Text

Chapter 1

1. Anselm Strauss, Shizuko Fagerhaugh, Barbara Suczek, and Carolyn Wiener (1985), *Social Organization of Medical Work*. Chicago: University of Chicago Press.
2. Carlos Angrisano, Diana Farrell, Bob Kocher, Martha Laboissiere, and Sara Parker (2007), *Accounting for the Cost of Healthcare in the United States*. San Francisco: McKinsey Global Institute.
3. Institute of Medicine (2000), *To Err Is Human: Building a Safer Health System*. Washington, DC: National Academy Press.
4. Sara R. Collins, Jennifer L. Kriss, Michelle M. Doty, and Sheila D. Rustgi (2008), *Losing Ground: How the Loss of Medical Insurance is Burdening Working Families*. New York: Commonwealth Fund.
5. Randal Cebul, James Rebitzer, Lowell Taylor, and Mark Votruba (2008), "Organizational Fragmentation and Care Quality in the U.S. Healthcare System," *Journal of Economic Perspectives*, 22 (4): 93–113.
6. Hoangmai H. Pham, Deborah Schrag, Ann S. O'Malley, Beny Wu, and Peter B. Bach (2007), "Care Patterns in Medicare and Their Implications for Pay for Performance," *New England Journal of Medicine*, 356 (11): 1130–1139.
7. Institute of Medicine Committee on Quality of Healthcare in America (2003), *Crossing the Quality Chasm: A New Healthcare System for the 21st Century*. Washington, DC: National Academy Press.

8. Anne-Marie J. Audet, Michelle M. Doty, Jamil Shamasdin, and Stephen J. Schoenbaum (2005), *Physicians' Views on Quality of Care: Findings from the Commonwealth Fund National Survey of Physicians and Quality of Care*. New York: Commonwealth Fund.

9. For a guide to mapping and improving work processes in healthcare settings, see Institute for Healthcare Improvement (2005), *Going Lean in Healthcare*, Innovation Series. These insights have been transferred from other industries through the work of individuals such as James Womack, founder and president of the Lean Enterprise Institute. See James Womack, Daniel Jones, and Danel Roos (1990), *The Machine That Changed the World: The Story of Lean Production*. New York: Harper Perennial; and James Womack and Daniel Jones (2005), *Lean Solutions: How Companies and Customers Create Value and Wealth Together*. New York: Free Press. I will return to these mapping tools in Chapter 19 in the discussion of implementation.

10. Adam Smith (2007), *The Wealth of Nations*. New York: Harriman House (first published in 1776).

11. Jody Hoffer Gittell (2003), *The Southwest Airlines Way: Using the Power of Relationships to Achieve High Performance*. New York: McGraw-Hill.

Chapter 2

12. Thomas Malone and Kevin Crowston (1994), "The Interdisciplinary Study of Coordination," *Computing Surveys*, 26 (1): 87–119, defined coordination as the management of task interdependencies.

13. Jody Hoffer Gittell (2006), "Relational Coordination: Coordinating Work through Relationships of Shared Goals, Shared Knowledge and Mutual Respect," in *Relational Perspectives in Organizational Studies: A Research Companion*, eds. Olympia Kyriakidou and Mustafa Ozbilgin, Cheltenham, UK: Edward Elgar.

14. Karl E. Weick and Karlene Roberts (1993), "Collective Mind in Organizations: Heedful Interrelating on Flight Decks," *Administrative Science Quarterly*, 38: 357–381; Jody Hoffer Gittell (2000), "Organizing Work to Support Relational Coordination," *International Journal of Human Resource Management*, 11 (3): 517–534; Samer Faraj and Lee Sproull (2000), "Coordinating Expertise in Software Development Teams," *Management Science*, 46: 1554–1568; Samer Faraj and Yan Xiao (2006), "Coordination in Fast Response Organizations," *Management Science*, 52 (8): 1155–1169; Beth A. Bechky (2006), "Gaffers, Gofers and Grips: Role-Based Coordination in Temporary Organizations, *Organization Science*, 17 (1): 3–21; and Paul Adler and Seok-Woo Kwon (2007), "Social Capital: Prospects for a New Concept," *Academy of Management Review*, 27 (1): 17–40.

15. Jane Dutton (2003), *Energize Your Workplace: How to Create and Sustain High-Quality Connections at Work*. San Francisco: Jossey-Bass.

16. Joyce Fletcher (1999), *Disappearing Acts: Gender, Power and Relational Practice at Work*. Cambridge, MA: MIT Press. See also Jean Baker Miller (1978), *Toward a New Psychology of Women*. Boston: Beacon Hill Press.

17. Mary Catherine Beach and Thomas Inui (2006), "Relationship-Centered Care: A Constructive Re-Framing," *Journal of General Internal Medicine*, 21: S3–8. See also Dana Gelb Safran, William Miller, and Howard Beckman (2006), "Organizational Dimensions of Relationship-Centered Care," *Journal of General Internal Medicine*, 21: S9–15.

18. Relational coordination is focused on relationships between roles rather than individual role inhabitants, as in the role-based coordination discussed in James D. Thompson (1968), *Organizations in Action: Social Science Bases of Administrative Theory*. New York: McGraw-Hill, and Beth A. Bechky (2006), "Gaffers, Gofers and Grips: Role-Based Coordination in Temporary Organizations, *Organization Science*, 17 (1): 3–21. Role-based relationships are explored more generally by Deb Meyerson, Karl E. Weick, and Roderick Kramer (1996), "Swift Trust and Temporary Groups," in *Trust in Organizations: Frontiers of Theory and Research*. eds. Roderick Kramer and T. R. Tyler. Thousand Oaks, CA: Sage.

19. Peter Senge (2006), *The Fifth Discipline: The Art and Practice of the Learning Organization*. New York: Doubleday Business.

Chapter 3

20. This study was reported in Jody Hoffer Gittell, Kathleen Fairfield, Benjamin Bierbaum, Robert Jackson, Michael Kelly, Richard Laskin, Stephen Lipson, John Siliski, Thomas Thornhill, and Joseph Zuckerman (2000), "Impact of Relational Coordination on Quality of Care, Post-Operative Pain and Functioning, and Length of Stay: A Nine Hospital Study of Surgical Patients," *Medical Care*, 38 (8): 807–819.

21. *Managed Care Digest* (2000), http://www.managedcaredigest.com/edigests/hm2000/hm2000c01s07g01.html.

22. We measured relational coordination by adapting a survey that originally was developed to measure coordination of the flight departure process. See Jody Hoffer Gittell (2000), "Organizing Work to Support Relational Coordination," *International Journal of Human Resource Management*, 11 (3): 517–534. This measure indicates the average strength of ties among care providers from five functions surveyed in each of the nine orthopedic departments ($n = 336$ care providers). Questions included the frequency, timeliness, accuracy, and problem-solving focus of communication in addition to the strength of shared goals, shared knowledge, and mutual respect. Cronbach's alpha among the seven dimensions of these coordination ties was 0.86, suggesting a reasonably high level of internal index reliability.

23. We sent surveys to all eligible care providers in the five core disciplines who had clinical or administrative responsibilities for joint replacement patients

during the study period: physicians, nurses, physical therapists, social workers, and case managers (known in some departments as care coordinators). Surveys were mailed to all eligible care providers initially during the second month of the study period, with one repeat mailing during the study period for nonrespondents. Providers were asked to comment on the ongoing day-to-day coordination occurring in their units. We received responses from 338 of 666 providers, for an overall provider response rate of 51 percent.

24. Patients were selected at random from among those admitted to one of the nine hospitals for primary elective unilateral total joint replacement during the study period with a diagnosis of osteoarthritis. All patients were mailed surveys between 6 and 10 weeks after discharge. Nonrespondents were sent up to three surveys. We received 878 of 1,367 surveys sent to patients in the target population, for a response rate of 64 percent. To measure performance outcomes, we developed a service quality index based on 15 survey items regarding service quality in the inpatient hospital setting. Postoperative pain and functional status were assessed from the patient survey, using the 5 items relating to pain and 17 items relating to physical functioning from WOMAC, a validated osteoarthritis instrument.

We developed a quality of care index from the 25 questionnaire items pertaining to the patients' acute care experience. We excluded 10 items with the potential response "not applicable" because of a large number of missing values. Those items were of the nature "Did you get answers you could understand from the physician?" with the response option "Did not have any questions for the physician." Including those items resulted in a biased subsample of respondents with more questions and problems than the typical respondent. The 15 questionnaire items that remained were the patient's reported confidence and trust in his or her physicians, nurses, physical therapists, and case managers; knowledge of the identity of the physician, nurse, physical therapist, or case manager in charge of his or her care; belief that providers were aware of his or her medical history; belief that providers were aware of his or her condition and needs; belief that his or her providers supplied consistent information; belief that his or her providers worked well together; belief that he or she was treated with respect and dignity; satisfaction with his or her overall care; and intent to recommend the hospital to others. An equally weighted index with potential values from 1 to 5 was created from these 15 items.

25. Jon Chilingerian (2000), "Evaluating Quality Outcomes against Best Practice: A New Frontier," in *The Quality Imperative: Measurement and Management of Quality in Healthcare*, eds. John R. Kimberly and Etienne Minvielle. London: Imperial College Press, pp. 141–167.

26. Margaret Gerteis, Susan Edgman-Levitan, Jennifer Daley, and Thomas Delbanco (1993), *Through the Patient's Eyes: Understanding and Promoting Patient-Centered Care*. San Francisco: Jossey-Bass.

27. Marsha Gold and Judith Wooldridge (1995), "Surveying Customer Satisfaction to Assess Managed Care Quality: Current Practices," *Healthcare Financing Review*, 16 (4): 155–173; Don Berwick (1996), "The Year of 'How': New Systems for Delivering Healthcare," *Quality Connections*, 5 (1): 1–4; and John Kenagy, Don Berwick, and Miles Shore (1999), "Service Quality in Healthcare," *Journal of the American Medical Association*, 281: 661–665.

28. Postoperative pain and functional status were assessed from the patient questionnaire, using the 5 items relating to pain and 17 items relating to physical functioning from WOMAC, a validated osteoarthritis instrument. The WOMAC is a self-administered instrument that was designed for three dimensions—pain, stiffness, and physical functioning—associated with osteoarthritis of the hip and knee. See N. Bellamy, W. W. Buchanan, C. H. Goldsmith, J. Campbell, and L. W. Stitt (1988), "Validation Study of WOMAC: A Health Status Instrument for Measuring Clinically Important Patient Relevant Outcomes to Anti-Rheumatic Drug Therapy in Patients with Osteoarthritis of the Hip or Knee," *Journal of Rheumatology*, 15: 1833–1840. This instrument has been shown to be useful in assessing outcomes after hip or knee replacement. The pain items query patients about amount of pain or degree of difficulty with functioning (five potential responses from none to severe) experienced in the last 48 hours during common activities. We did not utilize the stiffness scale. To minimize missing values, we included the responses of all patients who completed at least 80 percent of the items in each of the indexes. We assigned the mean of the nonmissing values for each item to missing values for that item. The resulting indexes of postoperative pain and functional status have potential values ranging from 1 to 100.

29. Length of stay was calculated from the hospital records for each patient as the number of whole days between the date of admission and the date of discharge.

30. Control variables for this study included patient age, comorbidities, overall mental health, preoperative pain, preoperative functioning, surgical procedure (hip versus knee arthroplasty), number of days between surgery and questionnaire completion, marital status, race, and sex. Patient age and sex were determined from hospital records. Comorbid conditions were assessed in the patient questionnaire with a series of questions asking patients whether they had heart disease, high blood pressure, diabetes, ulcer or stomach disease, kidney disease, anemia or another blood disease, cancer, depression, or back pain. The resulting index of comorbidities was computed as the number of comorbid conditions reported by the respondent. The SF–36 is a brief, internally consistent, and valid health-related quality of life instrument. It is organized into eight dimensions: physical function, role function (physical), role function (emotional), bodily pain, social functioning, mental health, vitality, and general health perceptions.

Overall mental health was assessed in our patient questionnaire by using the mental health component, which has been shown to be sensitive to clinical change after joint replacement. The mental health items were averaged to construct a score of overall mental health, an approach that has been validated elsewhere. Preoperative pain and functioning were measured in the same way as postoperative pain and functioning, using the WOMAC instrument, with the same treatment of missing values. We asked patients to report the date on which they were completing the questionnaire to determine the number of days between surgery and questionnaire completion. We also queried patients about race and marital status in the questionnaire.

In addition to patient characteristics, we collected measures of the volume of total joint replacements conducted in each hospital in the six months before the study period. Previous research has identified positive effects of the volume of procedures on clinical outcomes whether due to the effects of learning or due to economies of scale.

31. Roger Hallowell, Leonard Schlesinger, and Len Zornitsky (1996), "Internal Customer Satisfaction, Customer and Job Satisfaction: Linkages and Implications for Management," *Human Resource Planning*, 192: 20–31. See also Janine Nahapiet and Sumantra Ghoshal (1998), "Social Capital, Intellectual Capital and the Organizational Advantage," *Academy of Management Review*, 232: 242–266; Paul Adler and Seok Woo Kwon (2002), "Social Capital: Prospects for a New Concept," *Academy of Management Review*, 27 (1): 17–40; and Wayne Baker (2000), *Achieving Success through Social Capital*. San Francisco: Jossey-Bass.

32. To understand the argument from organizational psychologists that high quality relationships are a source of well-being for people at work, see William Kahn (1998), "Relational Systems at Work" in *Research in Organizational Behavior*, eds. Barry M. Staw and Larry L. Cummings. Greenwich, CT: JAI Press, vol. 20, pp. 39–76; Michelle Williams and Jane Dutton (1999), "Corrosive Political Climates: The Heavy Toll of Negative Political Behavior in Organizations," in *The Pressing Problems of Modern Organizations: Transforming the Agenda for Research and Practice*, eds. Robert E. Quinn, Regina M. O'Neill, and Linda St. Clair. New York: American Management Association, pp. 3–30; Jane E. Dutton (2003), *Energize Your Workplace: How to Create and Sustain High-Quality Connections at Work*. San Francisco: Jossey-Bass; and Jane E. Dutton and Belle Rose Ragins (2007), *Exploring Positive Relationships at Work: Building a Theoretical and Research Foundation*. Philadelphia, PA: Lawrence Erlbaum.

33. Jane E. Dutton and Emily D. Heaphy (2003), "Coming to Life: The Power of High Quality Connections at Work," in *Positive Organizational Scholarship: Foundations of a New Discipline*, eds. Kim S. Cameron, Jane E. Dutton, and Robert E. Quinn. San Francisco: Berrett-Koehler.

34. Care provider job satisfaction was scored on a five-point scale from "very satisfied" to "very dissatisfied." Although there has been a trend toward the use of multi-item scales, a recent study of the efficacy of single-item measures of job satisfaction shows a strong correlation between single-item measures of overall job satisfaction and scales measuring overall job satisfaction. To learn more about the results of this study, see J.P. Wanous, A.E. Reichers and M.J. Hudy (1997), "Overall Job Satisfaction: How Good are Single-Item Measures?" *Journal of Applied Psychology*, 82 (2): 247–252.

35. Cronbach's alpha for the relational coordination construct was 0.85, suggesting a reasonably high level of internal index reliability.

36. Statistical analyses confirmed that there were significant differences between hospitals in the strength of relational coordination. Using one-way analysis of variance, I found cross-hospital differences in relational coordination that were significant at the 99.9 percent level. See Exhibit 2–4 for hospital-level means for relational coordination.

37. Statistical analyses confirmed that cross-hospital differences in performance variables were significant at the 99.9 percent level.

38. Random-effects models, also known as mixed, hierarchical linear, or multi-level models, were used to accommodate the multi level structure of the data. Patient served as the unit of analysis, with hospital as the random effect. Regression coefficients, standard errors and the overall *R*-squared for random-effects models reflect statistical associations both within and across hospitals.

39. The impact of relational coordination on length of stay and service quality is significant at the 99.9 percent level. The impact of relational coordination on post-operative freedom from pain is significant at the 95 percent level, while the impact of relational coordination on post-operative mobility is significant at the 85 percent level. The higher the level of significance, the more certain that changes in relational coordination will result in changes to the performance measures in question.

40. This study is reported in Jody Hoffer Gittell, Dana Beth Weinberg, Adrienne Bennett, and Joseph A. Miller (2008), "Is the Doctor In? A Relational Approach to Job Design and the Coordination of Work," *Human Resource Management*, 47 (4): 729–755, though the analyses reported here go beyond what was reported in that paper.

41. A total of 1,800 provider responses were received out of 2,727 surveys sent, for an overall provider response rate of 66 percent. Responses were dropped if they referred to the care of a patient who was "observation only" and therefore not technically admitted to the hospital (a fact that often was not known until after the patient already had been discharged, owing to delays in payer decision making). We also dropped responses that did not complete the questions regarding coordination with the physician on the team. We were left with 893 complete provider responses regarding the care of 335 patients.

42. Exploratory factor analysis suggested that relational coordination was best characterized as a single factor with the following loadings: frequency 0.6759, timeliness 0.8725, accuracy 0.8566, problem solving 0.8943, shared goals 0.9053, shared knowledge 0.8596, and mutual respect 0.9057, with an eigenvalue of 5.13 and no cross-loadings greater than 0.20. Cronbach's alpha for this measure of relational coordination was relatively high at 0.87, suggesting a reasonably high level of internal index reliability.

43. Excess length of stay was measured as the difference between the patient's actual length of stay and the Massachusetts state average for a comparable patient. We created this measure by using three steps. First, using 3M's APR-DRG grouper software, we classified each patient into a diagnostic group and within that diagnostic group assigned a severity of illness measure between 1 and 4 that was based on the patient's secondary diagnoses. Using a reference database of all acute care hospitalizations (836,126) in Massachusetts in 2003, we created a normative case-mix measure equal to the mean length of stay for patients in the larger population who were in the same severity of illness and diagnostic group; we used this normative severity of illness measure as a case-mix adjuster in all of our models. To create the excess length of stay variable, we rounded the average length of stay for each patient profile to the nearest integer (since the length of stay data supplied by the hospital was recorded as an integer) and subtracted it from the patient's actual length of stay to create a comparison of the efficiency of care with the state average for a comparable patient. Thus, the dependent variable is the difference between actual and expected length of stay. The total cost measure was available through the hospital's activity-based cost accounting system. We also estimate models with a log-transformed value for total costs.

44. Each of these measures is dichotomous (e.g., patient was readmitted in seven days, yes or no), and each was available from the hospital information system.

45. To create a continuous measure of severity that could be used across diagnoses, we used a reference database of all acute care hospitalizations (836,126) in Massachusetts in 2002 to create a measure equal to the mean length of stay for patients in the larger population who were in the same diagnostic group (based on APR-DRG classification derived from primary diagnosis) and severity of illness group (between 1 and 4 based on secondary diagnosis). For example, the severity of illness measure for a level 3 pneumonia patient is 5.2, the statewide average length of stay for patients in that class. Though our models include only the outcomes of patients in the target hospital, the statewide sample is used as a basis for risk adjustment because of the benefits of a larger sample for risk adjustment.

46. The impact of relational coordination on length of stay is significant at the 99.9 percent level. The impact of relational coordination on total costs

and thirty-day readmissions is significant at the 99 percent level, and the impact of relational coordination on seven-day readmissions is significant at the 95 percent level. The higher the level of significance, the more certain that changes in relational coordination will result in changes in the performance measures in question.

47. This study was reported in Jody Hoffer Gittell, Dana Beth Weinberg, Susan Pfefferle, and Christine Bishop (2008), "Impact of Relational Coordination on Job Satisfaction and Quality Outcomes: A Study of Nursing Homes," *Human Resource Management Journal*, 18 (2): 154–170.

48. Susan Eaton (2000), "Beyond Unloving Care: Linking Human Resource Management and Patient Care Quality in Nursing Homes," *International Journal of Human Resource Management*, 11 (3): 591–616. See also B. Bowers, B. Fibich, and N. Jacobson (2001), "Care-as-Service, Care-as-Relating, Care-as-Comfort: Understanding Nursing Home Residents' Definitions of Quality," *The Gerontologist*, 41 (4): 539–545; and R. I. Stone, S. C. Reinhard, B. Bowers, D. Zimmerman, C. D. Phillips, C. Hawes, J. A. Fielding, and N. Jacobson (2002), *Evaluation of the Wellspring Model for Improving Nursing Home Quality*, New York: Commonwealth Fund.

49. Factor analysis showed that all five items loaded onto a single factor with an eigenvalue of 2.73 and factor loadings between 0.5719 and 0.8353. This simplified relational coordination index that we tailored to the nursing home setting achieved a Cronbach's alpha of 0.86, suggesting a reasonably high level of internal index reliability. All these indicators were consistent with the previous studies that used the original validated instrument.

50. Using a brief cognitive screen, we excluded residents who were unable to give informed consent. Resident surveys were conducted through interviews with a research assistant experienced in issues of dementia and cognitive impairment. Resident interviews were conducted in a space of the resident's choice to allow for maximum privacy and comfort. Residents were offered a nonmonetary incentive at the completion of the survey. We received responses from 105 of 123 eligible residents approached, for a response rate of 85 percent, with a range of 48 percent to 100 percent in each facility.

51. We used a 14-item measure based on 14 questions from across these seven domains as found in R. A. Kane, R. L. Kane, B. Bershadsky, H. Degenholtz, and K. C. Kling (2002), *Recommendations on Short Quality of Life Measures for Potential Incorporation into the Nursing Home Minimum Data Set*. Baltimore, MD: Centers for Medicare and Medcaid Services. We adapted the survey by offering two response categories ("mostly yes" and "mostly no") that were based on testing which suggested greater ease of response by elderly residents. Factor analysis using the principal factors method showed that 13 of the 14 items loaded onto one factor with an eigenvalue of 3.16 and factor loadings between 0.2887 and 0.7559. We dropped one item— "Do you feel your possessions are safe in this nursing

home?"—due to a factor loading of less than 0.20. From the remaining 13 items we created a single index called "resident quality of life" with a Cronbach's alpha of 0.69, suggesting a reasonably high level of internal index reliability.

52. Nursing aide job satisfaction was scored on a five-point scale from "very satisfied" to "very dissatisfied." Although there has been a trend toward the use of multi-item scales, a recent study of the efficacy of single-item measures of job satisfaction shows a strong correlation between single-item measures of overall job satisfaction and scales measuring overall job satisfaction. To learn more about the results of this study, see J.P. Wanous, A.E. Reichers and M.J. Hudy (1997), "Overall Job Satisfaction: How Good are Single-Item Measures?" *Journal of Applied Psychology*, 82 (2): 247–252.

53. Random effects models, also known as mixed, hierarchical linear, or multilevel models, were used to accommodate the multilevel (resident/facility or nursing aide/facility) structure of the data, with facility as the random effect. The impact of relational coordination on resident quality of life was assessed by using random effects linear regression with the quality of life index as the dependent variable (n = 93 residents for whom quality of life and covariates were available) and facility (n = 15) as the random effect. We included resident characteristics (age, length of stay, and gender) and facility characteristics (facility size and ownership status) as covariates. We present standardized regression coefficients and p values. The impact of relational coordination on nursing aide job satisfaction was assessed by using random effects linear regression with job satisfaction as the dependent variable (n = 231 nursing aides for whom job satisfaction and covariates were available) and facility (n = 15) as the random effect. Again, relational coordination is a facility-aggregate score calculated from individual index scores (n = 15). We included nursing aide characteristics (age, tenure, gender, language, and education), and facility characteristics (facility size and ownership status) as covariates.

54. The impact of relational coordination on resident quality of life is significant at the 99 percent level. The impact of relational coordination on nursing aide job satisfaction is significant at the 99.9 percent level. The higher the level of significance, the more certain that changes in relational coordination will result in changes in the performance measures in question.

55. The results of this study were reported in Jody Hoffer Gittell (2003), *The Southwest Airlines Way: Using the Power of Relationships to Achieve High Performance*. New York: McGraw-Hill, Chapters 3 and 4.

56. At each site, I administered the survey in person on a single day the employees working the morning shift. All surveys were conducted on weekdays between Tuesday and Thursday to avoid disrupting the operations and increase the number of surveys completed because passenger loads were typically lighter on those three days. Respondents typically required 20 minutes to complete

the survey. The survey was pretested in one site by administering a pilot survey to several members of each of the five target functions. Based on the pilot survey and a debriefing afterward, the wording of the questions was simplified considerably. Respondents were asked to answer the questions with respect to each of the 12 functions involved in flight departures, including the functions that were not surveyed: pilots, flight attendants, freight agents, mechanics, cabin cleaners, caterers, and fuelers. Responses were captured on a five-point Likert-type scale. Cronbach's alpha for the relational coordination construct was 0.80, suggesting a reasonably high level of internal index reliability.

57. Gate time is costly because it represents time that an aircraft is occupying valuable gate space and not earning revenue. Long gate times reduce the return on both the aircraft and the gate. Based on lost revenues from the aircraft alone, I have shown that a five-minute reduction in gate time resulted in an average annual savings of $1.6 billion, or $4,700 per employee, for the 10 major U.S. airlines over a one-year period. See Jody Hoffer Gittell (1995), "Cost/Quality Tradeoffs in the Departure Process? Evidence from the Major US Airlines," *Transportation Research Record*, 1480: 25–36.

58. These variables were chosen on the basis of advice from industry experts at MIT's Flight Transportation Lab and were included in a model of flight departure performance developed and tested in an earlier study of the flight departure process. See Jody Hoffer Gittell (1995), "Cost/Quality Tradeoffs in the Departure Process? Evidence from the Major US Airlines," *Transportation Research Record*, 1480: 25–36.

59. Statistical analyses confirmed that there were significant differences between airlines in the strength of relational coordination and that in addition there were significant differences between the sites within airlines. Using one-way analysis of variance, I found cross-airline differences in relational coordination that were significant at the 99.9 percent level. Jointly testing the significance of cross-airline and cross-site differences, I also found cross-site differences in relational coordination that were significant at the 99.9 percent level.

60. Statistical analyses confirmed that cross-site differences in product and performance variables were significant at the 99.9 percent level.

61. Random effects models, also known as mixed, hierarchical linear, or multilevel models, were used to accommodate the multilevel structure of the data. Site/month served as the unit of analysis, with site as the random effect. Regression coefficients, standard errors, and the overall R-squared for random effects models reflect statistical associations both within and across sites.

62. The impact of relational coordination on turnaround time, staffing productivity, and customer complaints is significant at the 99.9 percent level. The impact of relational coordination on flight delays is significant at the

99 percent level, and the impact of relational coordination on baggage losses is significant at the 95 percent level. The higher the level of significance, the more certain that changes in relational coordination will result in changes in the performance measures in question.

63. James Heskett, Earl Sasser, and Christopher Hart (1990), *Service Breakthroughs: Changing the Rules of the Game.* New York: Free Press.

64. James D. Thompson explains how task interdependence affects coordination requirements in his classic 1967 book *Organizations in Action: Social Science Bases of Administrative Theory.* New York: McGraw-Hill. Linda Argote (1982) explains how uncertainty affects coordination requirements in "Input Uncertainty and Organizational Coordination in Hospital Emergency Units," *Administrative Science Quarterly,* 27: 420–434, and Paul Adler (1995) explains how time constraints affect coordination requirements in "Interdepartmental Interdependence and Coordination: The Case of the Design/Manufacturing Interface," *Organization Science,* 6: 147–167.

Chapter 4

65. This chapter draws extensively on the arguments made in Jody Hoffer Gittell, Rob Seidner, and Julian Wimbush (2009), "A Relational Model of How High Performance Work Systems Work," *Organization Science,* forthcoming.

66. High performance work practices—work practices that leverage the ability of frontline workers to create value—have been found to explain differences in many types of performance outcomes. For the impact on manufacturing quality, see John Paul MacDuffie (1995), "Human Resource Bundles and Manufacturing Performance: Organizational Logic and Flexible Production Systems in the World Auto Industry," *Industrial and Labor Relations Review,* 48: 173–188. For the impact on patient mortality, see Michael West, Carol Borrill, Jeremy Dawson, Judy Scully, Matthew Carter, et al. (2002), "The Link between the Management of Employees and Patient Mortality in Acute Hospitals," *International Journal of Human Resource Management,* 13: 1299–1311. For the impact on worker productivity, see Ann P. Bartel (1994), "Productivity Gains from the Implementation of Employee Training Programs," *Industrial Relations,* 33: 411–425, and D. K. Datta, J. P. Guthrie, and P. M. Wright (2005), "HRM and Labor Productivity: Does Industry Matter?" *Academy of Management Journal,* 48 (1), 135–145. For the impact on equipment reliability, see Mark A. Youndt, Scott Snell, James W. Dean, Jr., and David P. Lepak (1996), "Human Resource Management, Manufacturing Strategy, and Firm Performance," *Academy of Management Journal,* 39 (4): 836–866, and Casey Ichniowski, Kathryn Shaw, and Giovanna Prennushi (1997), "The Effects of Human Resource Practices on

Manufacturing Performance: A Study of Steel Finishing Lines," *American Economic Review*, 87: 291–313. For the impact on financial performance, see Mark Huselid (1995), "The Impact of Human Resource Management on Turnover, Productivity and Corporate Financial Performance," *Academy of Management Journal*, 38: 635–672; John E. Delery and D. Harold Doty (1996), "Modes of Theorizing in Strategic Human Resource Management: Tests of Universalistic, Contingency, and Configurational Performance Predictions," *Academy of Management Journal*, 39 (4): 802–835; and Christopher J. Collins and Ken Smith (2006), "Knowledge Exchange and Combination: The Role of Human Resource Practices in the Performance of High-Technology Firms," *Academy of Management Journal*, 49 (3), 544–560.

67. High performance work practices—work practices that leverage the ability of frontline workers to create value—have been found to explain performance differences in many different industries. For impacts in the apparel industry, see John T. Dunlop and David Weil (1996), "Diffusion and Performance of Modular Production in the U.S. Apparel Industry," *Industrial Relations*, July, pp. 334–355. For impacts in the steel industry, see Casey Ichniowski, Kathryn Shaw, and Giovanna Prennushi (1997), "The Effects of Human Resource Practices on Manufacturing Performance: A Study of Steel Finishing Lines," *American Economics Review*, 87: 291–313. For impacts in call centers, see Rose Batt (1999), "Work Design, Technology and Performance in Customer Service and Sales," *Industrial and Labor Relations Review*, 52 (4): 539–564. For impacts in airlines, see Jody Hoffer Gittell (2003), *The Southwest Airlines Way: Using the Power of Relationships to Achieve High Performance*. New York: McGraw-Hill. For impacts in banks, see Ann P. Bartel (2004), "Human Resource Management and Performance Outcomes: Evidence from Retail Banking," *Industrial and Labor Relations Review*, 57: 181–203, and O. C. Richard and N. B. Johnson (2004), "High Performance Work Practices and Human Resource Management Effectiveness: Substitutes or Complements?" *Journal of Business Strategy*, 21 (2): 133–148. For impacts in high-technology firms, see Christopher J. Collins and Ken Clark (2003), "Strategic Human Resource Practices, Top Management Team Social Networks, and Firm Performance: The Role of Human Resource Practices in Creating Organizational Competitive Advantage," *Academy of Management Journal*, 46: 740–751.

68. For evidence regarding bundles of mutually supportive work practices, see John Paul MacDuffie (1995), "Human Resource Bundles and Manufacturing Performance: Organizational Logic and Flexible Production Systems in the World Auto Industry," *Industrial and Labor Relations Review*, 48: 173–188; John T. Dunlop and David Weil (1996), "Diffusion and Performance of Modular Production in the U.S. Apparel Industry," *Industrial Relations*, July,

pp. 334–355; Casey Ichniowski, Kathryn Shaw, and Giovanna Prennushi (1997), "The Effects of Human Resource Practices on Manufacturing Performance: A Study of Steel Finishing Lines," *American Economics Review*, 87: 291–313; Rose Batt (1999), "Work Design, Technology and Performance in Customer Service and Sales," *Industrial and Labor Relations Review*, 52 (4): 539–564; and Keld Laursen (2002), "The Importance of Sectoral Differences in the Application of Complementary HRM Practices for Innovation Performance," *International Journal of Economics and Business*, 9: 139–156.

69. Human capital arguments for high performance work practices have been made by Gary Becker (1975), *Human Capital*. New York: Columbia University Press; Rose Batt (1999), "Work Design, Technology and Performance in Customer Service And Sales," *Industrial and Labor Relations Review*, 52 (4): 539–564; Vance H. Fried and Robert D. Hisrich (1994), "Toward a Model of Venture Capital Investment Decision-Making," *Financial Management*, 23 (3): 28–37; Michael Gibbert (2006), "Generalizing about Uniqueness: An Essay on an Apparent Paradox in the Resource-Based View," *Journal of Management Inquiry*, 15: 124–134; Ian C. MacMillan, Lauriann Zemann, and P. N. Subbanarasimha (1987), "Criteria Distinguishing Successful from Unsuccessful Ventures in the Venture Screening Process," *Journal of Business Venturing*, 2: 123–138; Scott A. Snell and James W. Dean (1992), "Integrated Manufacturing and Human Resource Management: A Human Capital Perspective," *Academy of Management Journal*, 35: 467–504; and Tyzoon T. Tyebjee and Albert V. Bruno (1984), "A Model of Venture Capitalist Investment Activity," *Management Science*, 30: 1051–1066.

70. Commitment arguments for high performance work practices have been made by Eileen Appelbaum, Thomas Bailey, Peter Berg, and Arne L. Kalleberg (2000), *Manufacturing Advantage: Why High Performance Work Systems Pay Off*. Ithaca, NY: ILR Press; Jeffrey B. Arthur (1992), "The Link between Business Strategy and Industrial Relations Systems in American Steel Minimills," *Industrial and Labor Relation Review*, 45: 488–506; Casey Ichniowski, Kathryn Shaw, and Giovanna Prennushi (1997), "The Effects of Human Resource Practices on Manufacturing Performance: A Study of Steel Finishing Lines," *American Economic Review*, 87: 291–313; T. A. Mahoney and M. R. Watson (1993), "Evolving Modes of Workforce Governance: An Evaluation," in, eds., *Employee Representation: Alternatives and Future Directions*, eds. Bruce E. Kaufman and Morris M. Kleiner Madison: Industrial Relations Research Association, University of Wisconsin, pp. 135–168; Paul Osterman (1988), *Employment Futures: Reorganization, Dislocation and Public Policy*. New York: Oxford University Press; Anne S. Tsui, Jones L. Pearce, Lyman V. Porter, and Angela Tripoli (1997), "Alternative Approaches to the Employee-Organization Relationship: Does Investment in Employees Pay Off?" *Academy of Management Journal*, 40 (5):

1089–1121; and Anne S. Tsui, Jones L. Pearce, Lyman V. Porter, and J. P. Hite (1995), "Choice of Employee-Organization Relationship: Influence of External and Internal Organizational Factors," in *Research in Personnel and Human Resource Management*, ed. G. R. Ferris. Greenwich, CT: JAI Press, vol. 13, pp. 117–151.

71. David E. Bowen and Cheri Ostroff (2004), "Understanding HRM-Firm Performance Linkages: The Role of the 'Strength' of the HRM System," *Academy of Management Review*, 29: 203–221.

72. The argument for a relational approach to high performance work systems is found in Jody Hoffer Gittell, Rob Seidner, and Julian Wimbush (2009), "A Relational Model of How High Performance Work Systems Work," *Organization Science*, forthcoming. We describe a unique kind of high performance work system that builds relational coordination across key work groups. See also Randal Cebul, James Rebitzer, Lowell Taylor, and Mark Votruba (2008), "Organizational Fragmentation and Care Quality in the U.S. Healthcare System," *Journal of Economic Perspectives*, 22 (4): 93–113. These authors argue that high performance work systems can play an important role in overcoming the fragmentation of care, though they don't believe that such systems are likely to emerge in the absence of an employment relationship between the physician and the hospital. We address the importance of a physician employment relationship in Chapter 10 in our discussion of job design.

73. Michael Piore (1992), *The Social Embeddedness of Labor Markets and Cognitive Processes*, Keynote Address, European Association of Labor Economists, Warwick, England, p. 20.

74. Charles Heckscher (1994), "Defining the Post-Bureaucratic Type," in *The Post-Bureaucratic Organization*, eds. Charles Heckscher and Ann Donnellon. Thousand Oaks, CA: Sage, p. 24.

75. Carrie R. Leana and Harry J. Van Buren (1999), "Organizational Social Capital and Employment Practices," *Academy of Management Review*, 24: 538–555.

76. W. Randy Evans and Walter D. Davis (2005), "High-Performance Work Systems and Organizational Performance: The Mediating Role of Internal Social Structure," *Journal of Management*, 31: 758–775.

77. Jon Gant, Casey Ichniowski, and Kathryn Shaw (2002), "Social Capital and Organizational Change in High-Involvement and Traditional Work Organizations," *Journal of Economics, Management and Strategy*, 11: 289–328.

78. Christopher J. Collins and Kevin Clark (2003), "Strategic Human Resource Practices, Top Management Team Social Networks, and Firm Performance: The Role of Human Resource Practices in Creating Organizational Competitive Advantage," *Academy of Management Journal*, 46: 740–751. See also Christopher J. Collins and Ken Smith (2006),

"Knowledge Exchange and Combination: The Role of Human Resource Practices in the Performance of High-Technology Firms," *Academy of Management Journal*, 49 (3), 544–560.

79. Timothy Vogus (2006), "What Is It about Relationships? A Behavioral Theory of Social Capital and Performance," *Labor and Employment Relations Proceedings*, pp. 164–173.

80. To measure this high performance work system, we measured 10 of the 12 work practices that constitute it, as described in the following chapters. We then combined those 10 measures into a single standardized index. An additive scaling method was used in which each measure was standardized with a mean of 0 and a standard deviation of 1 so that each of the 10 work practices in the high performance work system index was equally weighted. Cronbach's alpha for the high performance work system index was 0.87.

Chapter 5

81. Paul R. Lawrence and Jay W. Lorsch (1968), *Organization and Environment: Managing Differentiation and Integration*. Boston: Graduate School of Business Administration, Harvard University.

82. For arguments that selection should focus on personality traits, see David Day and Stanley Silverman (1989), "Personality and Job Performance: Evidence of Incremental Validity," *Personnel Psychology*, 25–36, and Mark N. Bing, James D. Whanger, H. Kristl Davison, and Jason B. Van Hook (2004), "Incremental Validity of the Frame of Reference Effect in Personality Scale Scores," *Journal of Applied Psychology*, 89 (1): 150–158. For arguments that selection should focus on emotional intelligence, see Phillip Bardzil and Mark Slaski (2003), "Emotional Intelligence: Fundamental Competencies for Enhanced Service Provision," *Managing Service Quality*, 13 (2): 97–115. For arguments that selection should focus on organizational fit, see Richard Kwiatkowski (2003), "Trends in Organizations and Selection," *Journal of Managerial Psychology*, 18 (5): 382–395, and Jennifer Chatman and Sandra Cha (2003), "Leading by Leveraging Culture," *California Management Review*, 45 (4): 20–35. For arguments that selection should focus more generally on attitudes conducive to teamwork, see Leonard Schlesinger and James Heskett (1991), "The Service-Driven Service Company," *Harvard Business Review*, Sept.–Oct., pp. 71–80, and Peter Cappelli and Nicolai Rogovsky (1994), "New Work Systems and Skill Requirements," *International Labour Review*, 133 (2): 205–220.

83. Jody Hoffer Gittell (2003), *The Southwest Airlines Way: Using the Power of Relationships to Achieve High Performance*. New York: McGraw-Hill, Chapter 7.

84. To measure selection for teamwork, we asked administrators about selection criteria for physicians, nurses, and physical therapists, probing

whether cross-functional teamwork ability was considered an important selection criterion. This variable was coded from 0 to 2 for each of these three work groups, with 0 indicating that cross-functional teamwork ability was not considered, 1 indicating that it was considered to some extent, and 2 indicating that it was a consistent criterion for selection. Statements such as "usually," "some of us," and "I look for" were interpreted to mean "teamwork ability was considered to some extent," whereas a statement such as "this is how we do it here" was interpreted to signify that "teamwork ability was a consistent criterion for selection." We then combined the three variables into a single standardized index. An additive scaling method was used in which each variable was standardized with a mean of 0 and a standard deviation of 1 so that each variable in the selection for teamwork index was equally weighted. Cronbach's alpha for the selection for teamwork index was 0.75.

85. Random effects models, also known as mixed, hierarchical linear, or multilevel models, were used to accommodate the multilevel structure of the data. The patient served as the unit of analysis, with the hospital as the random effect. Regression coefficients, standard errors, and the overall R-squared for random effects models reflect statistical associations both within and across hospitals.

86. In the final column of Exhibit 5–3, we tested whether selection for teamwork affects performance through its effect on relational coordination. We aggregated relational coordination to the hospital level and entered it into the model for surgical performance, along with the selection for teamwork index. We found that the coefficient on the selection for teamwork index becomes insignificant when relational coordination is added to the model, suggesting that selection for teamwork influences surgical performance through its effect on relational coordination. We then used the Sobel test to determine whether the association between selection for teamwork and surgical performance is reduced significantly when relational coordination is added to the model and found that again, the results were supportive of mediation. These methods are documented in Reuben A. Baron and David A. Kenny (1986), "The Moderator-Mediator Variable Distinction in Social Psychological Research: Conceptual, Strategic and Statistical Considerations," *Journal of Personality and Social Psychology*, 51: 1173–1182, and David P. MacKinnon, Chondra M. Lockwood, Jeanne M. Hoffman, Stephen G. West, and Virgil Sheets (2002), "A Comparison of Methods to Test Mediation and Other Intervening Variable Effects," *Psychological Methods*, 7: 83–104.

Chapter 6

87. James G. March and Herbert A. Simon (1958), *Organizations*. New York: Wiley; Paul R. Lawrence and Jay W. Lorsch (1968), *Organization and*

Environment: Managing Differentiation and Integration. Boston: Graduate School of Business Administration, Harvard University. See also Robert H. Chenhall (2005), "Integrative Strategic Performance Measurement Systems, Strategic Alignment of Manufacturing, Learning and Strategic Outcomes: An Exploratory Study," *Accounting and Organizational Sociology*, 30 (5): 395.

88. J. Edward Deming (1986), *Out of the Crisis.* Cambridge, MA: MIT Press. See also Amy Edmondson (1996), "Learning from Mistakes Is Easier Said Than Done: Group and Organizational Influences on the Detection and Correction of Human Error," *Journal of Applied Behavioral Science*, 32 (1): 5–32; and Jody Hoffer Gittell, "Paradox of Coordination and Control," *California Management Review*, 42 (3): 177–183.

89. P. Triolo, K. Hansen, Y. Kazzaz, H. Chung, and S. Dobbs (2002), "Improving Satisfaction through Multidisciplinary Performance Improvement Teams," *Journal of Nursing Administration*, 32 (9): 448–254. See also Jody Hoffer Gittell (2000), "Paradox of Coordination and Control," *California Management Review*, 42 (3): 177–183.

90. Edward Locke and Gary Latham (1990), *A Theory of Goal Setting and Task Performance.* Englewood Cliffs, NJ: Prentice-Hall. See also Richard Saavedra, P. Christopher Earley, and Lyn Van Dyne (1993), "Complex Interdependence in Task-Performing Groups," *Journal of Applied Psychology*, 78: 61–72.

91. Don M. Berwick, A. Blanton Godfrey, and Jane Roessner (2002). *Curing Healthcare.* San Francisco: Jossey-Bass.

92. To measure cross-functional performance measurement, we asked administrators about the quality assurance process and the utilization review process in their hospitals, probing whether each of these processes was focused on identifying the single function that was responsible for a quality or utilization problem or whether the focus was more cross-functional. These two variables were coded on a scale of 1 to 5, with 1 indicating a purely functional approach and 5 indicating a highly cross-functional approach. Interviewees also were asked whether these two performance measurement processes were focused on affixing blame or on solving problems. These two variables were coded on a scale of 1 to 5, with 1 indicating a purely blaming focus and 5 indicating a purely problem-solving focus. We then combined the four variables into a single standardized index. An additive scaling method was used in which each variable was standardized with a mean of 0 and a standard deviation of 1 so that each variable in the cross-functional performance measurement index was equally weighted. Cronbach's alpha for the cross-functional performance measurement index was 0.91.

93. Random effects models, also known as mixed, hierarchical linear, or multilevel models, were used to accommodate the multilevel structure of the

data. The patient served as the unit of analysis, with the hospital as the random effect. Regression coefficients, standard errors, and the overall R-squared for random effects models reflect statistical associations both within and across hospitals.

94. In the final column in Exhibit 6–3, we tested whether cross-functional performance measurement affects performance through its effect on relational coordination. We aggregated relational coordination to the hospital level and entered it into the model for surgical performance, along with the cross-functional performance measurement index. We found that the coefficient on the cross-functional performance measurement index becomes insignificant when relational coordination is added to the model, suggesting that cross-functional performance measurement influences surgical performance through its effect on relational coordination. We then used the Sobel test to determine whether the association between cross-functional performance measurement and surgical performance is reduced significantly when relational coordination is added to the model and found that again, the results were supportive of mediation. These methods are documented in Reuben A. Baron and David A. Kenny (1986), "The Moderator-Mediator Variable Distinction in Social Psychological Research: Conceptual, Strategic and Statistical Considerations," *Journal of Personality and Social Psychology*, 51: 1173–1182, and David P. MacKinnon, Chondra M. Lockwood, Jeanne M. Hoffman, Stephen G. West, and Virgil Sheets (2002), "A Comparison of Methods to Test Mediation and Other Intervening Variable Effects," *Psychological Methods*, 7: 83–104.

Chapter 7

95. James G. March and Herbert A. Simon (1958), *Organizations*. New York: Wiley.

96. Ruth Wageman and George Baker (1997), "Incentives and Cooperation: The Joint Effects of Task and Reward Interdependence on Group Performance," *Journal of Organizational Behavior*, 18 (2): 139–158.

97. Edward Locke (2004), "Linking Goals to Monetary Incentives," *Academy of Management Executive*, 18 (4): 130–134.

98. Todd R. Zenger and William S. Hesterly (1997), "The Disaggregation of Corporations: Selective Intervention, High-Powered Incentives, and Molecular Units," *Organization Science*, 8 (3): 209–222. See also Ruth Wageman (1995), "Interdependence and Group Effectiveness," *Administrative Science Quarterly*, 40: 145–180; Ruth Wageman and George Baker (1997), "Incentives and Cooperation: The Joint Effects of Task and Reward Interdependence on Group Performance," *Journal of Organizational Behavior*, 18 (2): 139–158; and James P. Guthrie and Elaine C. Hollensbe (2004), "Group Incentives and Performance: A Study of Spontaneous Goal Setting, Goal Choice and Commitment," *Journal of Management*, 30 (2): 263–285.

99. To measure cross-functional rewards, we asked administrators about the criteria for rewards for physicians, nurses, and physical therapists, probing whether rewards were based purely on individual performance or were based on some cross-functional performance criteria as well. This variable was coded from 0 to 2. For nurses and physical therapists, 0 indicated no rewards, 1 indicated individual rewards only, and 2 indicated some cross-functional team rewards. For physicians, 0 indicated individual rewards only, 1 indicated surplus sharing with the hospital, and 2 indicated risk sharing with the hospital. We then combined the three variables into a single standardized index. An additive scaling method was used in which each variable was standardized with a mean of 0 and a standard deviation of 1 so that each variable in the cross-functional rewards index was equally weighted. Cronbach's alpha for the cross-functional rewards index was 0.64.

100. Random effects models, also known as mixed, hierarchical linear, or multilevel models, were used to accommodate the multilevel structure of the data. The patient served as the unit of analysis, with the hospital as the random effect. Regression coefficients, standard errors, and the overall R-squared for random effects models reflect statistical associations both within and across hospitals.

101. In the final column of Exhibit 7–3, we tested whether cross-functional rewards affect performance through their effect on relational coordination. We aggregated relational coordination to the hospital level and entered it into the model for surgical performance, along with the cross-functional rewards index. We found that the coefficient on the cross-functional rewards index becomes insignificant when relational coordination is added to the model, suggesting that cross-functional rewards influence surgical performance through their effect on relational coordination. We then used the Sobel test to determine whether the association between cross-functional rewards and surgical performance is reduced significantly when relational coordination is added to the model and found that again, the results were supportive of mediation. These methods are documented in Reuben A. Baron and David A. Kenny (1986), "The Moderator-Mediator Variable Distinction in Social Psychological Research: Conceptual, Strategic and Statistical Considerations," *Journal of Personality and Social Psychology*, 51: 1173–1182, and David P. MacKinnon, Chondra M. Lockwood, Jeanne M. Hoffman, Stephen G. West, and Virgil Sheets (2002), "A Comparison of Methods to Test Mediation and Other Intervening Variable Effects," *Psychological Methods*, 7: 83–104.

102. David Dranove, David P. Kessler, Mark B. McClellan, and Mark Satterthwaite (2003), "Is More Information Better? The Effects of 'Report Cards' on Healthcare Providers," *Journal of Political Economy*, 111 (3): 555–588.

Chapter 8

103. Richard Walton and John Dutton (1967), "The Management of Interdepartmental Conflict: A Model and Review," *Administrative Science Quarterly*, 73–83. See also Lisa H. Pelled, Kathleen M. Eisenhardt, and Kathleen R. Xin (1999), "Exploring the Black Box: An Analysis of Work Group Diversity, Conflict and Performance," *Administrative Science Quarterly*, 44: 1–28.

104. Karen A. Jehn (1995), "A Multi-Method Examination of the Benefits and Detriments of Intra Group Conflict," *Administrative Science Quarterly*, 40 (2): 256–282. See also Karen A. Jehn and Elizabeth A. Mannix (2001), "The Dynamic Nature of Conflict: A Longitudinal Study of Intragroup Conflict and Group Performance," *Academy of Management Journal*, 44: 238–251.

105. Jody Hoffer Gittell (2000), "Organizing Work to Support Relational Coordination," *International Journal of Human Resource Management*, 11 (3): 517–534, and Jody Hoffer Gittell (2003), *The Southwest Airlines Way: Using the Power of Relationships to Achieve High Performance*. New York: McGraw-Hill.

106. Peter Jordan and Ashlea Troth (2004), "Managing Emotions during Team Problem Solving," *Human Performance*, 17 (2): 195–219.

107. Patrice M. Mareschal (2003), "Solving Problems and Transforming Relationships: The Bifocal Approach to Mediation," *American Review of Public Administration*, 33 (4): 423–449. See also Tim Porter-O'Grady (2004), "Constructing a Conflict Resolution Program for Healthcare," *Healthcare Management Review*, 29 (4): 278–284.

108. To measure cross-functional conflict resolution, we asked administrators about conflict resolution processes, probing whether any formal cross-functional conflict resolution process was in place for physicians, nurses, or physical therapists. This variable was coded from 0 to 1 for physicians, nurses, and physical therapists, where 0 indicated that the work group had no access to a formal cross-functional conflict resolution process and 1 indicated that the work group did have access. We then combined these three variables into a single standardized index. An additive scaling method was used in which each variable was standardized with a mean of 0 and a standard deviation of 1 so that each variable in the cross-functional conflict resolution index was equally weighted. Cronbach's alpha for the cross-functional conflict resolution index was 0.79.

109. Random effects models, also known as mixed, hierarchical linear, or multilevel models, were used to accommodate the multilevel structure of the data. The patient served as the unit of analysis, with the hospital as the random effect. Regression coefficients, standard errors, and the overall R-squared for random effects models reflect statistical associations both within and across hospitals.

110. In the final column of Exhibit 8–3, we tested whether cross-functional conflict resolution affects performance through its effect on relational coordination. We aggregated relational coordination to the hospital level and entered it into the model for surgical performance, along with the cross-functional conflict resolution index. We found that the coefficient on the cross-functional conflict resolution index becomes insignificant when relational coordination is added to the model, suggesting that cross-functional conflict resolution influences surgical performance through its effect on relational coordination. We then used the Sobel test to determine whether the association between cross-functional conflict resolution and surgical performance is reduced significantly when relational coordination is added to the model and found that again, the results were supportive of mediation. These methods are documented in Reuben A. Baron and David A. Kenny (1986), "The Moderator-Mediator Variable Distinction in Social Psychological Research: Conceptual, Strategic and Statistical Considerations," *Journal of Personality and Social Psychology*, 51: 1173–1182, and David P. MacKinnon, Chondra M. Lockwood, Jeanne M. Hoffman, Stephen G. West, and Virgil Sheets (2002), "A Comparison of Methods to Test Mediation and Other Intervening Variable Effects," *Psychological Methods*, 7: 83–104.

Chapter 9

111. J. Richard Hackman and Gregory Oldham (1980), *Work Redesign*. New York: Addison-Wesley. See also Richard Walton and J. Richard Hackman (1986), "Groups under Contrasting Management Strategies." In *Designing Effective Work Groups*, ed. Paul Goodman and associates. San Francisco: Jossey-Bass; Richard Walton (1985), "From Control to Commitment in the Workplace," *Harvard Business Review*, March-April, pp. 76–84; and Richard Walton and Leonard Schlesinger (1979), "Do Supervisors Thrive in Participative Work Systems?" *Organizational Dynamics*, 7 (3): 25–38.

112. Douglas McGregor (1960), *The Human Side of Enterprise*. New York: McGraw-Hill. See also Rensis Likert (1961), *New Patterns of Management*. New York: McGraw-Hill.

113. Lyman Porter and Edward Lawler (1964), "The Effects of 'Tall' versus 'Flat' Organization Structures on Managerial Job Satisfaction," *Personnel Psychology*, pp. 135–148.

114. Jody Hoffer Gittell (2001), "Supervisory Span, Relational Coordination and Flight Departure Performance: A Reassessment of Post-Bureaucracy Theory," *Organization Science*, 12 (4): 467–482. These results also are reported in Jody Hoffer Gittell (2003), *The Southwest Airlines Way: Using the Power of Relationships to Achieve High Performance*. New York: McGraw-Hill.

115. To measure supervisory staffing, we measured the ratio of supervisors to frontline care providers in each of the nine hospitals for nurses, physical

therapists, and physicians. We then combined these three variables into a single standardized index. An additive scaling method was used in which each variable was standardized with a mean of 0 and a standard deviation of 1 so that each variable in the supervisory staffing index was equally weighted. Cronbach's alpha for the supervisory staffing index was 0.82.

116. Random effects models, also known as mixed, hierarchical linear, or multilevel models, were used to accommodate the multilevel structure of the data. The patient served as the unit of analysis, with the hospital as the random effect. Regression coefficients, standard errors, and the overall R-squared for random effects models reflect statistical associations both within and across hospitals.

117. In the final column of Exhibit 9–3, we tested whether supervisory staffing affects performance through its effect on relational coordination. We aggregated relational coordination to the hospital level and entered it into the model for surgical performance, along with the supervisory staffing index. We found that the coefficient on the supervisory staffing index becomes insignificant when relational coordination is added to the model, suggesting that supervisory staffing influences surgical performance through its effect on relational coordination. We then used the Sobel test to determine whether the association between supervisory staffing and surgical performance is reduced significantly when relational coordination is added to the model and found that again, the results were supportive of mediation. These methods are documented in Reuben A. Baron and David A. Kenny (1986), "The Moderator-Mediator Variable Distinction in Social Psychological Research: Conceptual, Strategic and Statistical Considerations," *Journal of Personality and Social Psychology*, 51: 1173–1182, and David P. MacKinnon, Chondra M. Lockwood, Jeanne M. Hoffman, Stephen G. West, and Virgil Sheets (2002), "A Comparison of Methods to Test Mediation and Other Intervening Variable Effects," *Psychological Methods*, 7: 83–104.

Chapter 10

118. This chapter draws extensively from Jody Hoffer Gittell (2004), "Achieving Focus in Hospital Care: The Role of Relational Coordination," in *Consumer-Driven Healthcare: Implications for Providers, Payers and Policy-Makers*, ed. Regina Herzlinger. San Francisco: Jossey-Bass; and Jody Hoffer Gittell, Dana Beth Weinberg, Adrienne Bennett, and Joseph A. Miller (2008), "Is the Doctor In? A Relational Approach to Job Design and the Coordination of Work," *Human Resource Management*, 47 (4): 729–755.

119. Wickham Skinner (1974), "The Focused Factory," *Harvard Business Review*, May–June, pp. 113–121.

120. For the benefits of focus in manufacturing, see Thomas Brush and Aneel Karnani (1996), "Impact of Plant Size and Focus on Productivity: An Empirical Study," *Management Science*, 42 (7): 1065–1081, and Robert

Hayes, Steven Wheelwright, and Kim Clark (1988), *Dynamic Manufacturing: Creating the Learning Organization*. New York: Free Press. For the benefits of focus in service settings, see James L. Heskett, Christopher Hart, and W. Earl Sasser (1990), *Service Breakthroughs: Changing the Rules of the Game*. New York: Free Press; and James L. Heskett, W. Earl Sasser, and Leonard A. Schlesinger (1997), *The Service Profit Chain: How Leading Companies Link Profit and Growth to Loyalty, Satisfaction and Value*. New York: Free Press.

121. For evidence regarding positive outcomes of organizational focus, see Cynthia A. Montgomery and Birger Wernerfelt (1988), "Diversification, Ricardian Rents, and Tobin's q," *RAND Journal of Economics*, 194: 623–632; Frank R. Lichtenberg (1992), "Industrial De-Diversification and Its Consequences for Productivity," *Journal of Economic Behavior and Organization*, 18: 427–438; Robert O. Hoskisson and Richard A. Johnson (1992), "Corporate Restructuring and Strategic Change: The Effect on Diversification Strategy and R&D Intensity," *Strategic Management Journal*,13: 625–634; and Michael Lubatkin and Sayan Chatterjee (1991), "The Strategy-Shareholder Value Relationship: Testing Temporal Stability across Market Cycles," *Strategic Management Journal*, 12: 251–270.

122. Regina E. Herzlinger (1997), *Market-Driven Healthcare: Who Wins and Who Loses in the Transformation of America's Largest Service Industry*. Reading, MA: Addison-Wesley.

123. James L. Heskett (1989), *Shouldice Hospital*, Harvard Business School Case No. 683–068. Boston: Harvard Business School Publishing.

124. Tarun Khanna and Krishna Palepu (1997), "Why Focused Strategies May Be Wrong for Emerging Markets," *Harvard Business Review*, July–August, pp. 3–10; Poh-Lin Yeoh and Kendall Roth (1999), "An Empirical Analysis of Sustained Advantage in the Pharmaceutical Industry: Impact of Firm Resources and Capabilities," *Strategic Management Journal*, 207: 637–653; Danny Miller (1993), "The Architecture of Simplicity," *Academy of Management Review*, 181: 116–138; Diwkar Gupta and Mandyam M. Srinivasan (1998), "How Does Product Proliferation Affect Responsiveness?" *Management Science*, 447: 1017–1020; and Karl T. Ulrich and David J. Ellison (1999), "Holistic Customer Requirements and the Design-Select Decision," *Management Science*, 455: 641–658.

125. Donald E. Hatfield, Julia P. Liebeskind, and Tim C. Opler (1996), "The Effects of Corporate Restructuring on Aggregate Industry Specialization," *Strategic Management Journal*, 171: 55–72; Thomas Brush and Aneel Karnani (1996), "Impact of Plant Size and Focus on Productivity: An Empirical Study," *Management Science*, 42 (7): 1065–1081.

126. For a comparison of these two perspectives on job design, see Frederick P. Morgeson and Michael A. Campion (2002), "Minimizing Tradeoffs When

Redesigning Work: Evidence from a Longitudinal Quasi-Experiment," *Personnel Psychology*, 55 (3), 589–612. For more insight into the technical perspective on job design and the benefits of greater specialization, see Adam Smith (1991), *The Wealth of Nations*. New York: Knopf (originally published in 1776), and Frederick Winslow Taylor (1911), *The Principles of Scientific Management*. New York: Harper and Row. For more insight into the psychological perspective on job design and the benefits of reduced specialization, see Rensis Likert (1961), *New Patterns of Management*. New York: McGraw-Hill; Douglas McGregor (1960), *The Human Side of Enterprise*. New York: McGraw-Hill; J. Richard Hackman and Gregory Oldham (1980), *Work Redesign*. New York: Addison-Wesley; and Maureen L. Ambrose and Carol T. Kulik (1999), "Old Friends, New Faces: Motivation in the 1990s," *Journal of Management*, 25 (3), 231–292.

127. To measure job focus, we surveyed all care providers who were assigned to work with joint replacement patients and asked about the percentage of their time that was spent working with those patients as opposed to other patients. We then combined four variables (for physician, nurse, physical therapist, and care manager job focus) into a single standardized index. An additive scaling method was used in which each variable was standardized with a mean of 0 and a standard deviation of 1 so that each variable in the job focus index was equally weighted. Cronbach's alpha for the job focus index was 0.54.

128. Random effects models, also known as mixed, hierarchical linear, or multilevel models, were used to accommodate the multilevel structure of the data. The patient served as the unit of analysis, with the hospital as the random effect. Regression coefficients, standard errors, and the overall R-squared for random effects models reflect statistical associations both within and across hospitals.

129. In the final column of Exhibit 10–3, we tested whether job focus affects performance through its effect on relational coordination. We aggregated relational coordination to the hospital level and entered it into the model for surgical performance, along with the job focus index. We found that the coefficient on the job focus index becomes insignificant when relational coordination is added to the model, suggesting that job focus influences surgical performance through its effect on relational coordination. We then used the Sobel test to determine whether the association between job focus and surgical performance is reduced significantly when relational coordination is added to the model and found that again, the results were supportive of mediation. These methods are documented in Reuben A. Baron and David A. Kenny (1986), "The Moderator-Mediator Variable Distinction in Social Psychological Research: Conceptual, Strategic and Statistical Considerations," *Journal of Personality and Social Psychology*, 51:

1173–1182, and David P. MacKinnon, Chondra M. Lockwood, Jeanne M. Hoffman, Stephen G. West, and Virgil Sheets (2002), "A Comparison of Methods to Test Mediation and Other Intervening Variable Effects," *Psychological Methods*, 7: 83–104.

130. Randal Cebul, James Rebitzer, Lowell Taylor, and Mark Votruba (2008), "Organizational Fragmentation and Care Quality in the U.S. Healthcare System," *Journal of Economic Perspectives*, 22 (4): 93–113.

131. Robert M. Wachter and L. Goldman (1996), "The Emerging Role of 'Hospitalists' in the American Healthcare System," *New England Journal of Medicine*, 33 (5): 514–517; and Robert M. Wachter (2004), "Hospitalists in the United States: Mission Accomplished or Work in Progress?" *New England Journal of Medicine*, 350: 1935–1936.

132. Random effects models, also known as mixed, hierarchical linear, or multilevel models, were used to accommodate the multilevel structure of the data. The patient served as the unit of analysis, with the hospital as the random effect. Regression coefficients, standard errors, and the overall R-squared for random effects models reflect statistical associations both within and across hospitals.

133. Janet Coffman and Thomas G. Rundall (2005), "The Impact of Hospitalists on the Cost and Quality of Inpatient Care in the United States: A Research Synthesis," *Medical Care Research and Review*, 62 (4): 379–406.

Chapter 11

134. Thomas A. Kochan, Harry Katz, and Robert McKersie (1986), *The Transformation of U.S. Industrial Relations*. New York: Basic Books.

135. See J. Richard Hackman and Gregory Oldham (1980), *Work Redesign*. New York: Addison-Wesley.

136. Paul R. Lawrence and Jay W. Lorsch (1968), *Organization and Environment: Managing Differentiation and Integration*. Boston,: Graduate School of Business Administration, Harvard University.

137. Kim Clark and Takahiro Fujimoto (1991), *Product Development Performance: Strategy, Organization, and Management in the World Auto Industry*. Boston: Harvard Business School Press.

138. Gil Preuss (1997), "The Structuring of Organizational Information Capacity: An Examination of Hospital Care," *Academy of Management Best Paper Proceedings*.

139. Janice Klein (1991). "Craft Pride: The Key to World Class Maintenance," *Harvard Business School Working Paper*, No. 91–033.

140. Institute of Medicine Committee on Quality of Healthcare in America (2003), *Crossing the Quality Chasm: A New Healthcare System for the 21st Century*. Washington, DC: National Academy Press.

Chapter 12

141. Paul R. Lawrence and Jay W. Lorsch (1968), *Organization and Environment: Managing Differentiation and Integration*. Boston: Graduate School of Business Administration, Harvard University.

142. Jay R. Galbraith (1995), *Competing with Flexible Lateral Organizations*. Reading, MA: Addison-Wesley.

143. Susan A. Mohrman (1993), "Integrating Roles and Structure in the Lateral Organization." In Jay R. Galbraith and Edward E. Lawler, eds., *Organizing for the Future: The New Logic of Managing Complex Organizations*. San Francisco: Jossey-Bass. See also Thomas Davenport (1993), *Process Innovation*. Boston: Harvard Business School Press.

144. Kim Clark and Steven Wheelwright (1992), "Organizing and Leading 'Heavyweight' Development Teams," *California Management Review*, 34 (3): 9–28.

146. Thomas Davenport and Nitin Nohria (1994), "Case Management and the Integration of Labor," *Sloan Management Review*, 27 (1): 11–23.

147. Jody Hoffer Gittell (2000), "Organizing Work to Support Relational Coordination," *International Journal of Human Resource Management*, 11 (3): 517–534. See also Jody Hoffer Gittell (2003), *The Southwest Airlines Way: Using the Power of Relationships to Achieve High Performance*. New York: McGraw-Hill.

148. For more insight into the transition from primary nursing to case management, see Jody Hoffer Gittell (1998), *Beth Israel Deaconess Medical Center: Coordinating Patient Care*. Boston, MA: Harvard Business School Publishing.

149. Jody Hoffer Gittell (2002), "Coordinating Mechanisms in Care Provider Groups: Relational Coordination as a Mediator and Input Uncertainty as a Moderator of Performance Effects," *Management Science*, 48 (11): 1408–1426.

150. To measure cross-functional boundary spanners, we asked administrators about the caseloads and roles of the case managers who worked with joint replacement patients and whether the primary nursing model was in place on that unit, providing a second boundary spanner role. Caseload was measured as a continuous variable, and each of the case manager roles—coordination and planning for patient discharge—was coded as 0 to 1, with 0 indicating that the role was not expected and 1 indicating that the role was expected of case managers. Primary nursing was coded 1 if the model was in place and 0 if it was not. We then combined the four variables into a single standardized index. An additive scaling method was used in which each variable was standardized with a mean of 0 and a standard deviation of 1 so that each variable in the cross-functional boundary spanner index was equally weighted. Cronbach's alpha for the cross-functional boundary spanner index was 0.55.

151. Random effects models, also known as mixed, hierarchical linear, or multilevel models, were used to accommodate the multilevel structure of the data. The patient served as the unit of analysis, with the hospital as the random effect. Regression coefficients, standard errors, and the overall R-squared for random effects models reflect statistical associations both within and across hospitals.

152. In the final column of Exhibit 12–3, we tested whether cross-functional boundary spanners affect performance through their effect on relational coordination. We aggregated relational coordination to the hospital level and entered it into the model for surgical performance, along with the cross-functional boundary spanners index. We found that the coefficient on the cross-functional boundary spanners index becomes insignificant when relational coordination is added to the model, suggesting that cross-functional boundary spanners influence surgical performance through their effect on relational coordination. We then used the Sobel test to determine whether the association between cross-functional boundary spanners and surgical performance is reduced significantly when relational coordination is added to the model and found that again, the results were supportive of mediation. These methods are documented in Reuben A. Baron and David A. Kenny (1986), "The Moderator-Mediator Variable Distinction in Social Psychological Research: Conceptual, Strategic and Statistical Considerations," *Journal of Personality and Social Psychology*, 51: 1173–1182, and David P. MacKinnon, Chondra M. Lockwood, Jeanne M. Hoffman, Stephen G. West, and Virgil Sheets (2002), "A Comparison of Methods to Test Mediation and Other Intervening Variable Effects," *Psychological Methods*, 7: 83–104.

Chapter 13

153. James D. Thompson (1967), *Organizations in Action: Social Science Bases of Administrative Theory*. New York: McGraw-Hill; Jay R. Galbraith (1973), *Designing Complex Organizations*. Reading, MA: Addison-Wesley; and Andrew Van de Ven, Andre Delbecq, and R. Koenig, Jr. (1976), "Determinants of Coordination Modes within an Organization," *American Sociological Review*, 41: 322–338.

154. Richard Nelson and Sydney Winter (1981), *An Evolutionary Theory of Economic Change*. Cambridge, MA: Belknap/Harvard University Press; and B. Levitt and James March (1986), "Organizational Learning," *Annual Review of Sociology*, 14: 319–340.

155. J. Edward Deming (1986), *Out of the Crisis*. Cambridge, MA: MIT Press, and Paul Adler and Brian Borys (1994), "Two Types of Bureaucracy: Enabling and Coercive," *Administrative Science Quarterly*, 41: 62–89.

156. James D. Thompson (1967), *Organizations in Action: Social Science Bases of Administrative Theory*. New York: McGraw-Hill; and Andrew Van de

Ven, Andre Delbecq, and R. Koenig, Jr. (1976), "Determinants of Coordination Modes within an Organization," *American Sociological Review*, 41: 322–338.

157. Jay R. Galbraith (1973), *Designing Complex Organizations*. Reading, MA: Addison-Wesley, p. 320.

158. Paul Adler and Brian Borys (1994), "Two Types of Bureaucracy: Enabling and Coercive," *Administrative Science Quarterly*, 41: 62–89.

159. Martha A. Feldman and Anat Rafaeli (2002), "Organizational Routines as Sources of Connections and Understandings," *Journal of Management Studies*, 393: 309–331.

160. To measure cross-functional pathways, we examined the clinical pathways for total joint replacement patients in each hospital to determine which functional groups were included on those pathways, considering physicians, nurses, physical therapists, and case managers. These variables were coded 1 if the work group was included on the pathway and 0 if it was not. We also asked administrators what percentage of patients was kept on those pathways throughout their hospital stay, a continuous variable that ranged from 70 to 100 percent. We then combined these five variables into a single standardized index. An additive scaling method was used in which each variable was standardized with a mean of 0 and a standard deviation of 1 so that each variable in the cross-functional pathways index was equally weighted. Cronbach's alpha for the cross-functional pathways index was 0.71.

161. Random effects models, also known as mixed, hierarchical linear, or multilevel models, were used to accommodate the multilevel structure of the data. The patient served as the unit of analysis, with the hospital as the random effect. Regression coefficients, standard errors, and the overall *R*-squared for random effects models reflect statistical associations both within and across hospitals.

162. In the final column of Exhibit 13–3, we tested whether cross-functional pathways affect performance through their effect on relational coordination. We aggregated relational coordination to the hospital level and entered it into the model for surgical performance, along with the cross-functional pathways index. We found that the coefficient on the cross-functional pathways index becomes insignificant when relational coordination is added to the model, suggesting that cross-functional pathways influence surgical performance through their effect on relational coordination. We then used the Sobel test to determine whether the association between cross-functional pathways and surgical performance is reduced significantly when relational coordination is added to the model and found that again, the results were supportive of mediation. These methods are documented in Reuben A. Baron and David A. Kenny (1986), "The Moderator-Mediator Variable Distinction in Social Psychological Research: Conceptual, Strategic and

Statistical Considerations," *Journal of Personality and Social Psychology*, 51: 1173–1182, and David P. MacKinnon, Chondra M. Lockwood, Jeanne M. Hoffman, Stephen G. West, and Virgil Sheets (2002), "A Comparison of Methods to Test Mediation and Other Intervening Variable Effects," *Psychological Methods*, 7: 83–104.

Chapter 14

163. Andrew Van de Ven, Andre Delbecq, and R. Koenig, Jr. (1976), "Determinants of Coordination Modes within an Organization," *American Sociological Review*, 41: 322–338.

164. Linda Argote (1982), "Input Uncertainty and Organization Coordination in Hospital Emergency Units," *Administrative Science Quarterly*, 27: 420–434.

165. Erving Goffman (1961), *Encounters*. Indianapolis: Bobbs Merrill. See also Nitin Nohria and Robert G. Eccles (1992), "Face-to-Face: Making Network Organizations Work," in *Networks and Organizations*, eds. Nitin Nohria and Robert G. Eccles. Boston: Harvard Business School Press.

166. Faye G. Mangrum, Michael S. Fairley, and D. Lawrence Weider (2001), "Informal Problem-Solving in the Technology-Mediated Workplace," *Journal of Business Communication*, 38 (3): 315–336.

167. To measure cross-functional rounds, we asked administrators in our interviews about participation in physician rounds and nursing rounds, probing to determine which functional groups participated in those rounds and the consistency of their participation. These variables were coded on a scale of 0 to 2, with 0 indicating that the work group members did not participate in the rounds, 1 indicating that they participated sometimes, and 2 indicating that they participated usually or always. We then combined the six variables into a single standardized index. An additive scaling method was used in which each variable was standardized with a mean of 0 and a standard deviation of 1 so that each variable in the cross-functional meetings index was equally weighted. Cronbach's alpha for the cross-functional rounds index was 0.78.

168. Random effects models, also known as mixed, hierarchical linear, or multilevel models, were used to accommodate the multilevel structure of the data. The patient served as the unit of analysis, with the hospital as the random effect. Regression coefficients, standard errors, and the overall R-squared for random effects models reflect statistical associations both within and across hospitals.

169. In the final column of Exhibit 14–3, we tested whether cross-functional rounds affect performance through their effect on relational coordination. We aggregated relational coordination to the hospital level and entered it into the model for surgical performance, along with the cross-functional

rounds index. We found that the coefficient on the cross-functional rounds index becomes insignificant when relational coordination is added to the model, suggesting that cross-functional rounds influence surgical performance through their effect on relational coordination. We then used the Sobel test to determine whether the association between cross-functional rounds and surgical performance is reduced significantly when relational coordination is added to the model and found that again, the results were supportive of mediation. These methods are documented in Reuben A. Baron and David A. Kenny (1986), "The Moderator-Mediator Variable Distinction in Social Psychological Research: Conceptual, Strategic and Statistical Considerations," *Journal of Personality and Social Psychology*, 51: 1173–1182, and David P. MacKinnon, Chondra M. Lockwood, Jeanne M. Hoffman, Stephen G. West, and Virgil Sheets (2002), "A Comparison of Methods to Test Mediation and Other Intervening Variable Effects," *Psychological Methods*, 7: 83–104.

Chapter 15

170. Thomas Malone (2004), *The Future of Work: How the New Order of Business Will Shape Your Management Style, Your Organization and Your Life*. Cambridge, MA: Harvard Business School Press; Thomas Malone, Joanne Yates, and Robert I. Benjamin (1987), "Electronic Markets and Electronic Hierarchies," *Communication ACM*, 30: 484–497; Thomas Davenport (1993), *Process Innovation*. Boston: Harvard Business School Press; Eric Brynjolfsson and H. Mendelsohn (1993), "Information Systems and the Organization of Modern Enterprise," *Journal of Organizational Computing*, 3 (3): 245–255; Michael Tushman and David Nadler (1978), "Information Processing as an Integrating Concept in Organization Design." *Academy of Management Review*, 3 (3): 613–624; Shoshona Zuboff (1988), *In the Age of the Smart Machine: The Future of Work and Power*. New York: Basic Books; Thomas Davenport and James E. Short (1990), "The New Industrial Engineering: Information Technology and Business Process Redesign," *Sloan Management Review*, 31 (4): 11–27; Martin Lea, Tim O'Shea, and Pat Fung (1995), "Constructing the Networked Organization: Content and Context in the Development of Electronic Communications," *Organization Science*, 6: 462–478; and Wanda Orlikowski (1996), "Improvising Organizational Transformation over Time: A Situated Change Perspective," *Information Systems Research*, 7 (1): 63–92.
171. N. Venkatramen (1994), "IT-Enabled Business Transformation: From Automation to Business Scope Redefinition," *Sloan Management Review*, 35 (2): 73–87.
172. Adam Seth Litwin (2008), "Information Technology and the Employment Relationship: An Examination of the Adoption and Use of Electronic

Health Records," Ph.D. dissertation, Sloan School of Management, Massachusetts Institute of Technology.

173. Henry C. Lucas and Jack Baroudi (1994), "The Role of Information Technology in Organization Design," *Journal of Management Information Systems*, 10 (4): 9–24. For competing arguments, see Nitin Nohria and Robert G. Eccles (1992), "Face-to-Face: Making Network Organizations Work," in *Networks and Organizations*, eds. Nitin Nohria and Robert G. Eccles. Boston: Harvard Business School Press, and Joseph B. Walther (1996), "Computer-Mediated Communication: Impersonal, Interpersonal and Hyperpersonal Interaction," *Communication Research*, 21: 460–487.

174. To understand how information systems contribute to building weak ties rather than strong ties, see Morton Hansen (1999), "The Search-Transfer Paradox: The Role of Weak Ties in Integrating Knowledge across Organizational Subunits," *Administrative Science Quarterly*, 44 (1): 82–111. To understand the importance of strong ties for transferring complex or tacit knowledge, see Deborah Ancona and David Caldwell (1992), "Bridging the Boundary: External Activity and Performance in Organizational Teams," *Administrative Science Quarterly*, 37: 634–665, and Gerald Szulanski (1996), "Unpacking Stickiness: An Empirical Investigation of the Barriers to Transfer Best Practice within the Firm," *Strategic Management Journal*, 17: 27–43.

175. For the argument that information technology increases the need for interpersonal interaction, see R. P. Hummell (1994), *The Bureaucratic Experience*. New York: St. Martin's Press. For the argument that IT can structure and facilitate interaction, see Faye G. Mangrum, Michael S. Fairley, and D. Lawrence Weider (2001), "Informal Problem-Solving in the Technology-Mediated Workplace," *Journal of Business Communication*, 38 (3): 315–336; and Alan R. Dennis and Monica J. Garfield (2003), "The Adoption and Use of GSS in Project Teams: Toward More Participative Processes and Outcomes," *Management of Information Systems Quarterly*, 27 (2): 289–324.

176. To measure cross-functional information systems, we asked administrators in the interviews whether the hospital's information system included the following elements: lab results, insurance information, financial data, medical history, inpatient procedures, provider order entry, inpatient consult history, discharge summary, and patient's current condition and functioning. Each of these nine variables was coded 1 if it was included in the information system and 0 if it was not included. We then combined the nine variables into a single standardized index. An additive scaling method was used in which each variable was standardized with a mean of 0 and a standard deviation of 1 so that each variable in the cross-functional information systems index was equally weighted. Cronbach's alpha for the cross-functional information systems index was 0.68.

177. Random effects models, also known as mixed, hierarchical linear, or multilevel models, were used to accommodate the multilevel structure of the data. The patient served as the unit of analysis, with the hospital as the random effect. Regression coefficients, standard errors, and the overall R-squared for random effects models reflect statistical associations both within and across hospitals.

178. In the final column of Exhibit 15–3, we tested whether cross-functional information systems affect performance through their effect on relational coordination. We aggregated relational coordination to the hospital level and entered it into the model for surgical performance, along with the cross-functional information systems index. We found that the coefficient on the cross-functional information systems index becomes insignificant when relational coordination is added to the model, suggesting that cross-functional information systems influence surgical performance through their effect on relational coordination. We then used the Sobel test to determine whether the association between cross-functional information systems and surgical performance is reduced significantly when relational coordination is added to the model and found that again, the results were supportive of mediation. These methods are documented in Reuben A. Baron and David A. Kenny (1986), "The Moderator-Mediator Variable Distinction in Social Psychological Research: Conceptual, Strategic and Statistical Considerations," *Journal of Personality and Social Psychology*, 51: 1173–1182, and David P. MacKinnon, Chondra M. Lockwood, Jeanne M. Hoffman, Stephen G. West, and Virgil Sheets (2002), "A Comparison of Methods to Test Mediation and Other Intervening Variable Effects," *Psychological Methods*, 7: 83–104.

179. Randal Cebul, James Rebitzer, Lowell Taylor, and Mark Votruba (2008), "Organizational Fragmentation and Care Quality in the U.S. Healthcare System," *Journal of Economic Perspectives*, 22 (4): 93–113.

Chapter 16

180. Walter Powell (1990), "Neither Market Nor Hierarchy: Network Forms of Organization," *Research in Organizational Behavior*, 12: 295–336; Christine Oliver (1990), "Determinants of Inter-Organizational Relationships: Integration and Future Directions," *Academy of Management Review*, 15: 241–265; Catherine Alter and Jerald Hage (1993), *Organizations Working Together*. Newbury Park, CA: Sage; and Gianni Lorenzoni and Andrea Lipparini (1999), "The Leveraging of Interfirm Relationships as a Distinctive Organizational Capability: A Longitudinal Study," *Strategic Management Journal*, 20: 317–338.

181. Rosabeth M. Kanter (1989), *When Giants Learn to Dance*. New York: Simon & Schuster. See also Rosabeth M. Kanter (1988), "The New Alliances: How Strategic Partnerships Are Reshaping American Business," in

Business in the Contemporary World, ed. H. L. Sawyer. Lanham, MD: University Press of America.

182. For the advantages of partnering in the auto industry, see Matthias Holweg and Frits Pil (2004), *The Second Century: Reconnecting Customer and Value Chain through Build to Order*. Cambridge, MA: MIT Press, and Susan Helper, John Paul MacDuffie, and Charles Sabel (2000), "Pragmatic Collaborations: Advancing Knowledge While Controlling Opportunism," *Industrial and Corporate Change*, 9 (3): 443–487. For the advantages of partnering in the apparel industry, see Frederick Abernathy, John Dunlop, Janice Hammond, and David Weil (1999), *A Stitch in Time: Lean Retailing and the Transformation of Manufacturing—Lessons from the Apparel and Textile Industries*. New York: Oxford University Press.

183. Russell Johnston and Paul R. Lawrence (1988), "Beyond Vertical Integration—The Rise of Value-Adding Partnerships," *Harvard Business Review*, July–August, pp. 94–101.

184. Stephen Shortell, Robin Gillies, David Anderson, John Mitchell, and Karen Morgan (1993), "Creating Organized Delivery Systems: The Barriers and Facilitators," *Hospital and Health Services Administration*, 38: 447–466; Stephen Shortell, Robin Gillies, and Kelly Devers (1995), "Reinventing the American Hospital," *Milbank Quarterly*, 73 (2): 131–160; Keith G. Provan and H. Brint Milward (1995), "A Preliminary Theory of Inter-Organizational Network Effectiveness: A Comparative Study of Four Community Mental Health Systems," *Administrative Science Quarterly*, 40:1–33; and Dana Beth Weinberg, Jody Hoffer Gittell, R. William Lusenhop, Cori Kautz, and John Wright (2007), "Beyond Our Walls: Impact of Patient and Provider Coordination across the Continuum on Outcomes for Surgical Patients," *Health Services Research*, 42 (1): 7–24.

185. This section draws extensively from Jody Hoffer Gittell and Leigh Weiss (2004), "Coordination Networks within and across Organizations: A Multi-Level Framework," *Journal of Management Studies*, 41 (1): 127–153.

186. Jamie C. Robinson and Lawrence Casalino (1996), "Vertical Integration and Organizational Networks in Healthcare," *Health Affairs*, 15 (1): 7–22.

187. For a complete analysis of these results, see Cori Kautz, Jody Hoffer Gittell, R. William Lusenhop, Dana Beth Weinberg, and John Wright (2007), "Patient Benefits from Participating in an Integrated Delivery System: Impact on Coordination of Care," *Healthcare Management Review*, 32 (3): 1–11.

188. Joel Podolny (1994), "Market Uncertainty and the Social Character of Economic Exchange," *Administrative Science Quarterly*, 39: 458–483. See also Randal Cebul, James Rebitzer, Lowell Taylor, and Mark Votruba (2008), "Organizational Fragmentation and Care Quality in the U.S. Healthcare System," *Journal of Economic Perspectives*, 22 (4): 93–113.

189. For a complete analysis of these results, see Jody Hoffer Gittell, Farbod Hagigi, and Dana Weinberg (2009), "Modularity and the Coordination of Complex Work: The Case of Post-Surgical Patient Care," Heller School Working Paper, Brandeis University.

190. To analyze patterns of coordination, we used a matrix form of analysis known as design structure matrix or dependency structure matrix (DSM). See Donald Steward (1981), "The Design Structure Matrix: A Method for Managing the Design of Complex Systems," *IEEE Transactions Engineering Management*, 28 (3): 71–74, and Manuel E. Sosa, Steven D. Eppinger, and C. M. Rowles (2003), "Identifying Modular and Integrative Systems and Their Impact on Design Team Interaction," *Journal of Mechanical Design*, 125: 240–252. We formed a matrix with providers from the three stages of care—hospital, rehabilitation, and home care—down one side and providers from the same stages of care across the top. We added a final row and column for those parties who were expected to play the system integrator role in this setting: primary care physicians, informal caregivers, and managed care case managers. We surveyed 8 provider types about their coordination with 14 provider types, and so our matrix is asymmetric. Observations about the six provider types that were not surveyed and are reported only from the perspective of others, not from their own perspective, making this an asymmetric matrix of coordination ties. Still, all coordination ties in the matrix are measured from the perspective of at least one of the two providers in each relationship. In each cell of the matrix is the mean level of relational coordination on a five-point scale, reported by the provider type along the left axis with respect to the provider type along the top axis, regarding the particular patient about whose coordination the provider was being surveyed. The total number of observations for each provider category is shown in the bottom row of the matrix. We can see that of the total 519 surveys received, all 519 included responses about the surgeon who was responsible for the patient in question. By contrast, only 452 of the 519 surveys received included responses about the hospital care case manager who was responsible for the patient in question, 467 of the 519 surveys included responses about the hospital nurses who were responsible for the patient in question, and so on.

191. Dana Beth Weinberg, R. William Lusenhop, Jody Hoffer Gittell, and Cori Kautz (2007), "Coordination between Formal Providers and Informal Caregivers," *Healthcare Management Review*, 32 (2): 140–150.

Chapter 17

192. Random effects models, also known as mixed, hierarchical linear, or multilevel models, were used to accommodate the multilevel structure of the data. The patient served as the unit of analysis, with the hospital as the

random effect. Regression coefficients, standard errors, and the overall R-squared for random effects models reflect statistical associations both within and across hospitals.

193. In the final column of Exhibit 17–3, we tested whether this high performance work system affects performance through its effect on relational coordination. We aggregated relational coordination to the hospital level and entered it into the model for surgical performance, along with the high performance work system index. We found that the coefficient on the high performance work system index becomes insignificant when relational coordination is added to the model, suggesting that the high performance work system influences surgical performance through its effect on relational coordination. We then used the Sobel test to determine whether the association between the high performance work system and surgical performance is reduced significantly when relational coordination is added to the model and found that again, the results were supportive of mediation. These methods are documented in Reuben A. Baron and David A. Kenny (1986), "The Moderator-Mediator Variable Distinction in Social Psychological Research: Conceptual, Strategic and Statistical Considerations," *Journal of Personality and Social Psychology*, 51: 1173–1182, and David P. MacKinnon, Chondra M. Lockwood, Jeanne M. Hoffman, Stephen G. West, and Virgil Sheets (2002), "A Comparison of Methods to Test Mediation and Other Intervening Variable Effects," *Psychological Methods*, 7: 83–104.

Chapter 18

194. This chapter draws extensively from Jody Hoffer Gittell (2008), "Relationships and Resilience: Care Provider Responses to Pressures from Managed Care," *Journal of Applied Behavioral Science*, 44 (1): 25–47. Note that the high performance work system discussed in this chapter and elsewhere in this book is more comprehensive than the one presented in the journal article.

195. Dana Beth Weinberg (2003), *Code Green: Money-Driven Hospitals and the Dismantling of Nursing*. Ithaca, NY: Cornell University Press, p. 42.

196. The term *work stressors* is used throughout this chapter to encompass both job demands and situational constraints, following John Schaubroeck and Deryl E. Merritt (1997), "Divergent Effects of Job Control on Coping with Work Stressors: The Key Role of Self-Efficacy," *Academy of Management Journal*, 40 (3): 738–754.

197. Barry Staw, Lance Sandelands, and Jane Dutton (1981), "Threat-Rigidity Effects in Organizational Behavior: A Multi-Level Analysis," *Administrative Science Quarterly* 26: 501–524, and Linda Argote, Marlene Turner, and Mark Fichman (1989), "To Centralize or Not to Centralize: The Effects

of Uncertainty and Threat on Group Structure and Performance," *Organizational Behavior and Human Decision Processes*, 43: 58–74.

198. P. M. Elsass and G. F. Veiga (1997), "Job Control and Job Strain: A Test of Three Models," *Journal of Occupational Health Psychology*, 2: 195–211; H. Davidson, P. H. Folcarelli, S. Crawford, L. J. Duprat, and Joyce C. Clifford (1997), "The Effects of Healthcare Reforms on Job Satisfaction and Voluntary Turnover among Hospital-Based Nurses," *Medical Care*, 35: 634–645; and C. A. Woodward, H. S. Shannon, C. Cunningham, J. McIntosh, B. Lendrum, D. Rosenbloom, and J. Brown (1999), "The Impact of Re-Engineering and Other Cost Reduction Strategies on the Staff of a Large Teaching Hospital: A Longitudinal Study," *Medical Care*, 37: 556–569.

199. Jon Chilingerian (2008), "Origins of DRGs: A Technical, Cultural and Political Story," Heller School Working Paper, Brandeis University.

200. Robert A. Karasek, Jr. (1979), "Job Demands, Job Decision Latitude, and Mental Strain: Implications for Job Redesign," *Administrative Science Quarterly*, 24: 285–309.

201. Lawrence H. Peters and Edward J. O'Connor (1980), "Situational Constraints and Work Outcomes: The Influences of a Frequently Overlooked Construct," *Academy of Management Review*, 5: 391–397.

202. Gary P. Latham and Edward A. Locke (1979), "Goal Setting: A Motivational Technique that Works," *Organizational Dynamics*, 8 (2): 68–80.

203. Lawrence H. Peters, Edward J. O'Connor, and C. J. Rudolf (1980), "The Behavioral and Affective Consequences of Performance-Relevant Situational Variables," *Organizational Behavior and Human Performance*, 25 (1): 79–96.

204. Robert A. Karasek, Jr. (1979), "Job Demands, Job Decision Latitude, and Mental Strain: Implications for Job Redesign," *Administrative Science Quarterly*, 24: 285–309.

205. For findings that job control reduces the negative effects of work stressors, see Dale J. Dwyer and Daniel C. Ganster (1991), "The Effects of Job Demands and Control on Employee Attendance and Satisfaction," *Journal of Organizational Behavior*, 12 (7): 595–608; Penny Moyle and Katherine Parkes (1999), "The Effects of Transition Stress: A Relocation Study," *Journal of Organizational Behavior*, 20 (5): 625–646; Sharon K. Parker and Christine A. Sprigg (1999), "Minimizing Strain and Maximizing Learning: The Role of Job Demands, Job Control and Proactive Personality," *Journal of Applied Psychology*, 84 (6): 929–935; and John Schaubroeck and Laurence S. Fink (1998), "Facilitating and Inhibiting Effects of Job Control and Social Support on Stress Outcomes and Role Behavior: A Contingency Model," *Journal of Organizational Behavior*, 19 (2): 167–195.

For findings that job control reverses the negative effects of work stressors, see Robert A. Karasek, Jr. (1979), "Job Demands, Job Decision

Latitude, and Mental Strain: Implications for Job Redesign," *Administrative Science Quarterly*, 24: 285–309; Marilyn L. Fox, Dale J. Dwyer, and Daniel C. Ganster (1993), "Effects of Stressful Job Demands and Control on Physiological and Attitudinal Outcomes in a Hospital Setting," *Academy of Management Journal*, 38: 289–318; and Jia Lin Xie (1996), "Karasek's Model in the People's Republic of China: Effects of Job Demands, Control and Individual Differences," *Academy of Management Journal*, 39 (6): 1594–1618.

206. For evidence that individual self-efficacy and job fit should reduce the negative effects of work stressors, see Jeffrey R. Edwards (1996), "An Examination of Competing Versions of the Person-Environment Fit Approach to Stress," *Academy of Management Journal*, 39 (2): 292–339; Steve M. Jex and Paul D. Bliese (1999), "Efficacy Beliefs as a Moderator of the Impact of Work Pressure: A Multi-Level Study," *Journal of Applied Psychology*, 84 (3): 349–361; John Schaubroeck and Deryl E. Merritt (1997), "Divergent Effects of Job Control on Coping with Work Stressors: The Key Role of Self-Efficacy," *Academy of Management Journal*, 40 (3): 738–754; and Jia Lin Xie (1996), "Karasek's Model in the People's Republic of China: Effects of Job Demands, Control and Individual Differences," *Academy of Management Journal*, 39 (6): 1594–1618.

207. Steve M. Jex and Paul D. Bliese (1999), "Efficacy Beliefs as a Moderator of the Impact of Work Pressure: A Multi-Level Study," *Journal of Applied Psychology*, 84 (3): 349–361.

208. John R. Aiello and Kathryn J. Kolb (1995), "Electronic Performance Monitoring and Social Context: Impact on Productivity and Stress," *Journal of Applied Psychology*, 80 (3): 339–353.

209. Penny Moyle and Katherine Parkes (1999), "The Effects of Transition Stress: A Relocation Study," *Journal of Organizational Behavior*, 20 (5): 625–646, and John Schaubroeck and Laurence S. Fink (1998), "Facilitating and Inhibiting Effects of Job Control and Social Support on Stress Outcomes and Role Behavior: A Contingency Model," *Journal of Organizational Behavior*, 19 (2): 167–195.

210. Wanda J. Orlikowski and Joanne Yates (1994), "Genre Repertoire: The Structuring of Communicative Practices in Organizations," *Administrative Science Quarterly*, 39 (4): 541–574, and Stelia E. Anderson and Larry J. Williams (1996), "Interpersonal, Job and Individual Factors Related to Helping Processes at Work," *Journal of Applied Psychology*, 81 (3): 282–296.

211. Ingrid M. Nembhard and Amy Edmondson (2006), "Making It Safe: The Effects of Leader Inclusiveness and Professional Status on Psychological Safety and Improvement Efforts in Healthcare Teams," *Journal of Organizational Behavior*, 27 (7): 941–966. See also Dierdre Wicks (1998), *Nurses and Doctors at Work: Rethinking Professional Boundaries*. Buckingham, UK: Open University Press.

212. Dana Beth Weinberg (2000). *Why Are The Nurses Crying? Restructuring, Power and Control in an American Hospital*. Ph.D. dissertation, Harvard University, p. 45.

213. Kathleen M. Sutcliffe and Timothy Vogus (2003), "Organizing for Resilience," in Kim S. Cameron, Jane E. Dutton and Robert E. Quinn (eds.), *Positive Organizational Scholarship: Foundations of a New Discipline*. San Francisco: Berrett-Koehler Press.

214. Kim Cameron, David Bright, and Arran Caza (2004), "Exploring the Relationships between Organizational Virtuousness and Performance," *American Behavioral Scientist*, 47: 766–790; Jody Hoffer Gittell, Kim Cameron, Sandy Lim, and Victor Rivas (2006), "Relationships, Layoffs and Organizational Resilience: Airline Responses to Crisis of September 11," *Journal of Applied Behavioral Science* 42: 300–329; and Gretchen Spreitzer, Kathleen Sutcliffe, Jane Dutton, Scott Sonenshein, and Adam Grant (2005), "A Socially Embedded Model of Thriving at Work," *Organization Science*, 16: 537–549.

215. *Managed Care Digest Series* (2000). HMO/PPO Medicare-Medicaid Digest. Centers for Medicare and Medicaid Services.

216. Using one-way analysis of variance, we found significant cross-unit differences in this perceived work stressor ($p < 0.0001$) as well as significant cross-functional differences ($p = 0.0014$). When unit-level and function-level differences were considered jointly, unit-level differences remained significant: Unit-level differences were significant ($p < 0.0001$), and function-level differences were also significant ($p = 0.0268$). The intraclass correlation for this perceived work stressor was significantly greater than zero ($p < 0.05$). These results were consistent with treating this perceived work stressor as a unit-level construct.

217. In the third column of Exhibit 18–2, we tested whether managed care penetration affects relational coordination through its effect on work stress. We entered work stressors into the model for relational coordination, along with managed care penetration. We found that the coefficient on managed care penetration becomes insignificant when work stressors are added to the model, suggesting that managed care penetration influences relational coordination through its effect on work stressors. We then used the Sobel test to determine whether the association between managed care penetration and relational coordination is reduced significantly when work stressors are added to the model and found that again, the results were supportive of mediation. These methods are documented in Reuben A. Baron and David A. Kenny (1986), "The Moderator-Mediator Variable Distinction in Social Psychological Research: Conceptual, Strategic and Statistical Considerations," *Journal of Personality and Social Psychology*, 51: 1173–1182, and David P. MacKinnon, Chondra M. Lockwood, Jeanne M. Hoffman, Stephen G. West, and Virgil Sheets (2002), "A Comparison of Methods to Test Mediation and Other Intervening Variable Effects," *Psychological Methods*, 7: 83–104.

218. To test whether high performance work systems were adopted in response to managed care penetration or work stress, we ran Spearman's rank correlations between managed care penetration and high performance work systems and then between work stress and high performance work systems. Both correlations were insignificant ($p = 0.200$ and $p = 0.134$, respectively).

219. These results suggest a duality regarding effective responses to external threats. There appears to be a need for both reactive coping (through psychosocial reactions) and proactive structuring (through work practices). These findings are consistent with the view of organizational resilience presented by Aaron Wildavsky (1988), *Searching for Safety*. New Brunswick, NJ: Transition.

220. See Jody Hoffer Gittell, Kim Cameron, Sandy Lim, and Victor Rivas (2006), "Relationships, Layoffs and Organizational Resilience," *Journal of Applied Behavioral Science*, 42 (3): 300–329.

Chapter 19

221. Several researchers have demonstrated the importance of implementing bundles of mutually supportive work practices. See John Paul MacDuffie (1995), "Human Resource Bundles and Manufacturing Performance: Organizational Logic and Flexible Production Systems in the World Auto Industry," *Industrial and Labor Relations Review*, 48: 173–188; John T. Dunlop and David Weil (1996), "Diffusion and Performance of Modular Production in the U.S. Apparel Industry," *Industrial Relations*, July, pp. 334–355; Casey Ichniowski, Kathryn Shaw, and Giovanna Prennushi (1997), "The Effects of Human Resource Practices on Manufacturing Performance: A Study of Steel Finishing Lines," *American Economics Review*, 87: 291–313; Rose Batt (1999), "Work Design, Technology and Performance in Customer Service and Sales," *Industrial and Labor Relations Review*, 52 (4): 539–564; and Keld Laursen (2002), "The Importance of Sectoral Differences in the Application of Complementary HRM Practices for Innovation Performance," *International Journal of Economics and Business*, 9: 139–156.

222. Charles A. O'Reilly and Michael L. Tushman (2002), *Winning through Innovation: A Practical Guide to Organizational Change and Renewal*. Boston: Harvard Business School Press; David A. Nadler and Michael L. Tushman (1997), *Competing By Design: The Power of Organizational Architecture*. Oxford: Oxford University Press; and Raymond E. Miles and Charles C. Snow (1994), *Fit, Failure and the Hall of Fame: How Companies Succeed or Fail*. New York: Free Press.

223. Anita Tucker and Amy Edmondson (2003), "Why Hospitals Don't Learn From Failures: Organizational and Psychological Dynamics That Inhibit System Change," *California Management Review*, 45 (2): 1–18.

224. For a description of Plan Do Check Act approach, see J. Edward Deming (1986), *Out of the Crisis*. Cambridge, MA: MIT Press. For a description of

the Plan Do Study Act approach as applied to healthcare improvement, see Eugene C. Nelson, Paul B. Batalden and Marjorie M. Godfrey (2007). *Quality by Design: A Clinical Microsystems Approach*. San Francisco: Jossey-Bass

225. James M. Kouzes and Barry Z. Posner (2008), *The Leadership Challenge*. San Francisco: Jossey-Bass.

226. For a model of distributed leadership in the healthcare industry that includes worker representatives as key partners, see Thomas A. Kochan, Adrienne Eaton, Robert McKersie, and Paul Adler (2008), *Healing Together: The Labor-Management Partnership at Kaiser-Permanente*. Ithaca, NY: Cornell University Press; also addressed in Chapter 20. For further insights into distributed or shared leadership, see Deborah Ancona and H. Bresman (2007), *X-Teams: How to Build Teams that Lead, Innovate and Succeed*. Boston: Harvard Business School Press; Craig L. Pearce and J. A. Conger (2003), *Shared Leadership: Reframing the Hows and Whys of Leadership*. Thousand Oaks, CA: Sage; Craig L. Pearce and H. P. Sims, Jr. (2002), "Vertical versus Shared Leadership as Predictors of the Effectiveness of Change Management Teams: An Examination of Aversive, Directive, Transactional, Transformational and Empowering Leader Behaviors," *Group Dynamics: Theory, Research, and Practice*, 6: 172–197; J. B. Carson, Paul E. Tesluk, and J. A. Marrone (2007), "Shared Leadership in Teams: An Investigation of Antecedent Conditions and Performance," *Academy of Management Journal*, 50 (5): 1217–1234.

227. Charles Heckscher, Saul Rubinstein, Linda Flynn, Niclas Erhardt, and Boniface Michael (2008), "Collaboration and the Quality of Healthcare Delivery," Working Paper, Rutgers University.

228. For a guide to mapping and improving work process in healthcare settings, see Institute for Healthcare Improvement (2005), *Going Lean in Healthcare*, Innovation Series.

229. Jody Hoffer Gittell (2009), *Relational Coordination: Guidelines for Theory, Measurement and Analysis*, Heller School Working Paper, Brandeis University.

230. To analyze patterns of coordination, we used a matrix form of analysis known as design structure matrix or dependency structure matrix (DSM). See Donald Steward (1981), "The Design Structure Matrix: A Method for Managing the Design of Complex Systems," *IEEE Transactions Engineering Management*, 28 (3): 71–74, and Manuel E. Sosa, Steven D. Eppinger, and C. M. Rowles (2003), "Identifying Modular and Integrative Systems and Their Impact on Design Team Interaction," *Journal of Mechanical Design*, 125:240–252.

231. Michael Tushman and Charles O'Reilly (1997). *Winning Through Innovation: A Practical Guide to Leading Organizational Change and Renewal*. Boston, MA: Harvard Business School Press.

232. Jody Hoffer Gittell, Andrew von Nordenflycht, and Thomas A. Kochan (2004), "Mutual Gains or Zero Sum? Labor Relations and Firm Performance

in the Airline Industry," *Industrial and Labor Relations Review*, 57 (2): 163–179; Adrienne Eaton and Paula B. Voos (1992), "Unions and Contemporary Innovations in Work Organization, Compensation and Employee Participation," in *Unions and Competitiveness*, eds. Paula Voos and Larry Mishel. Armonk, NY: M. E. Sharpe. See also OECD, *1999 Employment Outlook*. New York: OECD Publishing.

233. Sandra Black and Lisa Lynch (2004), "What's Driving the New Economy: Understanding the Role of Workplace Practices," *Economic Journal*, 114 (493), F97–116. See also David Coats (1999), *Speaking Up! Voice, Industrial Democracy and Organisational Performance*. London: The Work Foundation.

234. Saul A. Rubinstein (2006), "Collaborative Community and Employee Representation," in *The Firm as Collaborative Community: Reconstructing Trust in the Knowledge Economy*, ed. Paul Adler and Charles Heckscher. Oxford: Oxford University Press, pp. 334–352; Eileen Appelbaum and Larry Hunter (2005), "Union Participation in Strategic Decisions of Corporations," in *Emerging Labor Market Institutions for the 21st Century*, ed. Richard Freeman and Larry Mishel. Cambridge, MA: National Bureau of Economic Research, pp. 265–291; and Thomas A. Kochan, Adrienne E. Eaton, Robert B. McKersie, and Paul Adler (2009), *Healing Together: The Kaiser Permanente Labor-Management Partnership*, Ithaca, NY: Cornell University Press.

Chapter 20

235. This chapter draws extensively upon Christine Bishop, Thomas Kochan, et al. (2008), *Labor Policy to Support Healthcare Reform*, unpublished report.

236. Joel Cutcher Gershenfeld and Thomas Kochan (2004), "Taking Stock: Collective Bargaining at the Turn of the Century," *Industrial and Labor Relations Review*, 58 (1): 2–26.

237. See *Report of the International Action Research Project*.

238. Gil Preuss and Ann Frost (2003), "The Rise and Decline of Labor-Management Cooperation: Lessons from Healthcare in the Twin Cities," *California Management Review*, 45 (2): 85–106.

239. Thomas A. Kochan, Adrienne E. Eaton, Robert B. McKersie, and Paul Adler (2008), *Healing Together: The Labor Management Partnership at Kaiser-Permanente*. Ithaca, NY: Cornell University Press.

240. Adam Seth Litwin (2008), "Quantifying the Line from Partnership to Performance at Kaiser Permanente," MIT Institute for Work and Employment Research Working Paper.

241. Adam Seth Litwin (2008), "Information Technology and the Employment Relationship: An Examination of the Adoption and Use of Electronic Health Records," Ph.D. dissertation, Sloan School of Management, Massachusetts Institute of Technology.

242. Adrienne E. Eaton, Saul A. Rubinstein, and Thomas A. Kochan (2008), "Balancing Acts: Dynamics of a Union Coalition in a Labor Management Partnership, *Industrial Relations*, 47 (1): 31.

243. Adrienne E. Eaton and Jill Kriesky (1999), "Organizing Experiences under Union-Management Neutrality and Card Check Agreements," Report to the Institute for the Study of Labor Organizations, Silver Spring, MD: George Meany Center for Labor Studies.

244. Lawrence Darmiento (2003), "Unions Step Up Drive to Organize Cedars' Nurses," *Los Angeles Business Journal*, January 27.

245. The case has been reported at various stages in the local newspaper, *Chico Enterprise Record*. See also Larry Mitchell, "Who's the Bully in the Enloe Battle," and Larry Mitchell, "Unions-Enloe Agree over Legal Battle," available at www.chicoer.com/indepth/enloe/ci-3528047 and 5140273. Bargaining information comes from Enloe News Releases available at www.enloeorg/news_and_publications/2008/2008–03–28.asp.

Chapter 21

246. Randal Cebul, James Rebitzer, Lowell Taylor, and Mark Votruba (2008), "Organizational Fragmentation and Care Quality in the U.S. Healthcare System," *Journal of Economic Perspectives*, 22 (4): 93–113.

247. Gail R. Wilensky, Nicholas Wolter, and Michelle M. Fischer (2006), "Gain Sharing: A Good Concept Getting a Bad Name?" *Health Affairs*, 26: 59 (emphasis added).

248. Diane R. Rittenhouse, Lawrence P. Casalino, Robin R. Gillies, Stephen M. Shortell, and Bernard Lau (2008), "Measuring the Medical Home Infrastructure in Large Medical Groups," *Health Affairs*, 27 (5): 1246–1259; and Ronald A. Paulus, Karen Davis, and Glenn Steele (2008), "Continuous Innovation in Healthcare: Implications of the Geisinger Experience," *Health Affairs*, 27 (5): 1235–1245.

See also Deloitte Center for Health Solutions (2008), "The Medical Home: Disruptive Innovation for a New Primary Care Model," http://www.deloitte.com/dtt/cda/doc/content/us_chs_MedicalHome_w.pdf. See also A.C. Beal et al. (2007), "Closing the Divide: How Medical Homes Promote Equity in Healthcare: Results from the Commonwealth Fund 2006 Healthcare Quality Survey," http://www.commonwealthfund.org/publications/publication_showhtm?doc_id=506814.

249. Randal Cebul, James Rebitzer, Lowell Taylor, and Mark Votruba (2008), "Organizational Fragmentation and Care Quality in the U.S. Healthcare System," *Journal of Economic Perspectives*, 22 (4): 93–113.

250. Paul Adler, Seok Woo Kwon, and Charles Heckscher (2008), "Professional Work: The Emergence of Collaborative Community," *Organization Science*, 19 (2): 359–376.

251. For the full report, see Institute of Medicine Committee on the Quality of Healthcare in America, 2001, p. 83 (as cited by Randal Cebul, et al., ibid.).

252. Randal Cebul, James Rebitzer, Lowell Taylor, and Mark Votruba (2008), "Organizational Fragmentation and Care Quality in the U.S. Healthcare System," *Journal of Economic Perspectives*, 22 (4): 93–113.

253. Mark R. Yessian and Martha B. Kvall (1991), "State Prohibitions on Hospital Employment of Physicians," Department of Health and Human Services, Office of the Inspector General, OEI-Ol–91–00770.

254. Amy Burroughs and Regina Herzlinger (1998), *Note on Healthcare Accountability*. Boston, MA: Harvard Business School Press, p. 1.

255. Randal Cebul, James Rebitzer, Lowell Taylor, and Mark Votruba (2008), "Organizational Fragmentation and Care Quality in the U.S. Healthcare System," *Journal of Economic Perspectives*, 22 (4): 93–113.

256. For the full report, see Institute of Medicine Committee on the Quality of Healthcare in America, 2001, p. 154 (as cited by Randal Cebul, et al., ibid.).

257. This section draws extensively from Christine Bishop, Thomas Kochan, et al. (2008), *Labor Policy to Support Healthcare Reform*, unpublished report.

258. Adrienne Eaton and Jill Kriesky (2001), "Union Organizing under Neutrality and Card Check Agreements," *Industrial and Labor Relations Review*, 55 (1): 42–59.

259. Greg Bamber, Jody Hoffer Gittell, Thomas A. Kochan, and Andrew von Nordenflycht (2009), *Up in the Air: How the Airlines Can Improve Performance by Engaging Their Employees*. Ithaca, NY: Cornell University Press.

260. Thomas A. Kochan, Adrienne Eaton, Robert McKersie, and Paul Adler (2008), *Healing Together: The Labor-Management Partnership at Kaiser-Permanente*. Ithaca, NY: Cornell University Press.

Notes for Exhibits

Exhibit 2-4 (page 21)

Exhibit 2-4 shows the results of a care provider survey that was administered in nine orthopedic surgical units, each one in a different hospital. Survey questions were asked about relational coordination among five functions: physicians, nurses, physical therapists, case managers, and social workers. Each number on the table indicates the inclusiveness of ties among care providers in that particular hospital unit, using a five-point scale. All relationship and communication dimensions were highly correlated with one another and were combined into a single index called relational coordination (n = 313 care providers).

Exhibit 3-1 (page 30)

Exhibit 3-1 shows the impact of relational coordination on surgical performance. The first model shows that doubling relational coordination predicts a 33% reduction in length of stay. Asterisks indicate the probability that a change in relational coordination will produce a change in surgical performance (*** = 99.9%, ** = 99%, * = 95%, + = 90%). Other variables included in each model but not shown here are patient gender, race, and marital status. All models are random effects regressions with the patient as the unit of analysis (n = 599 for length of stay, n = 588 for patient satisfaction, n = 539 for postoperative pain, n = 531 for postoperative mobility, and n = 552 for the surgical performance index), as hospital (n = 9) is the random effect. R-squared indicates the percent of between-hospital variation in performance that is explained by each model.

Exhibit 3-3 (page 32)

Exhibit 3-3 shows the impact of relational coordination on job satisfaction and the impact of job satisfaction on surgical performance. Job satisfaction models are random effects regressions with the care provider as the unit of analysis (n = 332). Surgical performance models are random effects regressions with the patient as the unit of analysis (n = 552) and the hospital (n = 9) as the random effect. Asterisks indicate the probability that a change in relational coordination will produce a change in surgical performance or job satisfaction (*** = 99.9%, ** = 99%, * = 95%, + = 90%). R-squared indicates the percent of between-hospital variation in performance that is explained by each model.

Exhibit 3-5 (page 36)

Exhibit 3-5 shows the impact of relational coordination on medical performance. Efficiency models are random effects regressions, and quality models are logistic random effects regressions, with the patient as the unit of analysis (n = 5,790) and the attending physician (n = 52) as the random effect. Asterisks indicate the probability that a change in relational coordination will produce a change in medical performance (*** = 99.9%, ** = 99%, * = 95%, + = 90%). R-squared is presented for the random effects regressions and indicates the percent of between-physician variation in performance that is explained by the model. Chi-squared is presented for the logistic random effects regressions and indicates the probability that the null hypothesis for the model is true.

Exhibit 3-6 (page 40)

Exhibit 3-6 shows the impact of relational coordination on long-term care performance. All models are random effects regressions with the resident (n = 93) or nursing aide (n = 231) as the unit of analysis and the nursing home (n = 15) as the random effect. Asterisks indicate the probability that a change in relational coordination will produce a change in long-term care performance (*** = 99.9%, ** = 99%, * = 95%, + = 90%). R-squared indicates the percent of between-home variation in performance that is explained by the model.

Exhibit 3-7 (page 42)

Exhibit 3-7 shows the impact of relational coordination on airline performance. Asterisks indicate the probability that a change in relational coordination will produce a change in airline performance (*** = 99.9%, ** = 99%, * = 95%, + = 90%). All models are random effects regressions with the site/month as the unit of analysis (n = 99) and the site (n = 9) as the random effect. R-squared indicates the percent of variation in performance that is explained by the model.

Exhibit 4-2 (pages 54–55)

All work practices in Exhibit 4-2 were measured at the level of the hospital (n = 9), focused on the care of joint replacement patients in the orthopedics department. Note that 2 of the 12 work practices in the high performance work system—flexible job boundaries and supply partnerships—were not measured quantitatively for this study.

Exhibit 5-1 (page 63)

Exhibit 5-1 shows the impact of selection for teamwork on relational coordination. The model shows that doubling the inclusiveness of selection for teamwork predicts a 12% increase in relational coordination. The care provider variables indicate the levels of relational coordination reported by each function relative to the levels reported by nurses. Asterisks indicate the probability that a change in selection for teamwork will produce a change in relational coordination (*** = 99.9%, ** = 99%, * = 95%, + = 90%). The model is a random effects regression with the care provider as the unit of analysis ($n = 336$) and the hospital ($n = 9$) as the random effect. R-squared indicates the percent of between-hospital variation in relational coordination that is explained by the model.

Exhibit 5-3 (page 64)

Exhibit 5-3 shows the impact of selection for teamwork on surgical performance. The first model shows that doubling the inclusiveness of selection for teamwork predicts a 15% reduction in length of stay. Asterisks indicate the probability that a change in selection for teamwork will produce a change in surgical performance (*** = 99.9%, ** = 99%, * = 95%, + = 90%). The final model shows that selection for teamwork influences surgical performance *through* its effect on relational coordination. Other variables included in each model but not shown here are patient gender, race, and marital status. All models are random effects regressions with the patient as the unit of analysis ($n = 599$ for length of stay, $n = 588$ for patient satisfaction, $n = 539$ for postoperative pain, $n = 531$ for postoperative mobility, and $n = 552$ for the surgical performance index) with the hospital ($n = 9$) as the random effect. R-squared indicates the percent of between-hospital variation in performance that is explained by each model.

Exhibit 6-1 (page 78)

Exhibit 6-1 shows the impact of cross-functional performance measurement on relational coordination. The model shows that doubling the strength of cross-functional performance measurement predicts a 17% increase in relational coordination. The care provider variables indicate the levels of relational coordination reported by each function relative to the levels. Asterisks indicate the probability that a change in cross-functional performance measurement will produce a change in relational coordination (*** = 99.9%, ** = 99%, * = 95%, + = 90%). The model is a random effects regression with the care provider as the unit of analysis ($n = 336$) and the hospital ($n = 9$) as the random effect. R-squared indicates the percent of between-hospital variation in relational coordination that is explained by the model.

Exhibit 6-3

Exhibit 6-3 shows the impact of cross-functional performance measurement on surgical performance. The first model shows that doubling the strength of cross-functional performance measurement predicts a 36% reduction in the length of stay. Asterisks indicate the probability that a change in cross-functional performance measurement will produce a change in surgical performance (*** = 99.9%, ** = 99%, * = 95%, + = 90%). The final model shows that cross-functional performance measurement influences surgical performance *through* its effect on relational coordination. Other variables included in each model but not shown here are patient gender, race, and marital status. All models are random effects regressions with the patient as the unit of analysis (n = 599 for length of stay, n = 588 for patient satisfaction, n = 539 for postoperative pain, n = 531 for postoperative mobility, and n = 552 for the surgical performance index) and the hospital (n = 9) as the random effect. R-squared indicates the percent of between-hospital variation in performance that is explained by each model.

Exhibit 7-1 (page 87)

Exhibit 7-1 shows the impact of cross-functional rewards on relational coordination. The model shows that doubling the inclusiveness of cross-functional rewards predicts an 18% increase in relational coordination. The care provider variables indicate the levels of relational coordination reported by each function relative to the levels reported by nurses. Asterisks indicate the probability that a change in cross-functional rewards will produce a change in relational coordination (*** = 99.9%, ** = 99%, * = 95%, + = 90%). The model is a random effects regression with care provider as the unit of analysis (n = 336) and hospital (n = 9) as the random effect. R-squared indicates the percent of between-hospital variation in relational coordination that is explained by the model.

Exhibit 7-3 (page 89)

Exhibit 7-3 shows the impact of cross-functional rewards on surgical performance. The first model shows that doubling the inclusiveness of cross-functional rewards predicts a 24% reduction in the length of stay. Asterisks indicate the probability that a change in cross-functional rewards will produce a change in surgical performance (*** = 99.9%, ** = 99%, * = 95%, + = 90%). The final model shows that cross-functional rewards influences surgical performance *through* its effect on relational coordination. Other variables included in each model but not shown here are patient gender, race, and marital status. All models are random effects regressions with the patient as the unit of analysis (n = 599 for length of stay, n = 588 for patient satisfaction, n = 539 for postoperative pain, n = 531 for postoperative mobility, and n = 552 for the surgical performance index), and the hospital (n = 9) as the random effect. R-squared indicates the percent of between-hospital variation in performance that is explained by each model.

Exhibit 8-1 (page 101)

Exhibit 8-1 shows the impact of cross-functional conflict resolution on relational coordination. The model shows that doubling the inclusiveness of cross-functional conflict resolution predicts an 18% increase in relational coordination. The care provider variables indicate the levels of relational coordination reported by each function relative to the levels reported by nurses. Asterisks indicate the probability that a change in cross-functional conflict resolution will produce a change in relational coordination (*** = 99.9%, ** = 99%, * = 95%, + = 90%). The model is a random effects regression with the care provider as the unit of analysis (n = 336) and the hospital (n = 9) as the random effect. R-squared indicates the percent of between-hospital variation in relational coordination that is explained by the model.

Exhibit 8-3 (page 103)

Exhibit 8-3 shows the impact of cross-functional conflict resolution on surgical performance. The first model shows that doubling the inclusiveness of cross-functional conflict resolution predicts a 30% reduction in length of stay. Asterisks indicate the probability that a change in cross-functional conflict resolution will produce a change in surgical performance (*** = 99.9%, ** = 99%, * = 95%, + = 90%). The final model shows that cross-functional conflict resolution influences surgical performance *through* its effect on relational coordination. Other variables included in each model but not shown here are patient gender, race, and marital status. All models are random effects regressions with the patient as the unit of analysis (n = 599 for length of stay, n = 588 for patient satisfaction, n = 539 for postoperative pain, n = 531 for postoperative mobility, and n = 552 for the surgical performance index), and the hospital (n = 9) as the random effect. R-squared indicates the percent of between-hospital variation in performance that is explained by each model.

Exhibit 9-1 (page 112)

Exhibit 9-1 shows the impact of supervisory staffing on relational coordination. The model shows that doubling the strength of supervisory staffing predicts a 19% increase in relational coordination. The care provider variables indicate the levels of relational coordination reported by each function relative to the levels reported by nurses. Asterisks indicate the probability that a change in supervisory staffing will produce a change in relational coordination (*** = 99.9%, ** = 99%, * = 95%, + = 90%). The model is a random effects regression with care provider as the unit of analysis (n = 336) and hospital (n = 9) as the random effect. R-squared indicates the percent of between-hospital variation in relational coordination that is explained by the model.

Exhibit 9-3 (page 113)

Exhibit 9-3 shows the impact of supervisory staffing on surgical performance. The first model shows that doubling the strength of supervisory staffing predicts a

33% reduction in length of stay. Asterisks indicate the probability that a change in supervisory staffing will produce a change in surgical performance (*** = 99.9%, ** = 99%, * = 95%, + = 90%). The final model shows that supervisory staffing influences surgical performance *through* its effect on relational coordination. Other variables included in each model but not shown here are patient gender, race, and marital status. All models are random effects regressions with the patient as the unit of analysis (n = 599 for length of stay, n = 588 for patient satisfaction, n = 539 for postoperative pain, n = 531 for postoperative mobility, and n = 552 for the surgical performance index) and hospital (n = 9) as the random effect. R-squared indicates the percent of between-hospital variation in performance that is explained by each model.

Exhibit 10-1 (page 119)

Exhibit 10-1 shows the impact of patient focused job design on relational coordination. The model shows that doubling the strength of patient focused job design predicts a 20% increase in relational coordination. The care provider variables indicate the levels of relational coordination reported by each function relative to the levels reported by nurses. Asterisks indicate the probability that a change in patient focused job design will produce a change in relational coordination (*** = 99.9%, ** = 99%, * = 95%, + = 90%). The model is a random effects regression with the care provider as the unit of analysis (n = 336) and the hospital (n = 9) as the random effect. R-squared indicates the percent of between-hospital variation in relational coordination that is explained by the model.

Exhibit 10-3 (page 121)

Exhibit 10-3 shows the impact of patient focused job design on surgical performance. The first model shows that doubling the strength of focused job design predicts a 19% reduction in length of stay. Asterisks indicate the probability that a change in patient focused job design will produce a change in surgical performance (*** = 99.9%, ** = 99%, * = 95%, + = 90%). The final model shows that patient focused job design influences surgical performance *through* its effect on relational coordination. Other variables included in each model but not shown here are patient gender, race, and marital status. All models are random effects regressions with the patient as the unit of analysis (n = 599 for length of stay, n = 588 for patient satisfaction, n = 539 for postoperative pain, n = 531 for postoperative mobility, and n = 552 for the surgical performance index) and the hospital (n = 9) as the random effect. R-squared indicates the percent of between-hospital variation in performance that is explained by each model.

Exhibit 10-4 (page 123)

Exhibit 10-4 shows the impact of the hospitalist job design on relational coordination within a single hospital. Because this study was conducted within a single hospital, relational coordination was measured across the different care providers assigned to each individual patient, allowing us to compare differences in relational coordination at the patient level within the same hospital. Asterisks indicate the probability that the hospitalist job design will produce a change in relational coordination (*** = 99.9%, ** = 99%, * = 95%, + = 90%). All models are random effects regressions with the patient as the unit of analysis (n = 312), with the physician (n = 49) as the random effect. R-squared indicates the percent of between-physician variation in relational coordination that is explained by the model.

Exhibit 10-5 (page 124)

Exhibit 10-5 shows patterns of relational coordination with physicians, residents, nurses, therapists, and case managers as reported by the care providers in the left-hand column. The first number in each cell is relational coordination for patients who had a hospitalist physician; the second number is relational coordination for patients who had a nonhospitalist physician. The unit of observation is the provider response about the coordination of care for a particular patient (n = 893). P values are shown in parentheses, indicating the probability that these differences in relational coordination are associated with the hospitalist job design, where a smaller p value suggests a higher probability.

Exhibit 10-6 (page 125)

Exhibit 10-6 shows the impact of hospitalist job design on medical performance within a single hospital. All models are random effects regressions with the patient as the unit of analysis (n = 6,699 for length of stay, n = 6,866 for total costs, n = 6,866 for mortality, n = 6,866 for readmits within 7 days, and n = 6,866 readmits within 30 days), and the physician (n = 116) as the random effect. Asterisks indicate the probability that a change in hospitalist job design will produce a change in medical performance (*** = 99.9%, ** = 99%, * = 95%, + = 90%). R-squared is presented for the random effects regressions and indicates the percent of between-physician variation in performance that is explained by each model. Chi-squared is presented for the logistic random effects regressions and indicates the probability that the null hypothesis for the model is true.

Exhibit 12-1 (page 146)

Exhibit 12-1 shows the impact of cross-functional boundary spanners on relational coordination. The model shows that doubling the strength of cross-functional boundary spanners predicts an 11% increase in relational coordination. The care provider variables indicate the levels of relational coordination reported by each function relative to the levels reported by nurses. Asterisks indicate the probability that a change in cross-functional boundary spanners will produce a change in relational coordination (*** = 99.9%, ** = 99%, * = 95%, + = 90%). The model is a random effects regression with the care provider as the unit of analysis (n = 336) and the hospital (n = 9) as the random effect. R-squared indicates the percent of between-hospital variation in relational coordination that is explained by the model.

Exhibit 12-3 (page 147)

Exhibit 12-3 shows the impact of cross-functional boundary spanners on surgical performance. The first model shows that doubling the strength of cross-functional boundary spanners predicts a 19% reduction in length of stay. Asterisks indicate the probability that a change in cross-functional boundary spanners will produce a change in surgical performance (*** = 99.9%, ** = 99%, * = 95%, + = 90%). The final model shows that cross-functional boundary spanners influence surgical performance *through* their effect on relational coordination. Other variables included in each model but not shown here are patient gender, race, and marital status. All models are random effects regressions with the patient as the unit of analysis (n = 599 for length of stay, n = 588 for patient satisfaction, n = 539 for postoperative pain, n = 531 for postoperative mobility, and n = 552 for the surgical performance index) and the hospital (n = 9) as the random effect. R-squared indicates the percent of between-hospital variation in performance that is explained by each model.

Exhibit 13-1 (page 157)

Exhibit 13-1 shows the impact of cross-functional pathways on relational coordination. The model shows that doubling the inclusiveness of cross-functional pathways predicts a 12% increase in relational coordination. The care provider variables indicate the levels of relational coordination reported by each function relative to the levels reported by nurses. Asterisks indicate the probability that a change in cross-functional pathways will produce a change in relational coordination (*** = 99.9%, ** = 99%, * = 95%, + = 90%). The model is a random effects regression with the care provider as the unit of analysis (n = 336) and the hospital (n = 9) as the random effect. R-squared indicates the percent of between-hospital variation in relational coordination that is explained by the model.

Exhibit 13-3 (page 159)

Exhibit 13-3 shows the impact of cross-functional pathways on surgical performance. The first model shows that doubling the inclusiveness of cross-functional pathways predicts a 23% reduction in length of stay. Asterisks indicate the probability that a change in cross-functional pathways will produce a change in surgical performance (*** = 99.9%, ** = 99%, * = 95%, + = 90%). The final model shows that cross-functional pathways influence surgical performance *through* their effect on relational coordination. Other variables included in each model but not shown here are patient gender, race, and marital status. All models are random effects regressions with the patient as the unit of analysis (n = 599 for length of stay, n = 588 for patient satisfaction, n = 539 for postoperative pain, n = 531 for postoperative mobility, and n = 552 for the surgical performance index) and hospital (n = 9) as the random effect. R-squared indicates the percent of between-hospital variation in performance that is explained by each model.

Exhibit 14-1 (page 167)

Exhibit 14-1 shows the impact of cross-functional rounds on relational coordination. The model shows that doubling the inclusiveness of cross-functional rounds predicts a 20% increase in relational coordination. The care provider variables indicate the levels of relational coordination reported by each function relative to the levels reported by nurses. Asterisks indicate the probability that a change in cross-functional rounds will produce a change in relational coordination (*** = 99.9%, ** = 99%, * = 95%, + = 90%). The model is a random effects regression with the care provider as the unit of analysis (n = 336) and the hospital (n = 9) as the random effect. R-squared indicates the percent of between-hospital variation in relational coordination that is explained by the model.

Exhibit 14-3 (page 168)

Exhibit 14-3 shows the impact of cross-functional rounds on surgical performance. The first model shows that doubling the inclusiveness of cross-functional rounds predicts a 26% reduction in length of stay. Asterisks indicate the probability that a change in cross-functional rounds will produce a change in surgical performance (*** = 99.9%, ** = 99%, * = 95%, + = 90%). The final model shows that cross-functional rounds influence surgical performance *through* their effect on relational coordination. Other variables included in each model but not shown here are patient gender, race, and marital status. All models are random effects regressions with the patient as the unit of analysis (n = 599 for length of stay, n = 588 for patient satisfaction, n = 539 for postoperative pain, n = 531 for postoperative mobility, and n = 552 for the surgical performance index) and hospital (n = 9) as the random effect. R-squared indicates the percent of between-hospital variation in performance that is explained by each model.

Exhibit 15-1 (page 182)

Exhibit 15-1 shows the impact of cross-functional information systems on relational coordination. The model shows that doubling the strength of cross-functional information systems predicts a 15% increase in relational coordination. The care provider variables indicate the levels of relational coordination reported by each function relative to the levels reported by nurses. Asterisks indicate the probability that a change in cross-functional information systems will produce a change in relational coordination (*** = 99.9%, ** = 99%, * = 95%, + = 90%). The model is a random effects regression with the care provider as the unit of analysis (n = 336) and the hospital (n = 9) as the random effect. R-squared indicates the percent of between-hospital variation in relational coordination that is explained by the model.

Exhibit 15-3 (page 183)

Exhibit 15-3 shows the impact of cross-functional information systems on surgical performance. The first model shows that doubling the strength of cross-functional information systems predicts a 30% reduction in length of stay. Asterisks indicate the probability that a change in cross-functional information systems will produce a change in surgical performance (*** = 99.9%, ** = 99%, * = 95%, + = 90%). The final model shows that cross-functional information systems influence surgical performance *through* their effect on relational coordination. Other variables included in each model but not shown here are patient gender, race, and marital status. All models are random effects regressions with the patient as the unit of analysis (n = 599 for length of stay, n = 588 for the patient satisfaction, n = 539 for postoperative pain, n = 531 for postoperative mobility, and n = 552 for the surgical performance index) and the hospital (n = 9) as the random effect. R-squared indicates the percent of between-hospital variation in performance that is explained by each model.

Exhibit 16-1 (page 205)

In Exhibit 16-1, the numbers in each cell indicate the strength of relational coordination between care providers. Row labels indicate the types of care providers who were surveyed, and column headings indicate the types of care providers they were surveyed about. Shaded areas indicate coordination within a stage of care; white areas indicate coordination between stages of care; cross-hatched areas indicate coordination by system integrators. The unit of observation is the provider response about the coordination of care for a particular patient (n = 519).

Exhibit 17-1 (page 211)

Exhibit 17-1 shows the impact of a high performance work system on relational coordination. The model shows that doubling the strength of this high performance work system predicts a 44% increase in relational coordination. The care provider variables indicate the levels of relational coordination reported by each function relative to the levels reported by nurses. Asterisks indicate the probability that a change in this high performance work system will produce a change in relational coordination (*** = 99.9%, ** = 99%, * = 95%, + = 90%). The model is a random effects regression with the care provider as the unit of analysis (n = 336) and the hospital (n = 9) as the random effect. R-squared indicates the percent of between-hospital variation in relational coordination that is explained by the model.

Exhibit 17-3 (page 212)

Exhibit 17-3 shows the impact of a high performance work system on surgical performance. The first model shows that doubling the strength of this high performance work system predicts a 68% reduction in length of stay. Asterisks indicate the probability that a change in this high performance work system will produce a change in surgical performance (*** = 99.9%, ** = 99%, * = 95%, + = 90%). The final model shows that this high performance work system influences surgical performance *through* its effect on relational coordination. Other variables included in each model but not shown here are patient gender, race, and marital status. All models are random effects regressions with the patient as the unit of analysis ($n = 599$ for length of stay, $n = 588$ for patient satisfaction, $n = 539$ for postoperative pain, $n = 531$ for postoperative mobility, and $n = 552$ for the surgical performance index) and the hospital ($n = 9$) as the random effect. R-squared indicates the percent of between-hospital variation in performance that is explained by each model.

Exhibit 18-1 (page 226)

Exhibit 18-1 shows the impact of managed care penetration and work stress on relational coordination. The care provider variables indicate the levels of work stress and relational coordination reported by each function relative to the levels reported by nurses. Asterisks indicate the probability that a change in the predictor variables will produce a change in relational coordination (*** = 99.9%, ** = 99%, * = 95%, + = 90%). All models are random effects regressions with the care provider as the unit of analysis ($n = 336$) and the hospital ($n = 9$) as the random effect. R-squared indicates the percent of between-hospital variation in work stress and relational coordination that is explained by each model.

Exhibit 19-2 (pages 239–240)

The survey in Exhibit 19-2 can be tailored to any work process by (1) referring in each question to the focal work process and (2) listing in the first column all functions that play an important role in that focal work process. For guidance on measuring and analyzing relational coordination data, as well as alternative sample surveys, see Jody Hoffer Gittell (2009), *Relational Coordination: Guidelines for Theory, Measurement and Analysis*, unpublished manuscript.

Exhibit 19-3 (page 241)

The matrix diagram in Exhibit 19-3 shows patterns of relational coordination with physicians, nurses, physical therapists, case managers, and social workers as reported by the care providers in the left-hand column for the nine-hospital study of surgical care. Insert scores from your relational coordination survey to identify the weak and strong links in your focal work process.

Exhibit 19-4 (pages 242–243)

The interview protocol in Exhibit 19-4 can be tailored to any work process by (1) relating each question to the focal work process and (2) asking each question with regard to the functions that play important roles in that focal work process. Additional work practices can be added as relevant.

Index

About the Author

Jody Hoffer Gittell, an award-winning professor of management and director of the MBA program at Brandeis University, has been studying the healthcare industry for over 10 years. Her work on healthcare has been widely published in influential academic journals. She is a highly sought-after speaker at healthcare industry events around the world. *Managing High Performance Healthcare* is the culmination of her 10 years of research in the field. She has also written similar studies of the airline industry, including *The Southwest Airlines Way: Using the Power of Relationships to Achieve High Performance* (2003).